# SEEING FOR OURSELVES

# SEEING FOR OURSELVES

## Case-Study Research
## by Teachers of Writing

Edited by

## Glenda L. Bissex
## Richard H. Bullock

**Heinemann**
Portsmouth, New Hampshire

**Heinemann Educational Books, Inc.**
70 Court Street     Portsmouth, NH   03801

LONDON   EDINBURGH   MELBOURNE   AUCKLAND
SINGAPORE   KUALA LUMPUR   NEW DELHI
IBADAN   NAIROBI   JOHANNESBURG
KINGSTON   PORT OF SPAIN

10  9  8  7  6  5  4  3  2  1

The editors thank *Language Arts* for permission to reprint "What Is a Teacher-Researcher?" by Glenda L. Bissex, originally published in the September 1986 issue. Copyright 1986 by the National Council of Teachers of English.

The following publishers have generously given permission to use quotations from copyrighted works:

"The Old Wife and the Ghost" by James Reeves. From *The Blackbird in the Lilac*. Published 1959 by E. P. Dutton. © James Reeves Estate. Reprinted by permission of The James Reeves Estate.
"Keep a Poem in Your Pocket" by Beatrice Schenk de Regniers. From *Something Special*. ©1958, 1986 by Beatrice Schenk de Regniers; reprinted by permission of the author.
"Things I Like" by Patricia Miles Martin. From *The Dog Next Door and Other Stories* of READING 360 by Theodore Clymer and others. ©Copyright 1969 Silver, Burdett & Ginn Inc. Used with permission.
"Night Song" by Myra Cohn Livingston. From *Whispers and Other Poems* by Myra Cohn Livingston. © 1958 by Myra Cohn Livingston. Reprinted by permission of Marian Reiner for the author.

**Library of Congress Cataloging-in-Publication Data**

Seeing for ourselves.

   Bibliography: p.
   1. English language—Composition and exercises—Study and teaching—Research.   2. English language—Rhetoric—Study and teaching—Research.   3. English language—Composition and exercises—Study and teaching—Case studies.   4. English language—Rhetoric—Study and teaching—Case studies.   I. Bissex, Glenda L.
II. Bullock, Richard H.
PE1404.S36   1987       808′.042′07       86–27153
ISBN 0-435-08436-4

Designed by Marie McAdam.
Printed in the United States of America.

# CONTENTS

*v*

# ACKNOWLEDGMENTS

When a book has reached the final stages, it is tempting to look back not only to the people who aided and encouraged us, but also to those whose work over the years influenced us and shaped our lives and thinking to make our work possible. To them we owe an immense debt. More immediately, we thank Timothy Perkins, former dean of Off-Campus Programs at Northeastern University, for providing the context and initial idea for this book.

That idea was made irresistible by the excitement all the teachers in the first year-long case-study course felt about their research. The quality of their work and that of the graduate class from which the four short-term studies were drawn convinced us that research by teachers not only improves teaching but also permits talented teachers to demonstrate their abilities in a professional context that transcends their own classrooms.

We are also indebted to Suzanne Robblee and Kinley Roby of Northeastern for their support of the project, and to patient typists Lisa Dwight, Dianne Fredrickson, Becky Gruber, and Julia Werbinski.

We thank Philippa Stratton, editor in chief at Heinemann, for her patience and amenableness.

Finally we thank our family and friends for sharing our excitement and putting up with us during the past year, and Barbara Bullock deserves special thanks for her support and encouragement of her preoccupied but loving husband.

# CONTRIBUTORS

and their present professional positions and locations

Carol S. Avery. Grade 1 Teacher, William Nitrauer School, Lancaster, Pennsylvania.

Glenda L. Bissex. Faculty, Adult Degree Program, Norwich University, Montpelier, Vermont, and Northeastern University Advanced Institute on Writing, Boston, Massachusetts.

Judith Boyce. Grade 5, 6, and 7 English and Reading Teacher, The Bromfield School, Harvard, Massachusetts.

Richard H. Bullock. Coordinator of Introductory Writing Programs, Northeastern University, Boston, Massachusetts.

Jacqueline Capobianco. English and Writing Teacher, Holy Cross High School, Waterbury, Connecticut.

Kathy Calkins. Literature and Latin Teacher, King Philip Junior High School, Norfolk, Massachusetts.

Elizabeth Cornell. Grade 1 Teacher, White River Elementary School, White River Junction, Vermont.

Alice DeLana. Art History Teacher, Miss Porter's School, Farmington, Connecticut.

Patricia Hanlon. Honors Instructor, Northeastern University, Boston, Massachusetts.

Jennifer Hicks. Part-time Instructor, Northeastern University, Boston, Massachusetts.

Kathleen Hogan. Graduate Student, Northeastern University, Boston, Massachusetts.

Susan Kaplan. Writing Facilitator and Grade 8 English Teacher, DeWitt Middle School, Ithaca, New York.

Eileen McCormack. Grade 5 Teacher, Charlotte Cross School, Lockport, New York.

Ferguson McKay. Professor of English, Lyndon State College, Lyndonville, Vermont.

Jane Richards. Grade 11 and 12 English Teacher, Marathon Central School, Marathon, New York.

Peggy Sheehan. English Composition, Literature, and Developmental Reading Instructor, Post College, Waterbury, Connecticut.

# INTRODUCTION

Over the past decade, a shift in the teaching of writing has been taking place from product-oriented, teacher-centered instruction to process-oriented, student-centered pedagogies. Along with this shift has come a revolutionary change in the research into the nature of writing and its teaching and learning, and a concomitant alteration of the role of the teacher of writing. Teachers at all levels who have studied students as they write have found that empirical research, with its treatment and control groups, its statistical analysis and reliance on numerical validity, offers little of value to them as they confront the wonder and mystery of children, adolescents, and adults struggling with meaning as expressed in writing. To counter this dissatisfaction, teachers have begun to do research on their own—but research based on a single student, or perhaps two or three, closely observed and interviewed, their writings kept and carefully studied.

Out of these studies of particular writers as they learn to manipulate written language is emerging some of our best knowledge of what writers do when they write, what students do when they learn to write, and what teachers do when they teach writing. Indeed, because of its focus on the activities of individual writers and learners, case-study analysis is arguably the most valid form of research into the highly individual and idiosyncratic processes of writing and learning to write.

There is more to it than that, however. The teachers who are conducting this research are changing the definition of teaching and of their roles as teachers. The classroom becomes a place of inquiry, where questions are explored in meaningful contexts and teacher and students collaborate to seek answers. No longer dispensers of curricula designed by "experts" from universities, textbook companies, or their school districts, these teachers become experts themselves, bringing knowledge and confidence to their teaching and showing that they are professional educators to be respected within schools and without. By becoming researchers, these teachers take control over their classrooms and professional lives in ways that confound the traditional definition of *teacher* and offer proof that education can reform itself from within. Teachers doing case-study analyses of their students present a powerful challenge to society's preconceptions of the nature of schooling, the role of teachers, and ultimately the seat of power in educational decision making.

*Seeing for Ourselves* presents the first extensive collection of such teacher-conducted case-study research. Based on studies by teachers attending Northeastern University's Institute on Writing and graduate students enrolled in Northeastern's English graduate program, this book offers a comprehensive overview of the sorts of research being conducted by teachers and teachers in training, as well as extensive information on the changes this research has caused in the teaching and professional lives of these teachers, both novice and veteran.

Thus, this book is in part celebratory, not only of these teachers and their completion of a major task, but also of this altered conception of what good teachers should be and do. More than that, though, it offers previously unpublished insights into writing and how it is learned.

Teachers will doubtless recognize some of their own questions here—questions like: How can I move students beyond writing about their trips to the shopping mall or last weekend's pajama party? (Calkins) How can I help students assume more responsibility for the mechanics of their writing? (Richards) How can I teach a student with a different learning style? (Avery) Should students always select their own topics for writing? (Hogan) As Hogan argues, there is no simple answer to this last question; but her exploration of it, and the explorations of other questions by other researchers, will help classroom teachers observe and think further about such questions themselves.

Case studies may not enable us to generalize about the teaching and learning of writing. But because a single exception disproves the universality of a rule, they are powerful instruments for challenging theories and assumptions—and some of these studies do just that. For example, on the basis of her application of an accepted model of the writing process to her careful observation of a single writer, Jennifer Hicks proposes a modified, more complex version of that model. Carol Avery's understanding of a student with learning difficulties challenges the prevalent assumption that all such students require instruction that is tightly teacher directed and broken down into small segments of information. Kathleen Hogan questions the benefit of self-selected topics for all students. Ferguson McKay's reflections on his own writing conferences challenge the notion of teaching as instruction.

These studies ask us to look at the many factors that influence a piece of writing: the writing environment (Cornell, Calkins), the characteristics of an individual writer's learning style (Avery, Hanlon, Kaplan), the nature of the writer's interaction with the teacher (McKay, Boyce), the writer's sense of audience (Hanlon, Calkins), the intricacies of the writing process (Hicks), and the teacher's expectations of where responsibility lies (Richards), to name some of the more prominent ones.

The studies also offer many ways of looking—of observing individual writers or the effects of a particular teaching approach in a particular classroom: critical analysis of taped writing conferences (McKay), formal and informal interviews with writers (Hanlon, Avery, Hogan), documentation of the writing environment (Cornell), structured introspection (Kaplan), detailed observation of a writer at work (Hogan, Avery), analysis of written texts (Hicks, Hanlon), and theoretically informed speculation (Hicks, McKay). Most case studies are enriched and deepened by information and insights gained through a combination of methods.

Both the range of factors these studies explore and the diversity of research strategies they employ will help teachers broaden their observations and reflections on their own experiences. That is the aim of this book. The case studies are presented not as models to be followed but as suggestive explorations. We hope that they will provide teachers who may be researching independently or in small groups with a sense of colleagueship in a community of fellow teacher-researchers. We hope that our convictions about the importance of such case-study research will support these teachers and the teachers of these teachers. Our descriptions of the courses out of which the case studies emerged are intended, like the studies themselves, to be suggestive rather than prescriptive.

In describing the growth of poetry writing in her first-grade classroom, Elizabeth Cornell speaks of the sharing of poetry as giving children that "I can do it, too" attitude. We hope that this book may inspire an "I can do it, too" attitude so that you, like the teachers who did these studies, can see for yourself.

# PART I

# Backgrounds of Teacher Research

# CHAPTER 1

# What Is a Teacher-Researcher?

*Glenda L. Bissex*

To dispel some traditional associations with the word *research*, I'll begin by saying what a teacher-researcher *isn't*.

A teacher-researcher doesn't have to study hundreds of students, establish control groups, and perform complex statistical analyses.

A teacher-researcher may start out not with a hypothesis to test but with a "wondering" to pursue: "I wonder how much my students think about their writing outside of class. Vicky mentioned today that she mentally revises compositions on the bus coming to school. What about the others now that they're writing on their own topics?"

A teacher-researcher does not have to be antiseptically detached. He knows that knowledge comes through closeness as well as through distance, through intuition as well as through logic.

When a teacher-researcher writes about what she's discovered, she need not try to make her writing sound like a psychology textbook. Her audience is herself, other teachers, her students, their parents, her principal, maybe even the school board—none of whom is likely to be upset by plain English and a personal style.

A teacher-researcher is not a split personality with a poem in one hand and a microscope in the other.

So what *is* a teacher-researcher?

A teacher-researcher is an observer

a questioner

a learner

and a more complete teacher.

*A teacher-researcher is an observer.* "Research means looking—and looking again," says Ann Berthoff. "This new kind of REsearch would not mean going after new 'data,' but rather REconsidering what is at hand. REsearch would come to mean looking and looking again at what happens in the classroom. We do not need new information; we need to think about the information we have" (31).

Marie Clay notes that "an interesting change occurs in teachers who closely observe. They begin to question educational assumptions" (91). One assumption that has been questioned by observers of children in classrooms (and of children before they enter school) is that learning to read precedes learning to write. Young children have been seen learning to read *while* they write, for example.

*A teacher-researcher is a questioner.* "Why is Terry unwilling to read?" "How are poor writers and readers different from good ones?" "Do they have different concepts of what writing and reading are all about?"

Problems can become questions to investigate, occasions for learning rather than lamenting. Everything that happens in a classroom can be seen as data to be understood rather than causes for blaming or congratulating ourselves or our students. Teachers are constantly making evaluative judgments, but that evaluative frame of mind narrows our vision. "I really enjoyed asking questions of my students," one teacher-researcher told me, "because it gave me more insight into those students."

New approaches to teaching are no longer just risks but opportunities for learning: "What would happen if I had a reading workshop in this class and we shared and conferenced books everyone chose to bring?"

*A teacher-researcher is a learner.* In my ideal school, principals ask teachers, "What did you *learn* today?" not "What did you *teach*?" Teacher-researchers have plenty to respond. (In this ideal school, principals are researchers too.)

It's no accident that the notion of teacher-researchers grew out of writing projects that actively engaged teachers in *doing* what they taught. And whatever our subject matter, isn't it *learning* that we teach? Just as classrooms become writing workshops, they also become learning workshops, where both teachers and students see themselves as learners, where teachers are learning from children (as Lucy Calkins did in *Lessons from a Child*), where teachers ask questions of themselves as well as of students, where teachers are models of learners.

Finally, a teacher-researcher is not, as I have said, a split personality but a *more complete teacher*. Teachers have asked whether it's possible to teach and do research at the same time. The very question reflects the separation we feel between knowing and doing, and the division within our educational systems between those who "know" (such as college teachers, who have classrooms yet are not considered "classroom teachers") and those who "do" (the teachers who are not trusted, and often do not trust themselves, to know what and how they should teach). "I can't tell you how much difference this has made to me," one teacher-researcher who had received some criticism of her teaching methods said to me. "I knew I was doing the right thing because I'd done the research." If teacher research had been on the horizon ten years ago, I might still be in a classroom myself rather than having been driven to choose between knowing and doing.

## REFERENCES

Berthoff, Ann E. *The Making of Meaning*. Montclair, N.J.: Boynton/Cook, 1981.

Calkins, Lucy McCormick. *Lessons from a Child*. Portsmouth, N.H.: Heinemann Educational Books, 1983.

Clay, Marie M. "Looking and Seeing in the Classroom." *English Journal* 71 (February 1982): 90–92.

# CHAPTER 2

# Why Case Studies?

Glenda L. Bissex

About ten years ago I did a case study describing five years of my son's development as a writer and reader. I had set out not to do a case study as such but simply to understand more about his learning in the only way I could see to do it. At the time I was a remedial reading teacher and had been for many years before that an English teacher. As a teacher and as a parent I was often, though unsystematically and sporadically, observing and thinking like a case-study researcher. Of course I was not conscious of this; it was simply the way I looked at individuals learning. Although I had not deliberated a choice of method in observing my son for what eventually became my doctoral research, I was soon enough confronted with professional opinions about my case-study approach that provoked me to become more aware of the meaning of the choice I had tacitly made. In my first interview for a teaching job in a college education department, my description of my case study was challenged with, "And what does that prove?" Yet to a faculty member at another college my work sounded "wonderful—just like Piaget!"

After my study was published, I received letters from beleaguered doctoral students in need of support for their own case-study research. Some wanted comradeship and confirmation; one had been warned of the dire effects observation might have on her own child; another's proposal had reportedly been rejected because observation and description of events in a natural classroom setting was not considered rigorous research. It was clear that the way people went about their research was a political issue, and one I felt increasingly responsible for understanding. I began to see how much was attached to that little matter of methodology—how it was related to what you researched and why you researched, to the kinds of questions you asked and the kind of answers that would satisfy, to the kind of relationship you felt with the subjects or objects of your inquiry, to your assumptions about knowledge and control, and even to your gender. The more I understood, the stronger the commitment I felt toward the implications of the research path I had been drawn to as a graduate student: observation of individuals in their normal environment.

It is not difficult to see why teachers have felt excluded from the world of traditional research. In the round-table discussion among teacher-researchers (part 3), Peggy Sheehan recalls how the term *research* used to make her think of statistics and control groups, which "turned me off completely." These have been part of the accepted methodology. A researcher formulated a hypothesis—for example, that students who had worked on sentence-combining exercises would write sentences with more subordination than students without such training. The study would be designed around two equivalent groups of students, differing only in that one had no experience with sentence combining. The researcher would specify what was to be counted (in this case the number of subordinating constructions per sentence of student writing) to measure the effect of the training. A statistical analysis of these figures would indicate the mathematical probability that the differences found between the two groups could exist by chance. If the probability was slight, the researcher could conclude that the sentence-combining practice made a difference. Finally, a report would be written, reviewing other research as background, describing how the study was done and on whom, and presenting the results and interpreting them.

The language of such reports usually signals that they are addressed to other university researchers, not to classroom teachers—even college English teachers. Listen to the beginning of an article reporting a study of some effects of audience on writing:

> Recent inquiry into the nature and processes of writing reflects the influence of cognitive developmental psychology (Barritt & Kroll, 1978). As the field of rhetoric describes the rhetor as accommodating message to purpose and occasion (Perelman & Olbrechts-Tyecca, 1969), and as sociolinguistics portrays the language user as switch-

ing among alternate codes in order to express social or pragmatic meaning (Blom & Gumperez, 1972), so does the cognitive developmental model postulate that the course of communicative development is marked by growth in social cognitive acuity enabling communicators to adapt messages to the internal states of their receivers (Flavell, Botkin, Fry, Jarvis & Wright, 1968). The study of audience awareness in written composition draws from these foundations (Britton, Burgess, Martin, McLeod & Rosen, 1975). (Rubin and Piché, 293)

Now listen to how Nancie Atwell begins her account of research she conducted in her eighth-grade classroom:

> One afternoon last September, five things happened within one fifteen-minute period that made me aware of a change at my school.
> Bob Dyer, principal at my school, put a Bette Lord novel in my mailbox with the note, "I think you and your kids might enjoy this."
> Underneath Lord's book was my copy of Francine Du Plessix-Gray's *Lovers and Tyrants*. Susan Stires, our resource room teacher, had returned it with the note, "God, can she write. Thank you for this."
> Under Francine was a message from Nancy Tindal, a kindergarten teacher: "Do you have some afternoon this week to respond to my Open House speech?"
> When I went back to my classroom, I found another note on the chalkboard from a former student who'd borrowed a novel the week before: "Hi. I was here but you weren't. I love *Portrait of Jenny*. Who *is* Robert Nathan? Your favorite freshperson, Amanda."
> And finally, Andy, another freshperson, came by with a copy of an interview with Douglas Adams that he'd promised me over the summer.
> It was only because these things happened so one on top of another that I noticed and considered what was going on here. (240)

Atwell goes on to show us how her study grew out of reflections on her experience as a teacher rather than out of previous research studies. She speaks in a personal voice, as one individual to another, rather than in the impersonal tone of one authority to another. She describes what she has seen in her classroom, not an experiment she has designed. Her observations focus on the reading development of two of her students, and as she shows us some of the letters they wrote her about the books they'd read, we see how their individual character, and not just a particular kind of training, shapes their learning. Her description of their growth takes the form of a story, because it *is* through narrative that people are revealed in action, learning and growing. The significance of two students' development cannot be measured statistically; the meanings Atwell sees emerge from her understanding about learning.

The opening paragraphs of these two articles announce that their research has been conducted in different worlds for different audiences. But, you might ask, is a study that describes what a teacher has seen in his or her classroom really research or just a slice of life?

There are many ways of *re*-searching—of looking again at something. While the term suggests the existence of a single process (commonly known as the scientific method), the reality of researching is not so monolithic. The experimental, statistical approach that Peggy Sheehan called to mind was handed down to psychology through the physical sciences. Psychological research (which includes educational research) is being influenced today by methods from field studies of human cultures (ethnography) and studies of animals in their natural settings (ethology), methods that emphasize describing rather than counting, and observing rather than experimenting. Yet psychology has its own alternative research tradition: the work of Piaget and Freud originated in case studies. Piaget's first cases were his own three children, whom he observed as they played with household objects. Parents who recorded their own children's early speech and who were trained in linguistics pioneered our understanding of children's language development.

A research approach appropriate, for example, in physics may not be appropriate to the study of human beings. "No individual is exactly like another. . . . Here is a fundamental difference between living individuals and atoms. Two atoms of the same kind are identical in every respect—they are completely alike. Two living beings of the same species never are completely identical" (Weisskopf, 218). Research methods appropriate to the study of living beings have struggled for respectability in the scientific community. As nature writer Sally Carrighar tells us,

> the field workers have had some handicaps in winning respect for themselves. For a long time they were considered as little better than amateur animal-watchers—certainly not scientists, since their facts were not gained by experimental procedures: they could not conform to the hard-and-fast rule that a problem set up and solved by one scientist must be tested by other scientists, under identical conditions and reaching identical results. Of course many situations in the lives of animals simply cannot be rehearsed and controlled in this way. The fall flocking of wild birds can't be, or the homing of animals over long distances, or even details of spontaneous family relationships.   (38)

Nor can the complex interactions in a classroom. Because living beings are unique, there are limits to the extent research enables us to predict and control the behavior of individuals, limits to the replicability of studies on living beings, and limits to the generalizability of the findings from such research.

Traditional research, even on human beings, has sought to make generalizations based on similarities in behavior. Large numbers of people are studied in order to wash out the effects of particular individual differences. Case studies, by contrast, enable us to see individuals as individuals; and when several individuals are compared, common traits as well as differences become apparent. "And what does that prove?" The challenge reasserts itself. Perhaps nothing to a scientist. But case studies can be seen to have their roots in the humanities as well as the sciences.

As novelist Marjorie Kinnan Rawlings said, "A man may learn a deal of the general from studying the specific, whereas it is impossible to know the specific by studying the general" (359). Through the lives of literary characters, we come to know other people in a way that is different from the knowledge gained through abstraction and generalization. Literature assumes that the lives of its characters partake of human universals; if not, why should we feel engaged with its characters? While case studies do not provide the generalizability of large numbers or of experiments that can be readily duplicated, they are more true to life in their revelation of individuals in action and their reflection of the complexities of those individuals and actions.

Traditional research in education has tried to isolate and measure the effect of single factors, such as practice in sentence combining, over a large population of subjects. Case studies, by looking intensively at individuals, encompass *many* factors that influence their behavior. When a researcher's attention does not have to be directed toward identifying and counting a few predetermined items (such as subordinate clauses), it can be informed and guided by all the available data as they are gathered. Researchers can attend to information that is humanly significant though not mathematically measurable; they can, for example, ask a young writer what led to her choice of topic and thus understand the meaning of behavior from the child's point of view, not just tally it. "Quantitative research implies that one knows what to count," as psycholinguist William Labov points out, "and this knowledge is reached only through a long period of trial and approximation, and upon the basis of a solid body of theoretical constructs. By the time the analyst knows what to count, the problem is practically solved" (305).

Because science has aimed at establishing general laws that hold true regardless of context, experimenters—whether chemists or psychologists—have sought to remove the objects they study from the influence of any specific environment and observe them in pure form in laboratories. But human beings live and learn in particular contexts, such as families, classrooms, and cultures. We can neither live nor learn anywhere else. These contexts shape our experiences and what those experiences mean to us. Thus laboratory experiments do not yield a truthful, complete picture of human behavior, as Elliot Mishler argues in his wonderfully entitled article "Meaning in Context: Is There Any Other Kind?" In fact, a chemical laboratory and a psychologist's office are in themselves contexts, but contexts whose influence is not taken into account. When we observe individuals in their own environments, such as students and teachers in classrooms, part of what is observed *is* the context. Context then becomes, as Mishler puts it, a resource for understanding rather than an enemy of understanding. While the findings of research in context may be less universal, they provide a more holistic view than the results of laboratory experiments.

If case studies can't prove theories, they have the power to disprove them, as language researcher Jerome Harste argues:

It doesn't take much to disprove a theory—just a single exception. . . . In language research all phenomena are significant: for the theories we develop—if they are to have power—cannot wallow in frequency or convenience, but universality. It is for this reason that the case study is a powerful theoretical tool. Because all phenomena demand explanation, theories developed from this source have more generalizability rather than less. Now that's the opposite of what the profession as a whole seems to think. But experimental studies don't have generalizability. Experimental studies assume that exception is handled when it is termed "error" and statistically it can be shown that it is "insignificant." They think by labeling it "error" and "insignificant," it is *error* and *insignificant*. And so they trick themselves and confuse the profession with generalizations and models which end up explaining the behavior of no one. I'm not trying to be radical; I'm just trying to bring some standards back to the profession. A good model, now don't you agree, ought to at least be able to explain the behavior of one child before it gets implemented.   (368–69)

Research methods are not neutral tools; they embody assumptions about causation and control, about how knowledge is acquired, and about the researcher's relationship to what is being studied. For example, the many studies of the effectiveness of different methods of teaching reading, using experimental designs with control groups, assume that the crucial variable in learning is the instructional method, rather than the backgrounds or characteristics of the learners, the quality of interpersonal relationships in the classroom, or any other factor. This is a top-down vision of control, with students viewed as receivers of instruction, and learning as a product of external conditions. This assumption of external and controllable causation would seem to underlie all studies based on experimental and control groups. Yet observational studies of children's language development and preschool literacy have revealed children to be creators rather than mere recipients of their learning. This research approach allows individuals to be seen as actors and as interactors with their normal environment; it lets us view learners as in control of their own learning—as self-directed or interactive. It is no accident, then, that experimental research in education has focused largely on issues of *teaching* (i.e., external control), while observational studies have directed more attention toward *learning* (i.e., internal processes reflecting various educative influences including, of course, teaching).

Research methods also carry assumptions about the proper distance to be maintained between researchers and the objects of their research—about objectivity. We may envision a scientific researcher wearing a white coat, suggestive of the antiseptic environment of his researching. He may observe his material not directly but through specialized instruments, further maintaining his distance and objectivity. Reports of his findings contain lots of numbers which, being impersonal like the instruments, are seen as objective and factual, even though decisions about what to measure and why a particular problem is worth investigating involve subjective choices. There is knowledge to be gained through this kind of detachment, especially knowledge about the nonliving world; but objectivity is not the sole route to knowledge. There is knowledge of a different sort to be gained through empathy and involvement, through sympathetic observation that seeks to understand the experience of other persons rather than their behavior as objects. "An observer who is not emotionally involved will be unable to empathize, to see things from the perspective of his subject, and therefore will miss much of the meaning of what he sees. Consequently he will not know how to ask the right questions . . . and look in the right places," claims Paul Diesing in his book on research in the social sciences (280).

The notion that we can come to know people and human situations by distancing ourselves from them must seem as strange to a case-study researcher as to a literary storyteller, though both need at times to see their work through the eyes of an outsider in order to gain perspective. Our research tools should not hamper a full view of what we are researching. No single research design, no single angle of vision or set of assumptions, will enable us to see the whole picture. We need methods that will allow us to use our empathy and intuition while giving us the distance to look critically, as a writer alternates between the roles of involved creator and critical reader of his own work. Scientist Evelyn Fox Keller proposes the concept of "dynamic objectivity" in place of an objectivity that is static, detached, and controlling. "Dynamic objectivity aims at a form of knowledge that grants to the world around us its independent integrity but does so in a way that remains cognizant of, indeed relies on, our connectivity with that world. In this, dynamic objectivity is not unlike empathy, a form of knowledge of other persons that draws explicitly on the commonality of feelings and experiences in order to enrich one's understanding of another in his or her own right" (117). This sounds like the description of an ideal relationship between teachers and students as well as between teachers and their research.

The image of the white-coated scientific researcher I evoked was clearly, in my mind, that of a man. The differences between the research approach he stands for and the more humanistic, naturalistic, and holistic case study approach I have been describing seem to parallel the sex differences in values described by psychologists such as Carol Gilligan, who argues, in *In a Different Voice*, that male morality is based on separation, on distancing oneself from concrete situations in order to determine general, objective rules or principles, while feminine morality is based in a sense of connectedness to others and on judgments related to specific contexts. Since our society's concept of knowledge, and thus of the methods through which we gain knowledge, has been dominated by a scientific view embodying values associated with men, it is not surprising to find that women have been influential in opening up alternative research methodologies. I think especially of Patricia Carini's important theoretical work and the research she has nurtured for many years at the Prospect School in North Bennington, Vermont. Carini was one of the first to support teacher research in this country, guiding detailed classroom observations, long-term studies of individual children, and reflective conversations with teachers. This history of case-study research in psychology, including education—to which Freud, Piaget, and Erikson have contributed—as well as case-study research in the natural sciences, is replete with work by women. Janet Emig, a pioneer of case-study research in writing, concludes her essay on "Inquiry Paradigms and Writing" by stressing the importance of our choice of paradigms. What is involved, she holds, is "no less than how we choose to perceive the world and how we elect to define what is distinctly human about human life" (73).

In a speech entitled "Passionate Scholarship," psychologist Barbara DuBois extends this theme:

> Our models of inquiry, of science-making, are also models of reality: they reflect how we conceptualize what is, what is to be known, and how it is to be known.... And the science-making that is in fact based in *different* values than those prevailing in the culture at a given time, and that thus attempts to discover, explore and explain *different* realities, tends to be ignored—or attacked as "unscientific." This judgment can frequently be understood for what it really is: not in fact a judgment about science, but a charge of heresy.

Let us enlarge our gallery of images of researchers to include not only the white-coated scientist but also the naturalist in the salt marsh observing wild ducks, the parent carefully recording a child's monologues, the ethnographer in New Guinea observing and experiencing life in a different culture, and the teacher listening to tapes of his own writing conferences. If such research is a slice of life, it is a slice of carefully examined life.

Writing teacher Ferguson McKay (chapter 6) transcribes his tapes noting where he has talked too much and his instruction has silenced rather than informed a student. He is observing himself. His next writing conference will be different. "The research makes you become aware of what you do as a teacher," says fellow teacher-researcher Jacqueline Capobianco, although her case study focuses not on herself but on two of her junior-high students who were having trouble with school. A secondary teacher who set out to observe peer conferences told me, "I never knew I did all that stuff until I started recording it." As a researcher myself and in my work with teacher-researchers I have come to see the value of the research *process*. In traditional research the emphasis has been on results; in observational research the process *is* part of the result. "I learned. I became a listener. I saw the kids as individuals. The biggest thing I learned was to become a listener," reports Capobianco.

The *process* of observing even a single individual sensitizes us that much more to other individuals. As one teacher commented at the conclusion of her case study, "I focused on two children but I learned about twenty-three." In other words, the process of seeing in a certain way is generalizable. One characteristic of schools that has obstructed this kind of seeing is an evaluative mind set that readily leads teachers to respond to individuals and situations—and also to themselves—in terms of praise or criticism, approval or disapproval: grading rather than understanding. Case-study research is directed largely toward understanding; such descriptive research requires us to suspend judgment and just look. Researching in this way can be transforming because it changes the way we see others and ourselves. It can, in the very midst of being carried on, change the teaching of the researcher without years of waiting for reports of someone else's results or decades of waiting for the effects of university research to trickle down to classrooms.

First-grade teacher Carol Avery, author of "Traci" (chapter 5), who has done case-study observations in her classroom for several years, comments:

> There are no big conclusions coming out of the classroom researching process but there sure are some very powerful learnings. The whole process is open-ended. Researching does not bring answers but rather raises questions. It keeps opening doors. When I was a child I had a book and on the cover of that book was a little girl reading a book and so on. I think teacher researching is like that book cover. It offers the potential to keep going on and on. That's exciting to me.

Thus classroom-based case-study research by teachers becomes a powerful instrument for self-directed in-service education and staff development. Teachers can test out and put to use immediately what they learn through their research. In the course of studying her sixth-grade students' commonplace books, Judith Boyce (chapter 8) discovered that some students interpreted her questions, written in response to their entries, as criticisms. Since criticism was not her intention, she investigated responses to which students were more receptive and changed her teaching accordingly. And since she wasn't conducting an experiment in which conditions had to be held constant, she was free to make such changes and then take them into account in her later observations. "The kind of knowledge of a living system that case study methods provide is essentially suited to enabling a person to work within the system," claims Paul Diesing (264). Participant-observers, he continues, test the objectivity of their knowledge by seeing whether it is understandable to others in the system (the students in one's classroom or other teachers, for example) and by attempting to act on it.

Certain aspects of learning can be studied *only* by people engaged in teaching as they research, argues British teacher and researcher Michael Armstrong:

> It is characteristic of classroom research, indeed of most research into the processes of intellectual growth, that it excludes the act of teaching from its techniques of investigation. The research worker observes children and teachers, either in a natural setting or in a laboratory, and seeks to interpret, and sometimes to control, their behavior, but without attempting to participate directly in their activity. It is often assumed that the demands of scientific objectivity force this exclusion upon us as researchers. Yet its effect is to deprive us of vital sources of information and understanding: those sources which depend upon asking children questions and answering their questions, exchanging ideas with them, discussing each other's opinions, chatting and joking, trying to probe their intentions and appreciate their problems, offering help and responding to appeals for help—those sources, that is to say, which depend upon teaching.

It was for this reason that I felt I had to continue teaching children in order to investigate their learning. It seemed to me that the act of teaching was indispensable to the study of intellectual growth; that to refuse the opportunity to teach was greatly to diminish the prospect of understanding the understanding of children. My own interest, in any case, lay in discovering what insights were to be obtained from a research strategy that was almost the reverse of the normal procedure: from continuing, that is, to participate as a teacher in the life of the classroom while seeking to develop a degree of objectivity and a concern for close observation, analysis, and description adequate to the task of examining, in a more or less systematic way, the character and course of children's learning.   (53)

Although teachers may teach sizable groups of students, it is only individuals who learn; and it is the learning of each individual for which teachers are ultimately responsible. Thus an awareness of the individuals in their classroom and of the shapes of their learning is of prime importance for teachers. And when they closely observe individual students in their classrooms, they come to appreciate the many resources students utilize in learning, including but not limited to instruction. Teachers, and perhaps especially teachers of writing, are daily confronted with individual differences. Commercial teaching materials cannot take these differences into account; teachers cannot ignore them. Traditional research blurs and ignores individual differences in its search for similarities and generalizations. While generalizations can guide teachers, they may become meaningless or useless in any particular educational encounter with an individual student. As Kathleen Hogan remarks in her paper (chapter 11), case study "highlights the enormous complexity of one single writer, telling us how oversimplified most traditional approaches to teaching writing are."

Because of the varied individuals and settings and interactions involved, several teachers might carry on similar investigations in their classrooms and yet come out with different findings. This need not lead to discrediting some findings, as would be expected in the realm of traditional research with its demand for replicability, though we would want to be able to explain the differences. The main concern should be whether each teacher has learned something that will illuminate his or her particular teaching situation.

Yet if several teachers engaged in similar studies learn similar things, this should not be viewed as uselessly reinventing the wheel. The analogy does not fit. A mechanical invention that can be used by anyone is not like the understanding that we must all gain for ourselves through our own thinking. Understanding is not transferable, however much the thinking of others contributes to our own. This is why Piaget said that to understand is to reinvent.

At its worst, teacher research might reduce itself to an uncritical documentation of a teacher's preferences—a selective gathering of evidence to support a preconceived conclusion. This hazard is not unique to participant-observer research. Teacher-researcher Ferguson McKay (whose study of writing conferences appears in chapter 6) comments that "if you observe yourself as well as the students, you can prevent slanting the evidence—getting the results you predicted." Observing what they *do* may lead teacher-researchers to discover what they *know*— to make their knowledge-in-action visible to themselves and to others.

A new body of educational research is already building up, one that informs us about teaching and learning from the inside, as experienced and understood by teachers and their students. May the result of this research never become the generation of even more prescriptions to be laid on other teachers but rather a heightening of awareness on the part of the teacher-observers themselves and their colleagues and thus an increase in their responsiveness and effectiveness as teachers and learners. Every teacher whose research is included here was changed by that research.

We need to discuss not only *what* we see but *how* we see, realizing that choices exist. Research methods provide selective lenses, sharpening our focus on some things while excluding others from view. Methodologies and their acceptability also raise the political issue of who is empowered to see—to research, to know, and to be known as an authority. Richard Bullock reflects on that issue in the next chapter.

## REFERENCES

Armstrong, Michael. "A Seed's Growth." In *What's Going On? Language/Learning Episodes in British and American Classrooms, Grades 4–13*, edited by Mary Barr, Pat D'Arcy, and Mary K. Healy. Montclair, N.J.: Boynton/Cook, 1982.

Atwell, Nancie. "Writing and Reading Literature from the Inside Out." *Language Arts* 61 (March 1984): 240–52.

Carini, Patricia. *Observation and Description: An Alternative Methodology for the Investigation of Human Phenomena*. Grand Forks: University of North Dakota, 1975.

———. *The Art of Seeing and the Visibility of the Person*. Grand Forks: University of North Dakota, 1979.

Carrighar, Sally. *Wild Heritage*. New York: Ballantine Books, 1965.

Diesing, Paul. *Patterns of Discovery in the Social Sciences*. Chicago: Adline Atherton, 1971.

DuBois, Barbara. "Passionate Scholarship." Paper presented to the First National Women's Studies Association, Lawrence, Kansas, June 1979.

Emig, Janet. *The Web of Meaning: Essays on Writing, Teaching, Learning, and Thinking*. Montclair, N.J.: Boynton/Cook, 1983.

Gilligan, Carol. *In a Different Voice*. Cambridge, Mass.: Harvard University Press, 1982.

Harste, Jerome; Carolyn Burke; and Virginia Woodward. *Children, Their Language and World: Initial Encounters with Print*. Final NIE report. Bloomington: Indiana University, 1981.

Keller, Evelyn Fox. *Reflections on Gender and Science*. New Haven: Yale University Press, 1985.

Labov, William. "The Study of Language in Its Social Context." In *Language and Social Context*, edited by Pier Paolo Giglioli. Harmondsworth, England: Penguin Books, 1972.

Mishler, Elliot G. "Meaning in Context: Is There Any Other Kind?" *Harvard Educational Review* 49 (February 1979): 1–19.

Rawlings, Marjorie Kinnan. *Cross Creek*. New York: Charles Scribner's, 1942.

Rubin, Donald L., and Gene L. Piché. "Development in Syntactic and Strategic Aspects of Audience Adaptation Skills in Written Persuasive Communication." *Research in the Teaching of English* 13 (December 1979): 293–316.

Weisskopf, Victor F. *Knowledge and Wonder*. Garden City, N.Y.: Doubleday, Anchor Books, 1966.

## ANNOTATED BIBLIOGRAPHY
## OF SELECTED CASE STUDIES

These studies suggest the range of designs possible within the case-study approach. They look at single individuals or a small number of individuals, or, as in Nancie Atwell's article, interactions between individuals. They also extend the notion of a case to the unit of a particular classroom or community. They demonstrate various ways of organizing and focusing case studies. The subjects of these studies are persons of many backgrounds and ages, from young children through mature adults, including a researcher studying herself (Joanna Field). I have listed only studies that I feel are of interest and value in themselves, particularly to teachers of writing.

Armstrong, Michael. *Closely Observed Children*. London: Writers and Readers Publishing Cooperative Society, 1980. (Available in the United States through Boynton/Cook Publishers, Montclair, N.J.) A teacher-researcher documents the learning of children in one primary-school classroom during one year, with particular attention to writing, art, pattern, and play.

Atwell, Nancie. "Writing and Reading Literature from the Inside Out." *Language Arts* 61 (March 1984): 240–52. An eighth-grade teacher examines the growth of two students' personal responses to reading.

Bissex, Glenda L. *GNYS AT WRK: A Child Learns to Write and Read*. Cambridge, Mass.: Harvard University Press, 1980. A parent-researcher describes one child's development, from age five through ten, as seen through his activities at home and at school.

———. "The Child as Teacher." In *Awakening to Literacy*, edited by Hillel Goelman, Antoinette Oberg, and Frank Smith. Portsmouth, N.H.: Heinemann Educational Books, 1984. The learning styles of two young children from different family backgrounds are described and compared.

Calkins, Lucy McCormick. *Lessons from a Child*. Portsmouth, N.H.: Heinemann Educational Books, 1983. While this study focuses on the writing development of one third grader, it also discusses the teacher and the classroom.

Carini, Patricia F. *The School Lives of Seven Children: A Five Year Study*. Grand Forks: North Dakota Study Group on Evaluation, University of North Dakota, 1982. Carini documents seven modes of learning in seven children, prekindergarten through third grade, and includes useful suggestions for other researchers on ways of looking at learners.

Emig, Janet. *The Composing Processes of Twelfth Graders*. Urbana, Ill.: National Council of Teachers of English, 1971. This pioneering study of composing examines one writer in depth and seven others more briefly.

Field, Joanna. *On Not Being Able to Paint*. Los Angeles: J. P. Tarcher, 1958. In looking at her own struggles and discoveries as a learner, this psychoanalyst and educational researcher raises some fundamental questions about the creative process and about education.

Heath, Shirley Brice. *Ways with Words: Language, Life, and Work in Communities and Classrooms*. Cambridge: Cambridge University Press, 1983. The cases in this ethnographic study are two communities—a black working-class and a white working-class community—contrasted as environments in which children learn oral and written language at home and in school.

Johnston, Peter H. "Understanding Reading Disability: A Case Study Approach." *Harvard Educational Review* 55 (May 1985): 153–77. This close look at three adult readers, through interviews and observations, reveals much about social and psychological contributions to reading failure.

Perl, Sondra, and Nancy Wilson. *Through Teachers' Eyes: Portraits of Writing Teachers at Work*. Portsmouth, N.H.: Heinemann Educational Books, 1986. The authors present in-depth studies of six very different teachers and their classrooms, both elementary and high school.

Schaefer-Simmern, Henry. *The Unfolding of Artistic Activity*. Berkeley: University of California Press, 1948. This work offers intriguing studies of the artistic processes and development of mental defectives, delinquents, refugees, and business and professional people.

Selfe, Lorna. *Nadia: A Case of Extraordinary Drawing Ability in an Autistic Child*. New York: Harcourt Brace Jovanovich, 1979. This fascinating document raises the question, Why study a rare if not unique case? and suggests some reasons for doing so.

# CHAPTER 3

# A Quiet Revolution: The Power of Teacher Research

*Richard H. Bullock*

Walter Lippman, in a 1926 essay discussing majority rule and its relation to the Scopes trial in Tennessee, correctly asserted that "the votes of a majority have no intrinsic bearing on the conduct of a school. They are external facts to be taken into consideration like the weather or the hazard of fire. Guidance for a school can come ultimately only from educators." Yet sixty years later the majority—or community values, or local control, or the simple ignorance of parents who insist that their children be taught as they were taught—still dictates the agenda of most schools. The "back to basics" movement, with its plethora of reports and emphasis on drill, grammar study, and rote memorization; the conservative resurgence, with its desire to censor what students write as well as what they read; and, less dramatically, the resistance of school boards, parents' groups, and taxpayers to programs that the public perceives as innovative and therefore somehow threatening demonstrate the continuing influence of nonprofessionals on public education.

At the same time, professionals in the field of education who are not themselves classroom teachers heavily influence curricular decisions. The faculty of schools of education, heavily grounded in theory and statistical research methodology but too often lacking in primary or secondary teaching experience, not only prepare future teachers for their work in the classroom but also design teacher-preparation curricula, determining what these teachers need to know, and write, edit, and review many of the schools' textbooks, determining what the teachers will teach. School districts hire curriculum specialists to design curricula and administrators to ensure that teachers carry out the dictates of the curricula. In one way or another educational decisions are made from the top down and the outside in, and teachers carry out the educational programs designed for them by others.

Case studies and classroom-based research done by researchers who are themselves classroom teachers present a serious challenge to current and traditional education and to the public's definition of what teachers are and do. When teachers no longer depend on university-based research for their knowledge of students, they shift the locus of expertise from undergraduate and graduate schools removed from the day-to-day realities of teaching and learning to themselves as practicing teachers dealing in various ways with specific children. When they replace quantitative, positivistic research methods with case studies and careful observation, they alter the ways in which students are perceived, as individuals rather than as members of groups. When they replace curriculum guides and mandated textbooks written for a generalized student population with materials and methods they have found to be appropriate for and helpful to their students, they show that textbook publishers, with their necessary compromises to suit a broad market, and state- or district- or even schoolwide selection committees may not know how the students in their classrooms learn best. And when teachers assert their own expertise and demonstrate it through publishing research results growing out of their work in their classrooms, they force fundamental changes in themselves, their roles in the schools, and their place in society.

The changes classroom research makes in their lives are complex, exhilarating, and disturbing, as the participants in the round-table discussion in this volume (chapter 10) reveal. On the one hand, these teachers find classroom research exciting and self-validating. But on the other hand, in closely observing students as they go about their work, teacher-researchers find that they must also observe themselves, and the knowledge that results is disturbing as well as enlightening.

This sort of self-realization can often be painful, as these teachers can attest. Yet the rewards of working on classroom research clearly outweigh the anxieties and insecurities that result. By taking control over their students through studying them, teachers gain self-confidence, self-respect, and stronger self-images as teachers and as professionals. "There's a respect for what I'm doing that wasn't there before," confesses one researcher, and the pride in that statement says as much about her and her self-image as a competent teacher as it does about her effect on her school. Another declares, "I feel connected now"—connected with the profession in ways not available to teachers who passively accept the dictates and demands of others. Even when teachers become researchers for only a limited time, pursuing a firsthand research project at one stage in their career, the effects linger as they change the way they define their tasks and goals. Students and classes are no longer taken for granted but rather are seen as complex, vital entities that must be explored. When one researcher asserts, "I'll always do classroom research," she reveals her altered conception of the ways in which she has to approach her students: as individuals whose needs must be defined and met by her, not as groups to be defined by age, grade level, or scores on standardized tests, a homogeneous mass that behaves and performs according to various norms.

Teacher research demonstrates to teachers their power to assess students' needs and devise effective plans to meet those needs. In a teaching environment that constantly reinforces teachers' powerlessness and inability to act independently, teacher research provides individual teachers with proof of their own competence—a competence gained through diligent study and close observation. Doing classroom research demonstrates teachers' power to take control of their subject and their profession.

This is not to say that the renewal and confidence that grow out of classroom research are inevitably rewarded. The research presented in this volume, based on case studies of one or a few students, differs from the empirical, quantifiable research common in educational research and so may not be seen by some administrators or educational experts as research at all. The response of peers to the work is unpredictable too. As several teacher-researchers here attest, their colleagues found their research efforts threatening and even illegitimate, to the point that at least two researchers avoided mentioning their studies to fellow teachers, convinced that their efforts would be met with negative reactions. One felt that the others would dismiss her efforts as equivalent to the research done in university schools of education, which many teachers find irrelevant at best and insulting at worst. Another saw that her research activities posed a threat to the self-image of her co-workers; she avoided speaking of it because she recognized that in their eyes doing research in addition to her other duties, for no immediate monetary gain, would make the others "look bad." Here they were right; when one or two teachers in a school show that they care about their professional development beyond accumulating state-mandated credit hours, when they refuse to capitulate to the despair born of powerlessness that engenders attitudes of defensiveness and time serving, they do make their colleagues look bad, because they model professional behavior through seizing authority for their subject matter and activities.

At the same time, however, many educators understand the value of classroom research to the profession and to students. In some districts teachers may go on sabbaticals to conduct research, and in others grants are available for classroom research. The most important support comes not from money or time off, though; the teachers in this volume stress again and again the crucial importance of moral and intellectual support. One researcher's principal regularly asks how her research is coming along; another teacher is asked by her superintendent to share her findings with other teachers; a third finds for the first time other teachers who share an interest in his work. It is this sort of support that the round-table discussants mention again and again, for it is, as in all things, the approval of those we respect and love that motivates us; and while some teacher-researchers find support in their families, the greatest rewards for professional activities come from peers in the profession, along with the tangible rewards to be found in the teachers' own classrooms.

To rely on a teacher here and there, one in this school, one in that district, to achieve the meaningful changes in education that classroom research can bring is folly. As long as classroom research is seen as the province of the gifted few, who for whatever reason desire to go beyond their "normal duties" to investigate educational problems or students' minds, the teaching profession as a whole will continue on its present course. What must be achieved instead is an alteration in the ways in which teachers learn their profession and in the way schools are run. Currently most teachers attending teacher-training schools learn a great deal that has little or no bearing on their lives in the classroom; taught to rely on the studies of professional researchers and trained in how to behave in the classroom, they are given few tools with which to understand what they and their students are doing, let alone to achieve the role Miles Myers envisions for teacher-researchers "in the development of theory, in the explanation of why some lessons work and others do not" (2).

Instead, extensive training in techniques of classroom research should be part of every prospective teacher's college classroom training, and such research, carried out in the field over an extended period, should form a major requirement of the education curriculum. In graduate programs such as the Martha's Vineyard Institute on Writing, from which the first group of this volume's studies are drawn, year-long studies can be designed, monitored, and carried out through careful coordination between students teaching and pursuing their research independently, and an energetic and flexible research project adviser, who may have to rely on telephones and mail to keep track of students working hundreds of miles from the university. While the dangers of such tenuous academic arrangements are obvious, the advantages of doing such long-range and intensive studies in the context of the teachers' own classrooms are immense, as the teachers learn to do research not in a contrived situation limited by the restrictions of a standard undergraduate or graduate curriculum, and often by the students' lack of experience in the classroom, but in the course of doing their jobs, in the context in which their study has its ultimate meaning.

Such an arrangement approaches the ideal, in which learning and its application unfold simultaneously, but there are many circumstances under which this model cannot work. Undergraduate students learning to become teachers obviously have no classroom with which to work; even if they work as apprentice teachers or observers in a school, those roles differ greatly from the role they will assume as teachers in classrooms of their own and will alter the nature and results of their research as well. Further, most undergraduate and graduate curricula are based on the quarter or semester system, both of which discourage long-range investigations. Despite the difficulties, though, the basic element of classroom research, the close observation of individuals as they perform academic tasks, must be made part of the curriculum of every teacher-education program through courses devoted specifically to it. The second group of studies published here demonstrates the kinds of work that students faced with limited time can do to master research techniques and ways of seeing student behavior—techniques they can then take into their classrooms once they begin teaching. Beyond teaching techniques, these sorts of courses should impart a way of *thinking* about students and how they should be approached, about what teachers *do* in the classroom, and about what kinds of information are useful and valuable for teachers to read and to publish. Publishing—sharing results with colleagues, formally and informally—must be an ultimate base on which any classroom research course rests, as publication will determine both the scope of teacher-based classroom research and its integration into the professional lives of teachers.

This integration cannot stop at the teacher's own preparation, however. Schools must recognize the importance of ongoing research and alter their systems to accommodate it, and as with everything, accommodation requires time, money, and opportunity. Again and again the teacher-researchers represented in this volume complain that their biggest enemy was time: time to do the research and time to think about it, which for most had to be carved out of the part of their day left over after being at school and then working at home grading papers and preparing lessons for the next day. That time for reflection, for study, for professional activity that will enhance the educational experience of children and add to our knowledge should be provided by schools on a regular basis in ways by which teachers can examine their craft and art and subject *without leaving their classrooms*. Reduced course loads during research projects; paid leave to reflect on what happened; increased use of aides in elementary classrooms: these would provide a beginning. A further, deceptively simple improvement in teachers' lives might be to provide private offices, where they might spend time working and thinking without distraction. It seems curious to have to mention such a seemingly trivial proposal, but for too many teachers in too many schools, space must be shared with other teachers in department offices, or with the students themselves; the teacher wishing to think in solitude about work must leave it.

Of course, to make such changes in institutional structures requires money, and money is almost always in short supply in school districts. Acting as individual teachers, classroom researchers may get what they need through the very fact of their novelty. But what will convince administrators, school boards, and communities that classroom research is worth their support is a combination of increasing numbers of teachers doing classroom research, sharing what they have learned, demanding the respect due them, and the demonstrable improvement in teaching and learning that results from classroom research.

As classroom research by teacher-researchers spreads, whether or not it is supported by school systems, committed teacher-researchers will accomplish a manifold improvement in the teaching profession, in addition to improving our knowledge of how students learn and what works for them. Showing what teachers are capable of accomplishing pressures the less competent to improve or leave. Talking with other teachers and with school administrators about their work lessens the isolation felt by the single teacher in the closed classroom, creating a community of committed investigators. Teacher research provides unparalleled opportunities for staff development, enabling teachers to evaluate the results of their teaching and to look more critically at their own behavior, and encourages them to try new approaches. And demonstrating in those ways that teaching can be an intellectually exciting field rather than a refuge for the incompetent increases its allure. These factors, though, hinge on the effects of classroom research on a broader constituency, one that affects the nature of teaching and the conditions under which schools operate: the school administration and the community.

As teacher-researchers gain confidence in their ability through research and increased communication with their peers and with other researchers' results, they will face conflicts with principals, curriculum experts, and others who customarily decide what gets taught in the classroom and, through textbook selection, how the teaching is carried out, despite limited expertise in any discipline. As time goes by, teacher-researchers will prevail in more and more curricular decisions as they become recognized as authorities in their classrooms. In effect, the locus of academic planning will move from central administrations to the teaching staff, because expertise and authority will lie with the teachers.

The subversiveness of this assertion is difficult to emphasize, since one would expect teachers to know their subjects. The truth is, however, that teachers have never been trusted to know what they teach, and the notorious lack of rigor of college teacher-preparation curricula has provided a national teaching faculty that, like any other group in a complex society, lives up to expectations, by and large. The historical orientation of schools as structures governed from the top down has guaranteed that the substance of education is controlled not by professional educators from their own classrooms but by managers and legislators. When teachers assert their authority, they perforce demand the diminution of the power of the traditional managers and overseers of education, who are understandably unwilling to give up their power over personnel and budgets. Hence teacher-researchers must move carefully, convincing administrators and school boards by the results they achieve that everyone—students, teachers, and school systems—will benefit by such shifts of authority.

Like many simple acts, then, teacher research is finally revolutionary. Based on the results of her research project, one teacher quietly drops basal readers and their workbooks, saying "I didn't do one ditto." Another teacher, impressed by her newfound knowledge of her students' abilities, encourages her students to write essays on topics of their own choosing rather than relying on "story starters." A third, heartened by his participation in a network of fellow researchers, shares his students' essays with a few colleagues in the same school, who, astounded at the fluency and depth of the papers, begin to rethink their own pedagogy. And two others convince their principal that a certain textbook-workbook series should be replaced with blank notebooks and a story anthology by marshaling extensive documentation from professional literature to prove their point. These small acts, these little rebellions add up to a quiet assault on the entire educational hierarchy through the actions of individuals and the assertions by teachers in individual schools that they, not their supervisors or textbook companies, should determine the curricula for their subjects.

It is this quiet revolution that this collection of essays both celebrates and advertises. The teachers who present their findings in these pages had no intimation, when they began their work, that doing something so simple—watching a student or two, or a class, as they worked and learned over several months or weeks—would profoundly alter the way in which they regarded not only their students but themselves and their profession as well. Some did not realize how much they had changed until later, after their work on the case study itself had been completed. But this very absence of a preformulated agenda testifies to the nature of teacher research as a compelling and *natural* agent of change: doing classroom research changes teachers and the teaching profession from the inside out, from the bottom up, through changes in teachers themselves. And therein lies its power.

## REFERENCES

Lippmann, Walter. "Why Should the Majority Rule?" *Harpers Magazine* 152 (1926): 399, rpt. *The Essential Lippmann: A Political Philosophy for Liberal Democracy*, edited by Clinton Rossiter and James Lare. New York: Random House, 1963. 6–14.

Myers, Miles. *The Teacher-Researcher: How to Study Writing in the Classroom*. Urbana, Ill.: ERIC Clearinghouse on Reading and Communication Skills and National Council of Teachers of English, 1985.

# PART II

## Six Longitudinal Studies

# PREFACE

# Year-long, Classroom-based Case Studies

*Glenda L. Bissex*

Teachers who are sensitive observers of individual students in their classrooms, or of themselves as teachers and learners—and that includes many good teachers—are already doing informal case studies. But they may not have colleagues to share, support, and criticize their observations. Probably nothing compels them to record, write up, and in that process clarify those observations. Nor are they likely to have someone around to guide, prod, and give external validity to their efforts. The teachers, from first grade through college level, whose research is represented in this section were teachers who gained colleagues, a guide and nudger, and the necessity for writing through their participation in a year-long case-study course.

The case to be studied might be a single student or the teacher himself or herself; it might also be two or more students; or it might be a particular class and its response to a certain project or learning environment. All of these possibilities were, in fact, explored. But however many people were studied, they remained individuals, and their differences as well as their similarities were observed and valued.

Since we—the teachers participating in the course, along with myself, the guide and nudger—were all venturing into new territory and feeling our way along, I am not describing here a model course or one refined by years of teaching. This is simply the story of what happened to one group of teacher-researchers. I can envision alternative formats for such a course, each with its own distinct advantages and disadvantages. The case-study course was part of Northeastern University's Advanced Institute on Writing, which meets during the summer. Participants included teachers of writing from first grade through college level, from Lockport, New York, to Buies Creek, North Carolina. The main work of the first summer was the planning of each teacher's particular research project to be carried out during the academic year ahead.

Before that planning could proceed freely, we had to clear away a traditional conception of what "research" meant—namely, finding a question that had not previously been investigated and conducting the investigation by means of experimental and control groups. As the teachers came to accept their primary purpose as seeking to answer questions that directly affected them as teachers, they were more comfortable with their own concerns, which were further validated by the interest shown in them by other members of the case-study course. We discussed methods of observation and information gathering that would be compatible with their primary roles as teachers, such as observing and making field notes, interviewing, audio and video taping, and collecting writings for description and analysis. In addition to a common core of readings—examples of case studies—discussed during the summer meetings, each researcher compiled a bibliography of readings about her or his particular project area. During the winter, after they had done enough of their own researching to make more active use of the material, they would do this reading.

At the end of July we said our farewells with both a sense of excitement and an awareness of the long and uncharted year that stretched ahead. No teachers were from the same school or even the same city. I encouraged them to network with others who lived within a reasonable distance or who shared research concerns. Final drafts of all the case-study proposals were sent to each teacher-researcher as a first step in trying to maintain a sense of collegueship among the physically dispersed group. Aside from these, and our memories of the summer, the only official threads binding us together until the following July were our scheduled correspondence and report due dates, phone calls, and two reunion meetings. I knew from years of teaching in an external degree program for adults that students could work independently for six months and carry on an educational dialogue through the mails. But this would be a whole year.

What happened during that school year of researching is each teacher's story. Susan Kaplan's letters to me describe one teacher-researcher's experience. (For her study, "The Teacher as Learner," see chapter 4.) Susan is a junior-high teacher who was starting a sabbatical year. Her research proposal, in response to my guiding questions (in italics), looked like this:

*What is your central question?* How does a teacher function as a learner?

*What terms in the statement of your question will need to be defined?* Possibly the term "learner" will need definition since it is broader than the term "student" which is the more usual correlate with the term "teacher."

*What sub-questions will help you investigate your central question?*
What are the relationships between learning styles and teaching styles?
Are they conscious? Should they be?
Is time away from some tasks necessary for mastery of these tasks?
Do teachers learn from their students?
Does the experience of teaching improve one's interest in/capacity for learning?
Will observing oneself as learner increase empathy for other learners?
Will observing oneself as learner improve one's (my) outlook on teaching?
What methods for professional growth might be supportable based on my information/observation?—such as networking, time off, journal keeping.
Based on teachers' needs as learners, what are the best methods of presenting in-service education?
Can one increase one's capacity to learn? If so, how?

*What led you to ask this question?* I was led to ask this question primarily due to the circumstance of having a year's sabbatical leave and the desire to learn not only new information during this time, but enough about myself to see how I best learn, adapt, change, and grow. I also want to see what I've learned about myself as a teacher after I've been away from the classroom. I'm curious about how unique my observations about myself are in relationship to other teachers.

*Why do YOU think it's worth investigating? (If I understood x, then . . . )* If I better understood my own learning needs and style as well as that of other teachers, I *might*

a) be a more empathetic teacher.
b) find ways both inside and outside the classroom to keep me "fresh."
c) start/join one or more personal support groups of like-minded people to continue this personal growth process.
d) be more useful to administrators looking for improvement in teachers' professional growth.
e) be able to better utilize my time outside the classroom.
f) change careers.

*To whom else might this research be useful or interesting? (Mention everyone you can think of, including your mother, spouse, etc.)* This investigation is of definite interest to me. Members of the Ithaca Feminist Education Coalition have already expressed an interest in my process as well as my results. A friend (school psychologist) thinks this endeavor is useful and wants to discuss it. A few of the teachers I've asked for permission to interview were at least curious and expressed interest in thinking about themselves as learners. As stated, earlier, there's potential usefulness for administrators. I hope you think it's useful, Glenda.

*How will you seek to investigate the question? List all possible methods. When might you use each? (For example, continuously, at specified times of year, in a particular sequence.)*

a) Keep a learner/personal growth journal—to be written in regularly (I hope daily).
b) Interviews of teachers—I'd like to get as many as I can close to the start of the year when they are fresh from vacation. Also, I might need to speak to them again later to see if they have changed, or to gauge them against myself.
c) Interview log—keep a notebook in which the interviews are in a readable format. This will also contain my reactions to the interviewees' answers along with any connections I've made.
d) Possible teacher questionnaire.
e) Possible classroom or support group observations.

*What difficulties can you anticipate in your research?*

a) Getting honest answers about personal styles (e.g. will people say that they don't ever read or give reflective writing assignments if, indeed, they don't?)
b) Time/desire to keep accurate, readable records of all interviews.
c) Fear that I'll learn something key about myself (That's good!) but too late to relate it to others. (Overlooking items in interviews.)
d) Fear that I'll learn something key about myself that I won't like and I won't want to write about it or pursue it.
e) Ennui. Inertia.

I responded to the final draft of her proposal as I did to her later letters and progress reports by engaging in a conversation about the issues that interested me as well as advising her about her researching.

By October, when she wrote to me, Susan was deep enough into her study to find out—as the others were also discovering—just how messy researching can be: "My confusion is to the point where I'm uncertain if some of the things I have to report fall under the heading of a confirmation, surprise, or expectation." Her experiences and thoughts had led her to various conclusions:

1. It seems impossible for a person to settle on any *one* theory about anything of real importance (learning, spirituality, language, etc.).
2. I'm increasingly more convinced of the wisdom and importance of a humanities experience for my students. While a part of the day spent in "analysis" is good, a synthesis is the more profound (long-lasting) experience.
3. Reflective writing and interior dialogues greatly help me sort through a plethora of information.
4. Discussions (interpretive communities?) are my most important resource. Questioning and feedback are essential to real learning.
5. Learning is a process. (But will it aid or enrich the process in any way to analyze it, break it down and name all the steps?)
6. Both affective experience and empirical knowledge lead to (trigger?) the formation of connectedness, which is your "creative self." They are not mutually independent parts of a component organism. (Did I say that?)

I am also continually amazed at how long it takes me to break old patterns—and to establish new ones. I hope there is transfer and carry-over benefit to this process in my teaching next year. In other words, I hope this time helps me permanently break out of some real ruts.

I have confirmed—over and over—that what teachers (and learners) most lack is *support*. It is a recurrent theme and needs to be addressed on a mass scale as well as an individual one. (If they won't give it to you, you've got to go out and find some.)

I am surprised by the number of people who don't need—or at least express the need for reflexive learning and growth in "work-free" time. I'd like to know if this is a result of more physical stamina, not bringing the need to consciousness, or a real strategy that they have which might be transferred to others. (This last is my Neuro-linguistic Programming research coming through.)

I am being influenced greatly by my NLP research. It is so new, exciting, and controversial—and at the same time, some of it is so observedly true—that it is coloring my thinking about a great many things in the field of learning, education. I'm excited personally by this and don't think it will completely change my outcomes if I now change my research plan to include more outside reading and research. I still want the bulk of my findings to be based on observation and interview, but I need to bounce off of other people's theories. It is easier to compare and contrast learning styles than to invent them from scratch. If I read about a greater variety of theories, I will have a broader base of knowledge from which to work, and I will be less influenced by the one I have currently latched onto.

None of the case studies proceeded in a straight line. All the participants, as I had advised them to expect, made revisions of their original plans along the way. They revised, like Susan, as they discovered approaches to their research that they hadn't envisioned before they started. Or their initial data gathering led them to refocus their central question, as did Ferguson McKay, whose study appears in chapter 6. His original question—"What for me are effective methods to help writers see the need for details and then generate them?"—grew out of the kind of weakness he had noted in his students' writing the previous year. At the time of his case study he didn't get the type of students he'd expected. Instead he was dealing with "a large, vague group of problems visible both in an inability to write reasonably well and in an inability to get started and/or keep going on a piece." After a semester of exploratory research, he zeroed in on the teacher-writer relationship and dropped his concern for increased detail in writing in favor of any observable improvement in later drafts or in the writer's understanding of the process. His revised central question was, "What type of relationship between teacher and writer is most likely to help students who are struggling with the first steps in the writing process?" For Ferguson, discovering his question did not precede his research but rather was part of it. For other researchers, external events forced drastic changes. Judith Boyce had to scrap her proposal and start over again when she found that her students wouldn't have sufficient access to computers for her to study the effects of word processors on their writing. Some of her research, which focused instead on student commonplace books, is presented in chapter 8.

When Susan and I spoke on the phone in January, she reported gathering lots of data: she had interviewed twelve people, finding out much about herself and others, and about learning theories. The part of her study that dealt with other teachers was of less concern to her now. But she was frustrated because "it isn't coming together yet." Susan was by no means alone in this feeling. By midwinter most researchers were overwhelmed by all the data they'd collected—data that was not leading them toward a clear conclusion but rather seemed to point in many directions, or in none. I knew this disoriented feeling from my own research work. I had come through it, patterns had emerged from my material, and I believed that these teacher-researchers would likewise find meaning. But they could not believe this yet. Susan was afloat in a sea of ideas, possibilities, and questions about learning. She had observed herself as a learner, not only at lectures and workshops, as a researcher and writer, but in virtually every aspect of her life. Her observations were recorded in journals and in double-entry notebooks, with the right-hand pages for objective descriptions and the left for questions and interpretations. She had interviewed teachers. She had read a good deal and sought out varied theories of learning. Here is only some of what she distilled from those experiences and reported to me in February:

> Although a case study need not proceed by strict scientific method, I had certain hypotheses—some merely intuitions or personal prejudices—that I had wished to corroborate. They are stated here as dichotomies I hoped to resolve.

> 1. Sabbatical leaves are justifiable on the basis of personal and professional growth over time. My sabbatical leave stemmed from thoughts of leaving the profession.
> 2. People learn best when relaxed and given ample time to research, explore, digest new material. I perform best under pressure.
> 3. Most students seem to prefer teachers who have one approach to teaching (learning), state it at the outset, and stick to it all year. I always felt the best teachers were the ones who offered (not forced) several strategies for a given skill, allowing learners to experiment before settling on one that is best suited to them.
> 4. Teaching requires flexibility; personal preference and style should be modified to meet student needs. Most teachers teach to the learning style which best suits them (the teacher).
> 5. The structure and content in most schools overemphasize analysis. Learning is making connections: awareness, analysis, and synthesis need to be given more equal time/space.
> 6. Institutional individualization overemphasizes learning differences and deficits. Balance derives from attention to similarities and strengths.
> 7. Education seemed too cut off from life when it could become closer, if not life itself. There is comfort and security in the notion of education as preparation for life.
> 8. The field of education seems too subject to political whimsy; administrators, scholars, and government officials do not appear to be guided by a common philosophy. I did not have a philosophy guiding my teaching.

*Random Observations, Questions, Impressions, Confusions*

> Learning is often equated with memory. I do not watch myself remember; I watch myself connect, change, or grow.

> I have been looking up and toying with the terms "style," "strategy," and "technique." They seem to come up constantly in my reading and in my thinking, but I

don't yet know what, if any, their importance is to my research.

Whenever I have found a brief "test" to discover a learning style, I take it. Based on a few different theories, I can term myself an intuitive, sensory generalist, emotionally involved but explicitly structured, collaborative, eclectic learner.

As a classroom learner I need to be allowed to make connections. Classroom dialogue is most helpful. I have also discovered the joys of annotating, and double entry notebooks.

I love the pre-writing stage to the point of getting stuck in it. I avoid the writing stage by postponing it: There is always more research to do, more people to speak with, other points of view to be considered, more connections to be pondered. During the writing phase I tend to edit prematurely. I want all the patterns to emerge early on and my writing (and probably my life) suffers from this.

I resent classroom experiences which cut me off from people as resources. I realize that I want education to prepare me for life, not be it, if being it means that I must face all the tasks alone, getting feedback only in the end in the form of a grade, success or failure. I believe in product, but only after help with the process.

Oh, to keep remembering how I respond to praise and success! The positive comments on my writing will enable me to think about the negative ones.

From the study of creative visualization I have learned to change my internal state and have this manifest externally. Mapping goals helps enormously. I enjoy and profit from imagining my goals as fully represented. I want to try this with students.

It is difficult to break old habits. Bad patterns emerge when a new, difficult task is being tried. Awareness seems to be the key here, for both teacher and learner.

The two needs of teachers as echoed in my interviews are for time and support. Administrators seem to have forgotten about praise and success as the main motivators.

Most teachers seem to have one learning experience which they remember above all others, but only a few can make any connections between this experience and their current teaching practices. Even these connections don't appear to fall into any patterns.

Susan's one-year case study was threatening to become a lifetime project. Eventually she and others learned that what they already knew about writing applied to researching as well: you have to generate more material than you need and throw some away in order to get a product with shape and focus.

At an early spring meeting of almost the entire group, I became aware of a sense of disappointment among these researchers: they had not made breakthroughs or arrived at earth-shattering conclusions, and they felt that this meant failure. They were relieved to find that they were not alone in their feelings or falling short of some expectation I had for their studies. We talked about cutting off their data gathering in April so they'd have time to reflect on what they'd collected and write up their research reports. But how to organize all that data they were drowning in? Out of the combined probing and wisdom of our discussion, I developed these possibilities, each emphasizing a different aspect of the data:

1. Organize by the individuals studied. Tell all about one individual and then all about the other(s), perhaps making comparisons and contrasts as you go along, or at the end. This organization emphasizes individual characteristics and differences.

2. Organize your material by issues or categories. These might well coincide with your subquestions. This scheme will emphasize the answers to those questions.
3. Organize chronologically. This scheme would emphasize development or changes over time.

These schemes aren't necessarily mutually exclusive. For example, if you were describing two individual students throughout the year, you might choose to organize your report basically by scheme #1 (telling all about one individual and then about the other), but within the description of each individual your observations might be presented either chronologically or by categories, or even chronologically within categories (e.g., Karen's growth as a writer from September to April, as a conferencer over the same period, and finally as a reader).

The case-study reports arrived in my mailbox in June. Susan's was accompanied by a letter expressing her mixed feelings. "Done at last! Done at last! But am I, really? I have some thoughts on and questions about this paper." Most of the teacher-researchers found that the process of writing up their reports finally gave shape to their observations. "The greatest revelation was when I started writing and the pieces began to fit together," remarked Peggy Sheehan, who has more to say about her research experience in the round-table discussion (chapter 10). Susan was grieved that so many ideas she liked had to be omitted from her report:

Thoughts on the use of *repetition*. (Briefly, I always tried to avoid ever repeating myself as a teacher. Now I see it as a very valuable tool for emphasis in both teaching and writing—and other art forms. Aesthetically, it is comforting/reassuring. I think it has the same effect on students.)

Classical rhetoricians emphasized *honesty* and I see cause to return to this emphasis, if not to other strictures of classical rhetoric. Too much planning, too little feedback before "final" evaluation, and one-person audiences encourage dishonest, facile writing.

School as a place to prepare for life and not life itself. (Mainly I got insight from classes I took this year and how they were structured that "This is how it is in the real world" is a DIScouraging phrase even on the graduate level, ridiculous on the elementary/secondary level.) Why not do things over? Why not work with other people?

Also there are lots of learning/writing strategies which I have collected from my readings which I tried and liked. Some of them are hints, some heuristics, some actual exercises.

I did not list what I see as the most useful implementation of this information, mainly because I have no control over it. But I'd love to see a pre-service education course where the first 4–6 weeks had students engaged in this process of self-observation and recording. During this period, readings would be assigned (like those in *The Making of Meaning*) and students would record notes and reactions and questions in double-entry notebooks. The rest of the semester would work through traditional learning theories, but the students would react from a personal, first-hand knowledge.

Susan regretted making practically no use of the teacher interviews, although her proposal for a preservice course very possibly grew out of the disappointing results of those interviews.

I was unprepared for the exhilarating energy that seemed to lift this pioneer group of teacher-researchers right off the ground—and their guide and nudger with them—when they came together again in July to share their research with each other and with the new group of case studiers. In place of their earlier feelings of inadequacy and uncertainty as researchers, their bewilderment or disappointment with their work, was a sense of pride and excitement at what they and their fellow teacher-researchers had accomplished. Their enthusiasm was contagious, inspiring those who were about to embark on their own case studies. "I'll never stop doing classroom research!" exclaimed Jane Richards with a grin, as she reported on her study (see chapter 9). Indeed, the very setup of the case-study course with its year of independent work may have contributed to this feeling, which was widespread among the group. The following year Liz Cornell (see chapter 7), who was engaged in a new research project, commented that working alone so much had thrown her on her own resources and made her more independent. Carol Avery, still researching too, agreed that working alone makes you believe in yourself more, and, she reflected, the absence of frequent meetings and directing made it easier for her to continue researching in her classroom after she finished her study of Traci (chapter 5). She didn't feel lost when the course was over.

Having heard from still more of these case studiers about their current explorations, I know that this is not the end but the beginning of the story of one group of teacher-researchers.

# CHAPTER 4

# *T*he Teacher as Learner

*Susan Kaplan*

Since Susan Kaplan's letters have been quoted to illustrate how these long-term case studies evolved, it is fitting to lead off with her report. It is also fitting because this is a book about teachers as learners. Susan observed herself while actively engaged in four writing tasks involving subject-matter learning. Her observations resulted in a two-part portrait of herself as a learner, the first describing her learning style, the second analyzing her internal process. From this base of self-knowledge, she speculates on the benefits of "metalearning" for both teachers and students.

Susan entered into this research project seeking regeneration as a teacher during a sabbatical leave. "After thirteen years, I had a chance to master the three Rs: relaxation, refinement, and retooling. I knew I wanted to improve my skills, but in a way that involved less instruction, more independence. Creating my own research project might provide self-empowerment in ways that committee work and isolated experimentation had failed to do. I signed on [with the case-study course]. The group's first meeting dismayed me. We were asked to devise a research question which we could take back to our classrooms in September. Back? Classroom? Uh, oh. I seemed to be in the wrong place. But Glenda sees possibilities where the rest of us see obstacles. She was open to suggestion, exploration. She encouraged me to continue with the projects I had set out for myself—and to watch myself in the process. I did. And I learned. And I learned how I learned. And that's what the next year—and this paper—was about."

Susan ("happily") teaches seventh- and eighth-grade English and has ("delightedly") directed more than twenty-five plays and musicals in the Ithaca (New York) City School District. She holds a degree in speech and theater from Ithaca College and a master's in speech education. In addition to teaching, she has served as the writing facilitator at DeWitt Middle School and as drama reviewer for *Critique*, a monthly magazine of the arts in Tompkins County. Resting in her file cabinet are her manuscripts of unpublished plays and musicals.

The 1984–85 school year that once stretched languorously before me was over too soon. It was very different from the thirteen preceding years, all spent at the head of a class, teaching. A year's sabbatical leave afforded me time away from lesson plans, grade books, interim report letters, and ninety-nine computer-printed comments on student progress. But the doubts and questions I had about the nature and purpose of educating remained, minus the classroom "laboratory" in which to explore possible answers.

No, I had not been at a loss for ways to fill the time without a daily bell schedule: I had plans—lots of them—with space in between for ease of transition. Because there was much I wanted to learn and experience, I set out on the trail of—pardon the abused terminology—personal growth. My only hesitation was the fear that the journey would lead me so far away from the problems of teachers and students that I would choose not to find my way back in the fall.

In an attempt to pull together all my interests, I became a researcher in the unorthodox field of human science. My living room was my laboratory, my "personal growth" my data. Gathering and transforming that data into meaningful learning which I could share forced me to examine the workings of my mind. The question which focused the research was, How does a teacher function as a learner?

Observing myself as a learner was my primary task. Although there was a strangeness in objectifying myself in that way (focusing on myself meant forcing myself to be conscious of self where usually the opposite is the goal, especially for anyone, such as a teacher, who must stand in front of a group), the tasks seemed "a snap" in the fall. I was going to chart my "aha"s, the "clicks" familiar to readers of *Ms.* magazine. Early on, I discovered that little learning occurs in "aha"s. This discovery was corroborated by findings from my second task, which was to interview teachers about their teaching and learning.

## THE TASKS AT HAND

As a "learner" I was not always a "student" in the formal sense. I supplied my own curriculum—almost all of which included composing with words—even when the impetus stemmed from a university course. I planned to look at my growth as a writer in three areas: journal writing, play writing, and magazine writing. In order to have something to write about, I had to learn content as well.

I was keeping a journal mainly to record my insights into or changes in my composing process. It was to serve as an artifact of learning, my "click" book. The journal's intended audience was me; its contents were not to be made public except for selected quotes to be used in this research. Although keeping it required no content learning, I found myself reading various books on journals and diaries, some of which assigned exercises to improve or expand one's journal writing. The study itself involved reading about learning theory, classroom-based research, creativity, and research methodology.

In the second area, play writing, I undertook two very different chores. The first was to rework an original Broadway-style libretto I had completed with a musical collaborator. The purpose was to pare it down for an audience of children, to make it a more commercially viable product. The second play was also a collaboration, but nonmusical and begun from scratch. The motivation was not economic but a desire for personal expression. The plot derived from my coauthor's experience and involved episodes of madness.

The magazine article was a requirement in a graduate course. I wrote it under the guidance of a professor emeritus who also authored the textbook. I chose to write about neurolinguistic programming (NLP). Like any reporter I sought a "slant" for the story along with answers: What is it? Who is using it and why?

My starting premise, or hypothesis, was that writing begets writing, and that practice and improvement in any one of these areas would lead to improvement in the other areas. This idea was only partially borne out. As writing is not generic, neither is learning. It is often task specific and idiosyncratic. I had to account for this when observing myself attempting to master both skills and content.

In addition to the four writing tasks, I was involved in other "personal growth" activities in a more informal way. These included classes in various movement and relaxation techniques (yoga, Feldenkrais, Alexander), reading about and practicing creative visualization, and a program of weight control. Since, of course, I couldn't separate my learning into neat compartments, some of my observations stem from my "work" in these areas as well.

## DETERMINING DIRECTION: DIFFICULTIES AND DECISIONS

Settling on the tasks and content was not difficult, and for a few weeks I thought that going about my business—of learning, observing, interviewing, and recording—would yield sufficient data to constitute a study. But questions interrupted the process. What would I observe? Was I not learning all the time? If I hadn't had a "click" in two weeks, what evidence would I have of "learning?" What *is* "learning?"

In order to formulate answers to these questions, I retrieved information stored in my memory from my undergraduate years. In doing so, I recalled research on memorization of nonsense syllables from an educational psychology course. By remembering it, I "learned" it, but neither the memory nor the content was of value to me. I was not interested in "learning" as a linear process of gain, retain, retrieve. This had no relation to my desire to improve my writing skill or to get insight into my process of understanding or creating meanings. Sense, not nonsense, was one of my intended outcomes; understanding, not memorization, was another.

I further recalled studying the theories of Piaget and Bruner concerning common developmental trends among students. A little review reminded me that they had looked at characteristics in four domains: physical, social, emotional, and mental. This review was useful to me in two ways. First, in hindsight I recognized that theories had been put into practice by creating expectations of students at a certain age ("common trends"). The result made instruction more uniform, the outcome conformity. In observing myself, I wanted to concentrate more on uniqueness, ways in which I differed from other learners. I hoped this experience could help to make instruction more diverse, the outcome diversity. Articulating my bias helped me to keep it in check, to try less subjective reporting. Also, I recognized that in observing how one learns, it is unavoidable to uncover the converse: how one fails to learn. My successes ("clicks") would have little meaning without my failures ("thuds?").

When I made note of these initial musings, I saw the words *linear* (an acronym for "I learn"), *form*, and *shape* and knew that these would be invaluable to me. In what way remained to be seen. But in shaping the language—and noting its shape—I was "learning": gaining insight, changing perceptions, and motivating myself to go on. There might not be enough information for a short-answer test, but my research had direction.

Further direction came from bearing in mind my two subquestions: (1) Is knowledge (consciousness) of one's personal learning style/process of value to a teacher? learner? (2) What are the relationships between learning styles and teaching styles?

I hoped that observing myself and interviewing teachers in an attempt to answer my main question—How does a teacher function as a learner?—would result in data-based knowledge; to me, however, this would not be sufficient reason for having spent ten months on an activity. The value claims that would result from answering the two subquestions would extract purpose from the data. This was just cause. I was on my way.

## METHODOLOGY

My data collection took four forms: journal entries, self-inventories, subject-matter notebooks, and interview transcriptions. (As I underwent change—"learned"—so did the forms of record keeping.)

The journal entries recorded "clicks" and "thuds." They also included lists of events, particularly those related to the four forms listed above; but soon almost everything seemed to relate, and it became difficult to exclude any experience from the journal. My reactions to events were also noted with little effort to remain "objective." There were also questions which seemed to arise endlessly. In addition I used the journal to try exercises—or heuristics—suggested in my readings. For example, I used treasure maps as suggested in *Creative Visualization* (Gawain, 106–7) to help set goals. I used several techniques from *The New Diary* (Ranier) to try to get through obstacles to writing and learning. Drawings and diagrams of various sorts were based on such divergent writings as *A Life of One's Own* (Field) and *Educating* (Gowin). Finally, I tried to record feedback, both explicit and implicit, from collaborators, teachers, classmates, friends, and later, students.

In September I received a copy of *The Teaching and Learning Process* by Terry Blue. This NEA booklet provided several self-exploration exercises designed to give teachers an opportunity to evaluate their views on various components of the instructional model. As I read, I took each test. I used these again as posttests in May.

Other inventories come from *Meta-cation* (Jacobson) and *Discover* magazine (McKean, 40–41). I recorded my answers to these as I discovered them, but I did not posttest myself.

At first I decided to keep different subject-matter notebooks in order to separate my skill acquisition (writing tasks) from my fact accumulation (content). These notebooks initially contained just notes and/or quotes about a given subject. By the end of October, I had altered the nature of these books.

Two of the notebooks are double entry. In the "Learning Theory" notebook I copied quotations or paraphrased sections from my reading on the right-hand pages. On the facing pages I wrote reactions to or questions about the material written on the right. I might add to the personal responses on the left at any time. This notebook also includes correspondence with Glenda Bissex concerning progress and problems on case-study research. In the "Madness" notebook the right-hand pages include copied quotes, articles cut from periodicals, and notes from private discussion and public forums. The left side was used as in the "Learning Theory" notebook.

My play scripts are annotated so that my reactions are to the material as well as to reactions from other readers. Also, there are notes about what to change, expand, or leave—my prerogative since the material on both sides is self-generated.

Hoping that the answers would supply points of comparison or contrast, I devised a three-part questionnaire for teachers, which I administered in face-to-face interviews. I asked the questions and took notes as the interviewee spoke. There were no tapes or verbatim transcriptions. Part 1 contained questions about their teaching. Part 2 was a self-inventory about educational viewpoints which I adapted, with changes, from Blue's book. This was filled out by each respondent. Part 3 contained questions about opportunities for and types of learning experiences.

Beyond the inclusion of some anecdotes, the interview material was of little value in answering my three research questions. I had intended to match answers from parts 1 and 3 and note consistencies or discrepancies between learning and teaching styles. Part 3 was geared to discover if teachers have a fundamental philosophy guiding their teaching/learning activities. Because I had little experience in devising questionnaires, mine suffered from common amateurish problems. Most of the questions moved obliquely toward the information I wanted to gain. In order to draw conclusions from the responses, I would have to make inferential leaps, which could only lead to a faulty or false conclusion.

## OBSERVATIONS

To provide a framework for my observations, I selected a taxonomy by Rita and Kenneth Dunn. The Dunns delineate eighteen elements of learning style. Because I view this as a good but imperfect classification system, I took liberties by combining some of the elements (fifteen remain) and then by stretching some of the implied definitions to include overlooked aspects. Also, by placing unequal amounts of data in each category, I gave added weight to some areas. This was conscious, since I did not believe the elements to be of equal importance. The Dunns divided their eighteen elements into four categories: environmental, emotional, sociological, and physical.

### Environmental

This data I dealt with somewhat perfunctorily, as it was gathered with hindsight, after I had decided to use the Dunns' taxonomy, either from my memory or feedback from collaborators and friends. While I think that they are worthy of inclusion, these elements are of minor interest to me. They are:

(1) Sound—I work (write, study) best in quiet surroundings. Monotonous background noise is sometimes helpful; if I no longer hear it, I know I'm "inside" the material. I am very easily distracted by verbal stimuli—even access to a phone, stereo, or television set is a dangerous diversion.

(2) Light—I prefer incandescent to fluorescent light, but this factor is noted nowhere in my data. I feel that I can adapt readily to most normal lighting conditions and still learn.

(3) Temperature—Heat, especially artificial heat, makes me sleepy and unproductive. Also, falling barometric pressure makes it difficult for me to concentrate, and I rarely accomplish anything in periods before a storm.

(4) Design—My preference for formal or informal settings depends on the task I need to perform, although here too I feel able to adapt to either style. I did

discover that there are certain chairs or areas in my house in which I am unusually productive. Readings in NLP led me to believe that settings can be linked too strongly with particular activities and/or emotions, making it difficult to overcome these effects. For example, my desire for food seems to be "anchored" in my reclining chair. Try as I might to work in that seat, I make too many forays to the refrigerator. It's easier to change chairs than to "release" the anchor.

### Emotional

(5) Motivation/Persistence—I lumped these two elements together, since they seem to be getting at the same (elusive) trait. While I am uncomfortable with most labels (an emerging theme in discussions with my co-playwright on mental-health issues), a general tag of "motivated" or "unmotivated" seems insupportable for anyone, certainly for me.

Frequently it was difficult to assess whether my willingness to work (motivation? persistence?) was a cause or an effect of learning. For example, in December, while attending a public forum entitled "Issues in Mental Health," I thought that I finally understood the prevailing concerns on both sides of the issue (primarily ex-patients versus professionals, although the lines are not so clearly drawn) and the dilemmas both faced. The experience was almost a "click," but not quite because I had not decided which group I thought was right.

This juncture in my learning process recurred often and became of interest to me for two reasons. First, I found this state to be intrinsically motivating: I had "learned" something new, but the knowledge felt incomplete. (Closure for me implies evaluation.) In order to feel satisfied, I went home and wrote: thoughts and reactions in my "Madness" notebook, dialogue for our script. The act of writing as well as the rereading of my words added to my understanding. In other words, a learning experience motivated me to write, which helped me to make connections, which led to further learning. Motivation was both cause and effect in the learning process. Perhaps what is more important is that writing also was both a cause and an effect of learning.

Another reason why I focus on that juncture is that my tendency to evaluate has thwarted my learning as often as motivated it. This is evident in my composing process, which I described in a January entry in my journal:

> Although usually I enjoy the act—and product—of writing, I also practice avoidance of the act. Most frequently I dwell in the prewriting stage—thinking, discussing, reading, organizing ideas in my head. I wait until pressure from a collaborator or instructor—or some external force, such as a deadline—forces me to confront the blank page. Sometimes ideas start flowing then and proceed apace. But more often I interrupt the draft with editing. I tend to stop repeatedly, review, evaluate (finding faults), and revise what I've written to that point. This leads to many unfinished pieces.

So, am I motivated? There is data to support either a yes or a no answer, with but two examples cited. Is my motivation intrinsic or extrinsic? My curiosity and excitement (as in the mental-health episode) are diametrically opposed to my expressed need for pressure and deadlines. Am I persistent? Definitely. Sometimes. The one true answer, I think, is that motivation varies, even within one individual, depending upon the task, the perceived need of the learner, the setting, and probably a host of other factors.

I made several other observations about motivation/persistence—particularly about motivational strategies. Recurring frequently were notes on my positive response to praise. (I realize that this has been noted in most educational texts, but it's too important for a teacher to ever lose sight of it.) Expressions of encouragement and words of positive evaluation gave my increased energy to produce more and better work—whether reading, drafting, or revising. Conversely, I readily succumbed to perceived failure. A withering example was my sudden total loss of commitment after my professor tore into my final magazine article. Even after a semester of almost continual praise, this final act of discouragement led me to abandon the reworking of the article for publication.

The use of particular phrases by perceived authorities sometimes "de-motivated" me. For example, John Gardner in *The Art of Fiction* often embeds the phrase *of course* in statements about books "every" aspiring writer has read, or about subject area knowledge, which, "of course," you have already mastered. Ann Berthoff is also overly fond of "of course" and "as you know." Giving these two authors the benefit of the doubt, I assume that they use these phrases rhetorically to invite readers in, make them feel part of the inner circle. I thought, however, that these phrases exposed the writers' assumptions about me, and when I found myself an exception to the assumption (and clearly lacking), it stopped me cold. In fact I wrote nothing for a few weeks after reading a chapter in *The Art of Fiction*.

In contrast, my competitive nature was stimulated when the magazine-writing professor assigned an exercise with the caution, "Probably none of you can do this." Although I am sure that this approach would not always work, that challenge motivated me to produce one of my best compositions of the semester. Further, when I described this episode to an NLP practitioner during an interview, he suggested that I rely not so much on the strategy (challenging words) for motivation as on fully recalling the success it engendered. I have tried this procedure and it works! My ability to recall, in detail, past successes in a given endeavor has motivated me to get over obstacles and try again. (Yes, I am persistent.)

Finally, talking to someone about a topic, especially if there is a lively interchange which may include disagreement, often motivates me to read/research/write. This aspect is taken up more fully below, under sociological elements.

(6) Responsibility—I am generally a responsible learner. Some of this involves my reaction to extrinsic motivation: if I promise work to another, or if there is a

firm deadline, or if I think that anyone else is counting on my contribution, I feel compelled to complete my task. If, for some reason, I fail, I take responsibility for what I did not do or learn.

(7) Need for Structure—In this area too there are discrepancies which render classification of my style difficult. For instance, I prefer to be given specific directions and/or guidelines if the task I am working on is assigned to me. Since the material to be learned or the product by which I must prove that I learned did not originate with me and will be evaluated by the assigner, I like to have explicit instructions about what is expected. This desire is reiterated in my correspondence with Glenda Bissex (see the preface to this part).

Yet feedback from peers and teachers often refers to my creative response or originality. My musical collaborator was usually surprised by my ability to create tension by writing lyrics to his melodies so that the meaning ran counter to the tone he had established. My university professor registered surprise when I outlined the disorganization of an article he had assigned us to analyze.

In areas where I am more skilled—the verbal side—I can shake limits and produce something "creative." In areas where I am more limited—for example, scientific laboratory work—I need more structure and am less likely to produce original responses.

Desire for specificity does not override my need for choice. I especially appreciate being offered choices of strategy in all areas. For me this means modeling; I like to be shown how others have proceeded with similar tasks so that I may select the method most comfortable for me, or create a new method by combining elements from two or more models. In a classroom situation I am frustrated by attempts to keep students from knowing how their colleagues are proceeding. In my evaluation of the magazine class, I stated my resentment at being cut off from possible models among my peers in a learning situation.

A person's need for structure has implications for his or her ability to take risks, a point not addressed by the Dunns. An important theme I was exploring in my play writing was that of individuals facing their fears, specifically the fear of being different and of being out of control. During the period of this study, I made the connection between this theme and a similar one in the learning process. Learning too involves risk taking. If proof of learning is a product—knowledge that was not previously part of a person—then there must have been a time of not knowing. Not knowing, or ignorance, is usually thought of as shameful. There is some point in the process when I must face my own ignorance and shame in order to overcome it. This is early in the process and partly or wholly unconscious, but it is analogous to Carlos Castaneda's Don Juan stepping off the mountain into an abyss—a very heady and frightening prospect. Perhaps the Dunns omitted this issue because it falls in that fuzzy region between style and process, a distinction I will discuss later.

## Sociological

(8–11) Relating—This category concerns the ways in which students achieve best in response to other people. The Dunns provided six possible preferences: with peers, alone, in a pair, on a team, with an adult, or in a variety of patterns. In considering these categories in relation to myself as an adult learner, I collapsed the choices to four, combining "with an adult" with "in a pair," and "with peers" with "on a team."

My preference for collaboration should be clear to anyone reading about my projects and the methods by which I collected data. Both my plays were written collaboratively, although the condensing and restructuring was a solo effort, as yet incomplete. Journal writing and case-study research I undertook alone. Yet even in the independent projects, an element of collaboration emerges; even when working alone I created a dialectic. I interviewed people for both this study and my article on NLP. Double-entry notebooks and annotation were techniques that enabled me to establish dialogue with material.

I am capable of working alone, and actually prefer it when reading, drafting, or studying, but am happier when collaborating. The interaction and creative tension are energizing. In collaboration, feedback is frequent, focus is sharper, questions are more likely to receive answers.

## Physical

(12) Perceptual strengths—I became fascinated by the importance of perceptual styles during my research on NLP. The task of NLP is to discover the uniqueness of each person in how she or he experiences the world. This discovery relates to individual perception and sequencing in three modalities: visual, auditory, and kinesthetic. Because these modalities were key components in a body of knowledge I found pragmatic and compelling, I used several methods to try to ascertain my dominant sensory system.

My sociological orientation (described above) indicates a strong auditory component. I establish dialogues, need feedback, like to talk over projects with collaborators or interested third parties: all verbal/auditory activities.

A linguistic analysis yielded mixed results, with a slight emphasis on the kinesthetic mode. According to NLP, the use of certain "predicates" is indicative of internal processes. For example, *see*, *notice*, and *appear* are visual terms; *hear*, *loud and clear*, and *ring a bell* are auditory terms; and *feel*, *touchy*, and *smooth it over* are kinesthetic terms. In my speech I use kinesthetic predicates most frequently. In my writing the terms are more evenly distributed, with visual terms getting slightly more use.

I asked a few people to record my eye-movement responses to questions that required sensory recall, but the results, again, were inconclusive.

I listed my favorite activities, which include play directing, going to the movies and theater, cooking, listening to music, and dancing. These represent an appeal to all three modalities.

Finally I referred to one of the questions I had asked in my teacher interviews: Can you recall a best-ever learning experience? If so, tell about it. This elicited fascinating (if not always useful) responses. My recollection was of a dance class in which a different artistic creation was brought in and discussed in each session as a stimulus for our own choreography. The stimuli included recorded music, sculpture, paintings, instruments, and natural objects. The interrelationship of all the arts—and the common elements in creation—was a powerful lesson for me. While dance is primarily a kinesthetic art form, my other senses became actively employed in the learning process.

These observations and recollections led me to believe that I have no dominant modality and can adapt to a variety of sensory input.

(13) Intake—According to the Dunns, "A need to eat, drink, nibble, or chew, or snack when studying, concentrating, or trying to internalize is also part of how some people learn" (240). My dependence on food for gratification has lessened as I have worked through a weight-loss program. So I understand this need but feel that it can be interrupted or satisfied some other way. (The role of physical "anchors" in relation to food and study was briefly discussed above under Design.)

(14) Time of Day—I am a night person. All of my long spurts of productivity and creativity occur after supper, often into the wee hours. I like to read early in the morning and write late at night.

(15) Need for Mobility—Although I dislike feeling confined, I can sit still for long periods if necessary. I have no problem with either hyperactivity or short attention span.

After analyzing and assessing my learning characteristics according to the Dunns' a priori taxonomy, I had only a partial picture of how I function as a learner. I indicated mostly strong preferences or trends under each element, but I know that I can be flexible in almost all of these areas. In fact, my ability to adapt to circumstances is a trait I cherish above all those I have noted. What, then, is represented by those fifteen elements? They are elements of style—the observable, external manifestations of learning. Style is personal and idiosyncratic, but it is also mutable and often conscious. The fifteen elements present a picture that is all style but hints at substance. The substance of learning theory is process, the internal system of creating meaning from bits of information and chunks of knowledge. Process is also personal and rarely conscious but may also have elements that are generalizable or universal.

In seeking to know my learning process, I had to transform and/or arrange my data another way. I found no outline comparable to the Dunns'; there are visual constructs (models), however, that attempt to give the process a shape. I am sympathetic with the need to create a form for this knowledge, for forming is learning. But I cannot use the existing models to represent my process. The linear models represent the learning process as a unidirectional sequence, a chain with links added on to one end. If, as Piagetian theory states for children and NLP implies for adults, I have a specific, repeatable sequence for gaining knowledge, I have not as yet uncovered it.

A cyclical model shows a recurrence of elements and a continuity that don't allow for a fixed point of origin. These characteristics have greater resonance with my data, but I also reject a cyclical model because it still implies a repeatable sequence of events.

Bob Gowin uses a *Vee* to represent the structure of knowledge, a shape only partially useful for me. A *Vee* does show the narrowing that occurs as one focuses on a record or event, while at the other end it reveals the broadening as one "opens up" and allows the new (information/experience) to mingle with the old. Also the two sides represent a kind of tension that exists in the dialectical—a recurring component in my process. Gowin insists in his books that there is interaction between the two sides, and I applaud his mention of this element; but I do not see the interactive nature of learning represented in the structure. Also, the *Vee* is hierarchical, suggesting not only a sequential process but one that withholds power rather than granting it.

Before I provide a visual metaphor for my learning process, I want to record some of the elements that make it up. They are listed below in a linear sequence, but reordering, interruptions, recycling, omissions, and repetitions would render this a fictional sequence and unrepeatable.

1. Need—At some point of entry on a moving field, I sense a void, a gap, or a blur. There is an event I cannot recognize, understand, or connect to previous events.
2. Select—I choose whether to tend to the need or ignore it. (Sometimes I feel that the process is on "automatic pilot," but other times I see myself in control of the process.)
3. Focus—There is a period of narrowing attention, often when I pose a question to myself for which I have no answer. (Articulating the question increases clarity.)
4. Seek (Internal)—I search my memory for similarities to past events. If I retrieve something and externalize it (say it, draw it, write it down), I am more likely to return to this "bit" later. If I allow the "bits" to surface but I remain focused inward, I often "lose" them.
5. Seek (External)—I read/listen/watch/manipulate records and/or events. (I try to maintain Focus, but sometimes other Needs arise that take precedence. This interrupts any sequence and may recycle me through the listed elements one or more times.) The "bits" are either stored internally, stored externally (completely or partially written or taped), or "lost."
6. Connect—I manipulate answers to the question in relation to what I already

know. (There are aspects of personalization and transformation that make Connect different from Seek.)

7. Request—This is a seeking element also, but I am looking not for the answer but for an evaluation of my tentative answer. (My answer might be either well formed or blurry at the point of seeking feedback.)

8. Reflect—I try to get away from the question and become less focused. The reality of this component is sometimes "taken on faith"—the only method I have of affirming its occurrence is an "answer" that appears. The more usual result of Reflection (in a possible minisequence) is to . . .

9. Energize—I am refreshed to return to Seek or Connect. This component is often linked to motivation (discussed earlier as part of Style).

10. Analyze—I break down a tentative "answer" into its component parts. (This is almost always an unsatisfying but necessary element in my process—and look! We're in the midst of it again.)

11. Recapitulate/Access—I retrieve the sequence so far. For the most part, only the events that have been externalized are recapturable.

12. Evaluate—I place the element of critical assessment near the end of this list, although it is interspersed often (too often) throughout my process. (It usually serves as an interruption rather than an exit point. It frequently takes the form of self-censorship, which occurs in my desire for originality, rejection of repetition, or fight against shapelessness.)

13. Ask (the next question).

The verbs I chose to describe the elements of this process underscore its active nature. Because the elements can rearrange themselves and the learner can exert influence over the elements, the process is interactive as well. I felt a growing familiarity as I recognized recurring components, but surprise as the same components recurred in random, unique patterns.

My learning, therefore, is neither linear, cyclical, nor *Vee*-shaped. It is kaleidoscopic, with bits that are stored internally interacting with each other and an external source of light, set in motion by an observer (learner). It is a reflective process. Emergent patterns sometimes fade and then come into focus. The basic elements are finite and always the same (though all are not always used), but the results are new connections and transformation into different, often beautiful shapes.

So my flexible, eclectic learning style combines with my active, kaleidoscopic learning process to (tentatively) complete the portrait of one teacher as a learner.

## CONCLUSIONS

The question of usefulness still remains: Is consciousness of one's learning process/ style of value to a teacher? to a learner? In other words, why bother? My evaluative (read: critical) nature repeatedly interrupted periods of observation with this re-frain: Why bother? The problem seemed either too fabricated or too esoteric, the process too schizoid or narcissistic. Despite the elements of truth in some of these early doubts, I am glad that I persisted to the point of trying to integrate my observations with my readings.

In short, my answer is yes to both parts of the question, although I feel more certain (and have more support) about the value for teachers than for learners. Before I elaborate on the value, I need to interject a note of caution by returning to my doubts.

Watching myself in the act of learning led to a disorienting change in per-ception. The nature of the disorientation was akin to that which occurs in figure-ground reversal: at first it is fun to discover the two flip-flopping images, but then the organism yearns for integration. Sometimes the learner is in the foreground being watched, but then a consciousness creeps in asking, "Who is watching me?" If the answer comes back, "I am," then the observer is in the foreground. While the split—"going-meta" in NLP jargon—is consciousness expanding, it is tolerable only on a temporary basis. I am not trained in psychology, but the experience was sometimes weird enough that I could imagine problems resulting from being required to go into this state of disintegration. Nevertheless, I could envision enjoying the study of self to the point of getting stuck in it (narcissism). Those teachers who fail to look, however, are the ones most likely to get stuck.

I found the process of observing myself more humbling than egocentric. Pullias and Young recognize this as but one positive result of a personal-growth journey:

> If [a teacher] ceases to grow as a learner, he is in danger of becoming just a trainer who is arrested in his own development. . . . The teacher learns about himself and his own inadequacies and develops humility in the presence of a greater awareness of the far reaches of knowledge. Instead of merely transmitting information, he gets a re-flection of the meaning of knowledge and learns to teach with a purpose.   (205–6)

For a teacher, continued growth and insight (learning) are essential to achieving that sense of purpose.

The process itself gave me a greater appreciation for researchers in the social sciences. Every aspect of the method is more complex than in the physical sciences, from deciding where to focus to shaping the data into meaningful results. But I can also be a better evaluator of both case-study and experimental research. I am likely to look for new educational research, and to assess its "truthfulness" and practicality, at least for me. This outcome would be beneficial to any teacher.

Another useful change that I underwent concerned my viewpoint on human behavior. In the pretest inventory on this topic (Blue, 16), I agreed with almost all of the statements, even though they represented ideas from divergent philos-ophies. According to another self-test I took (McKean, 40–41), this result was indicative of my left-brain orientation. Blue's analysis didn't allow for such a quick labeling. He explained that the "quiz" represents the views of behaviorists and phenomenologists. and an inability to choose between the two orientations is a "common problem." He did, however, underscore the importance of the choice:

> The acceptance of either model to the exclusion of the other, or the nature of the combination one personally creates, may have important implications for one's everyday professional life. More importantly, teaching is an activity which should emerge from some conceptualization of how learning occurs. It is the responsibility of each individual to clarify his/her viewpoint on this process. (71)

I took Blue's admonition to heart and embarked on a study of learning theories. I learned from my reading, but not one or a combination of all these writings had the same impact as my own observations. The meaningfulness of firsthand learning is a lesson that cannot get too much reaffirmation for teachers. By the way, on my posttest I had joined the ranks of the phenomenologists. This is an orientation I can support because of the internal harmony I have experienced with its findings. When I act on my theories in the fall, I will retest their educational adequacy.

In *Educating*, Bob Gowin asks us to look at what we know and value "and try to understand how we got that way. When you have learned to do this for yourself, then you can begin to help your students to do the same thing" (150). Gowin echoes the Socratic injunction to "know thyself." In short, we cannot teach what we do not know. If we want to empower students by encouraging autonomous learning—the ultimate goal of educating in my view—we need to know more about the nature of learning and knowledge. And it is best to start with ourselves.

Knowledge of learning process has provided me with both a theoretical and a practical basis for curriculum selection. Materials need to be harmonious with the learning process while allowing for unique ways of perceiving experience. As a teacher I need to be even more flexible than the materials—flexible enough to discard them when they are not fulfilling their promise, or to supply alternatives to a few students who can't or won't adapt to the idiosyncrasies of the material.

My experience also gives me greater empathy for students. My return to the other side of the desk and my attempts at writing remind me how difficult and frustrating learning and composing often are. I have been thinking about the scariness of confronting one's own ignorance; that is what is mirrored on those blank papers. I would like to work on ways to ease that transition, to forestall shame or paralysis by anticipating its possibility. My observations further reinforce the notion that nothing succeeds like success and that praise must be sincere but frequent.

These are some of the benefits to teachers. But can students find value in studying their own learning process? Ann Berthoff acknowledges that consciousness of process is worthwhile for both groups when she writes that "we can learn or teach better if we know how learning any one thing is related to learning anything else." I add another cautionary note here: if we are to respect our uniqueness and individuality, we must make these connections for ourselves, and not assume that our method is universally generalizable. As (if?) more people not only analyze their learning styles and processes but also share their findings, I predict that similarities will be evident, but the differences will be startling. This may persuade us to have greater patience with the idiosyncrasies of students. Teachers will generate and value larger (internal) catalogues of strategies to stimulate and aid the learning process.

If consciousness of the learning process—or learning how to learn—is of value to a student, then the implication for educators is that this "skill" should be taught. If "metalearning" becomes part of the curriculum, teachers will be impelled to find some methods for understanding and articulating the process. Blue believes, and I concur, that "the quality of teaching can only be enhanced when teachers think through the question of the nature of the learning process they want to promote in students" (20).

Finally, I present an optimistic continuum based on more aware students (learners). Consciousness of how they learn should make schooling easier. Persons who can articulate their needs are more likely to have those needs met. Also, the element of "going inside" and tapping into internal resources may be a source of strength previously outside the awareness of many learners. This might lead naturally to a desire for externalizing knowledge—to hold it or share it—and writing is the most obvious method for achieving this purpose. Sharing these products may encourage more openness about individual differences, strengths, and weaknesses, which can only increase our humanity and help create a more tolerant society.

What are the relationships between learning styles and teaching styles? Before undertaking to answer this question, I must admit to the biases I had at the start of this study. When I formulated the question, I assumed that alignment of learning and teaching styles was both possible and desirable. If we matched learners with teachers and materials that favored their styles, many of our educational problems would be solved. Although my data directly assess neither the area of teaching style nor the question of alignment, working through this process has changed my attitude.

My assumption was first shaken by Joseph Williams, a guest lecturer at Cornell University from the University of Chicago. In a talk delivered to writing teachers (from kindergarten to graduate school) he spoke of various student learning styles in relation to their growth in writing. Williams indicated that during the period of mastering difficult new content, bad attitudes surface in writing. He acknowledged this as a phase of learning not to be dealt with foolishly by grouping students based on their apparent deficits or stylistic preferences ("relativists to the right; dualists to the left"). The implication was that as they learn, students are more likely to adapt and change.

Similarly, a few studies published in the January 1979 edition of *Educational Leadership* decried efforts to match teaching and learning styles. Richard Turner lauds the public-school system for not attempting this match.

If style is observable behavior based mainly on performance, it can be changed to adapt to situational demands. For teachers this means being cognizant of their usual style and willing to change it in order to adapt to the needs of learners. This should be a conscious goal for teachers and one they might encourage for students. I now recognize that curriculum, milieu, and style are elements that can be brought under my control. But I want any changes I make to be based on defensible theories of human learning, growth, and development.

An English teacher I interviewed recounted her "best-ever learning experience." A college professor brought in a cottage-shaped teapot as a horrible example of form not flowing from function. This experience had a lasting impact on her artistic and professional life and can serve as a metaphor for us as well. Teaching style is a form that must emerge from its function: to serve the educational needs of a variety of learners. Understanding learning process should lead to an increased willingness to acquire a variety of styles.

## REFERENCES AND RELATED SOURCES

Atwell, Nancie M. "Class-Based Writing Research: Teachers Learn from Students." *English Journal* (January 1982): 84–87.

———. "Writing and Reading Literature from the Inside Out." *Language Arts* 61, no. 3 (March 1984): 240–52.

Avery, Carol S. "Young Writers Learning to Read: Three Case Studies." Unpublished paper, Northeastern University Summer Institute on Writing, August 1983.

Berthoff, Ann E. *Reclaiming the Imagination*. Upper Montclair, N.J.: Boynton/Cook, 1984.

———. *The Making of Meaning*. Upper Montclair, N.J.: Boynton/Cook, 1981.

Bissex, Glenda, *GNYS AT WRK: A Child Learns to Write and Read*. Cambridge, Mass.: Harvard University Press, 1980.

Blue, Terry W. *The Teaching and Learning Process*. Washington, D.C.: National Education Association, 1981.

Brande, Dorothea. *Becoming a Writer*. Los Angeles: J. P. Tarcher, 1934.

Calkins, Lucy M. *Lessons from a Child: On the Teaching and Learning of Writing*. Portsmouth, N.H.: Heinemann Educational Books, 1983.

Clay, Marie M. "Looking and Seeing in the Classroom." *English Journal* (February 1982): 90–92.

DiYanni, Robert. *Connections: Reading, Writing, and Thinking*. Upper Montclair, N.J.: Boynton/Cook, 1985.

Dunn, Rita S., and Kenneth J. Dunn. "Learning Styles/Teaching Styles: Should They . . . Can They . . . Be Matched?" *Educational Leadership* 36, no. 4 (January 1979): 238–44.

*Educational Leadership* 36, no. 4 (January 1979).

Emig, Janet. *The Composing Processes of Twelfth Graders*. Urbana, Ill.: National Council of Teachers of English, 1971.

———. *The Web of Meaning: Essays on Writing, Teaching, Learning, and Thinking*. Upper Montclair, N.J.: Boynton/Cook, 1983.

Field, Joanna. *A Life of One's Own*. Los Angeles, Calif.: J. P. Tarcher, 1981. (Distributed by Houghton Mifflin, Boston, Mass.)

Fischer, Barbara Bree, and Louis Fischer. "Styles in Teaching and Learning." *Educational Leadership* 36, no. 4 (January 1979): 245–54.

Gardner, John. *The Art of Fiction*. New York: Alfred A. Knopf, 1984.

Gawain, Shakti. *Creative Visualization*. Toronto: Bantam Books, 1978, and *The Creative Visualization Workbook*. Mill Valley, Calif.: Whatever Publishing, 1982.

Gowin, D. Bob. *Educating*. Ithaca: Cornell University Press, 1981.

Graves, Donald H. "Writing Research for the Eighties: What Is Needed." *Language Arts* 58, no. 2 (February 1981): 197–206.

Jacobson, Sid. *Meta-cation*. Cupertino, Calif.: Meta Publications, 1983.

Kamler, Barbara. "One Child, One Teacher, One Classroom: The Story of One Piece of Writing." *Language Arts* 57, no. 6 (September 1980): 680–93.

Maslow, Abraham H. *Toward a Psychology of Being*. Princeton: Van Nostrand, 1962.

McKean, Kevin. "Of Two Minds: Selling the Right Brain." *Discover* 6, no. 4 (April 1985): 30–41.

Novak, Joseph D., and D. Bob Gowin. *Learning How to Learn*. Cambridge: Cambridge University Press, 1984.

Pullias, Earl V., and James D. Young. *A Teacher Is Many Things*. Bloomington: Indiana University Press, 1968.

Ranier, Tristine. *The New Diary: How to Use a Journal for Self-Guidance and Expanded Creativity*. Los Angeles: J. P. Thatcher, 1978.

*Theory into Practice* 19, no. 3 (Summer 1980): "Learning to Write: An Expression of Language. A journal of the College of Education, The Ohio State University.

# CHAPTER 5

# Traci: A Learning-Disabled Child in a Writing-Process Classroom

*Carol S. Avery*

Like "The Teacher as Learner," this study focuses on learning style. Carol Avery decided to study Traci because "she had already spent one year in my classroom, was going to be with me again, and was such a unique learner that I knew I could learn a lot from her." The research affirmed for Carol "something I have always believed but maybe never trusted enough: all kids (barring severe mental impairment or trauma) can learn to read—or even more basic, all kids can learn—and that a key ingredient in their learning is the environment which supports and maintains their natural momentum for growth."

Carol has taught first grade for ten years in the Manheim Township School District in Lancaster, Pennsylvania. She holds degrees in library and elementary education from Millersville University and has completed further graduate work in English and writing. She lives in Millersville with her husband and their younger son; their elder son is married. Before teaching first grade she was a school librarian, high school English teacher, and substitute teacher.

Since doing her case study, Carol continues to be a teacher-researcher. "I look at everything that happens in my classroom and write and write and write about it. My teaching keeps evolving as I write and see and discover and learn from my students. They are such wonderful teachers! I think the disciplined work with Traci established patterns for me that continue. The research experience validated this way of looking at and learning from what happens in my classroom. I find myself talking with my students not only about *what* we learn, but about *how* we learn."

I first met Traci when she visited my classroom in June preceding her September entry into first grade. She smiled demurely at me and snuggled under my arm, much like a three-year-old visiting her grandmother or favorite aunt, and was oblivious to the surrounding bustle of activity. A small cluster of children gathered around us and asked, "Who's she?"

When I asked Traci to respond, she produced a slurred jumble of indecipherable baby talk. Despite my assistance and encouragement, she could not enunciate her name clearly. I introduced her to the children. She smiled; they petted her affectionately as they might a toddler. She was shorter in stature than they, but it was more her demeanor and immature speech that placed her as a younger child in their minds. As Traci left the classroom, I sensed my own apprehension about her readiness for first grade in September.

Traci is classified learning disabled. Research by Donald Graves validates that the environment of a writing-process classroom has a profound effect on literacy development in young learners (Graves 1983). I myself had witnessed this growth in children when I implemented the process approach in my own classroom. Would this same environment meet the special needs of a learning-disabled child such as Traci, a child who might normally be separated from peers and the regular classroom? How well would the process approach serve a child with distinctive learning styles that demand particular teaching strategies and methods? Could that child remain with peers and function on an equal basis? How would the experience in a writing-process environment affect aspects of her learning other than writing?

Fall came, and Traci, along with her twenty-one classmates, was introduced to the procedures of a writing-process classroom. Each day the children drew in large journals of blank paper and wrote about their drawings. Some children wrote phrases or sentences using their own invented spelling. Others labeled pictures with letters to represent the initial sounds of words. Every writing period ended with a group session in which two or three children shared their writing.

Traci was bewildered. She could not locate her journal and needed daily restatement of expectations in order to proceed. Her writing consisted of scratchy drawings and indecipherable scribbles. Today, when I examine Traci's writing and recall her process during those days, I realize that Traci did understand the communicative function of written language. She was usually able to tell me what she had written, even though she rarely used alphabet letters except to write her name. She seemed unaware of the function of letters in communicating meaning. The significance of Traci's efforts is verified by the research of Harste, Woodward, and Burke into the early language understandings of young children (Harste et al. 1984).

This was the beginning of the two years Traci spent in my first-grade classroom, where I used a writing-process program adhering to the philosophies of Graves, Murray, Bissex, Calkins, and others. In this environment she was compatible with her classmates and functioned in a natural give and talk within the peer group. Traci was, and continues to be, distinctively different from her peers, yet astoundingly akin to them.

During the summer after Traci's first year, I became involved with a teacher-research project led by Glenda Bissex. A decision had been made for Traci to stay with me for another year, so I decided to study her learning process closely. I planned to log Traci's observable behaviors in the various aspects of school life, and I invited her mother to log Traci's activities at home. Records of Traci's writing and reading during both years would provide insights into her learning, as would tape-recorded conferences and interviews with her. My goal was to identify the key elements in Traci's learning process and to examine the relationship of writing process to her learning.

This article defines the essential components of the writing aspect of this classroom, describes Traci's evolution as a learner in this environment, and discusses the benefits of the process approach, especially writing process, for a child such as Traci.

## THE WRITING-PROCESS CLASSROOM

The writing-process classroom provides frequent blocks of time for children—even young children not yet reading—to compose. Initially, they use their knowledge of the alphabet to write words by listening to sounds and inventing their own spelling. The writing time is carefully structured and predictable. All the children know that each day there will be a regular time for writing. They know that they will select their own topics and receive responses to their writing. These components establish a writing community, a community that encourages each child to grow and to learn as an individual.

In Traci's classroom an hour was allotted each day to student writing. The time began with a short lesson by me on one specific skill or function of language. The writing time that followed had a studio atmosphere to it: each child wrote, discussed, revised, and edited his or her writing. At the end of this writing workshop, two or three children shared their writing with the entire group and received responses. An hour was a substantial portion of the school day, but it was time well spent. Much learning was accomplished during this time; required skills were taught, and as a result, other, more traditional modes of teaching these skills efficiently could be abandoned.

The children had an investment in their writing because they chose their own topics. The meaning they communicated was important to them because it consisted of personal experiences and knowledge. The responses they received to their writing, from both the teacher and peers, gave value not only to their writing efforts but to the personhood of each child and promoted investment in written communication. This in turn nurtured the process of written communication as well as the development of the individual writer. In this supportive atmosphere a community of writers was created.

## TRACI: THE FIRST YEAR

When Traci began first grade she was almost seven years old, but she was clearly at developmental and experiential levels well below the class norm. The other children adopted a "little sister" attitude toward her and were quick to rescue when she needed assistance. In many areas Traci clearly could not manage independently. They tied her shoes, sharpened her pencil, gathered her things at the close of school each day. While this was beneficial early in the year, it also proved to be a detriment to Traci's learning as the year progressed. Traci developed helpless behaviors in order to cope with overwhelming situations; she was competent in enlisting help with comments such as, "I can't. Will you do this for me?"

Silver describes this mechanism in learning-disabled persons as "passive-dependent. Initially the child avoids failure and unpleasant feeling by staying out of the situation that could result in failure. . . . A truly helpless child arouses sympathy in adults . . . [and] often makes people angry because the helplessness appears to be deliberate and contrived" (Silver 1984).

In November a school eye examination revealed Traci's vision to be 20/200. A new prescription for her glasses corrected this to 20/70, but the prognosis was that her vision would continue to deteriorate. Although Traci's learning difficulties are not caused by her eyesight, it became obvious that there might be some neurological connection between the vision and the learning impairments. She certainly was handicapped by poor vision in her early experiences. Harste, Woodward, and Burke discuss the important language learnings that young children extract from their environment in their preschool years (Harste et al. 1984). As a preschooler Traci probably did not see the golden arches of McDonald's until she was practically touching them. Letters in books and on billboards and signs were no doubt a blur to her. In school Traci held her head a few inches from the printed page, even after the new glasses had arrived.

In the beginning of the year Traci lacked self-confidence and needed continual support in order to understand classroom procedures. My daily, individual responses to her during the writing time were helpful but not adequate during the first weeks of school. Therefore, Traci spent a portion of the writing time each day in the resource room. The resource-room teacher and I collaborated to coordinate Traci's learning activities with those of the entire group, and she returned to the classroom each day for part of the writing time, especially the sharing time at the end of each session. After a few weeks Traci began to acclimate to procedures, and the resource-room support was phased out.

Once she understood the routines, Traci made remarkable progress. By the end of October she was writing letters in sequence to communicate meaning. Her poor coordination was a handicap in producing legible handwriting. Even Traci could not easily decipher what she had written, so I daily typed the message she wrote and pasted it under her words in her journal. She read these short sentences to me and the resource-room teacher each day. By November she was writing several sentences using correct letter-sound correlations in invented spelling and was even using conventional spelling for some words. By December she was reading print materials other than her own writing. Her favorite books were the final drafts of the children's best writing, revised and edited by the authors themselves and typed by me in standardized English. The pages were stitched into attractive covers and illustrated by the children. By Christmas, Traci had "published" two such books.

During the spring months Traci amazed everyone. She wrote and read with a passion and at year's end tested at a 2.8 grade level of reading achievement on the California Achievement Test.

Although she had made great strides in emotional and social development, Traci was still immature compared to her classmates. Her math achievement was extremely weak. In May it was decided to keep her in the first-grade writing-process environment for another year.

## TRACI: THE SECOND YEAR

### Writing

Traci came to school the first day bubbling and full of confidence. "Do you like my new shoes? Slip-ons!" she said as she pointed to her loafers. I recalled the struggles to keep her shoes tied the year before. "I'm glad I came to this class. Guess what I'm going to write about today! The beach. We went to the beach and guess what . . . a crab bited my toe! I been writing stories at home. Want me to bring some to show you?" Traci's mind was full and her thoughts tumbled out in rapid succession without waiting for responses.

I was struck by the amazing growth and maturity that had taken place in her since June. Her speech, though still filled with immature grammar and slurred pronunciations, was much easier to understand. She was eager, enthusiastic, and confident. Her familiarity with classroom procedures was obviously an asset for her, and as she moved through the day's activities, I noticed the poise with which she handled herself.

When Traci participated in a small writing group that first day, she wrote about the beach.

> This is the Bench.
> I Willy [really] Like it heRe
> I think This is goinng
> too have a goo time.
>
> Traci 9–5–84

Traci closely watched the other children, and when she saw the brevity of their initial writing efforts, she limited her own. She turned down an offer for a second piece of paper. It was obvious that Traci wanted her writing to match that of the other children.

A few days later, however, Traci was working independently at her desk, filling several pages during the writing hour. Once she began writing, she became deeply involved in the process, pausing only when she reached the bottom of each page to reread what she had written and to revise by lining out or inserting words or letters. Her drafts were more legible, her use of space was better organized, and her content clearer and better focused than it had been in June. During the first week she shared a piece about roller-skating with the class.

> all aumawt rollaskateinng By TRaci 9–6–84
> I now how to rola skate   This is how   fiRst you put one foot in frot AnD the ater foot goes in Bake   I fell a Kaper Time's   I fell on My Bute   Wien you go Dawn My hill you Miget foll I Din BuT get Back up AnD TRay aGene if you Do et tell My Moom She will wanch you if you Doet she will smill at you   The EnD

The other children, who had just begun writing one-sentence compositions, were impressed with Traci's writing and responded: "That's a good story." "You can write a *lot*!" "Yeah, that's a long story." "I like the part when you said you fell on your butt." Traci glowed as she magnanimously thanked her classmates. In the days and weeks that followed, she often brought in stories she had written at home. Sometimes these were formally shared with the group. Other times Traci conducted her own small sharing sessions during the free-play time when that began the school day. It was obvious that Traci was glad to be part of a writing community again and that she very much wanted responses to her writing.

In a September interview Traci readily acknowledged writing as her "best part of school." The regard and respect peers gave her writing further strengthened Traci's self-confidence. She led the way for the entire class in writing process during the fall months. Because she was familiar with procedures and the process of writing, she provided an excellent model for the other children as the classroom format was established. Kronick notes that in building self-esteem, it is important that the learning-disabled child be "ensured opportunities to excel in activities that are highly valued by his peer group" (Kronick 1981). Traci's competence established a trusted place for her in the writing community which, in turn, further increased her confidence.

On a typical day I closely observed Traci during the writing time.

> Sitting straight in her chair, she begins by reading yesterday's piece. When she comes to the end she says to no one in particular, "I want to scratch out 'The End.' " She does this; I anticipate she will add to the piece. But she sits still for only a minute, then gets up and goes to the pencil sharpener. On the way back she stops at Christy's desk to listen to Christy read her piece. "It's a nice story," Traci responds, and Christy explains how she will organize her piece. Traci nods, returns to her own seat, and rereads her story. "The End," she says as she rewrites the words. She puts her pencil down, looks at me, and says, "Mrs. Avery, I'm going to write a picture here." She picks up her pencil and says, "Mrs. Avery, I just figured something out. I'm going to write this whole story about going to the New Holland fair tonight and I'm not going to draw a picture. I think I'll just try something different." Traci begins to write. She stands on her right foot, puts her left knee on the chair and leans over the desk to write. After a few minutes she sits down, pats the paper as she whispers to herself, then stands again as she starts to write. This time her head goes down to rest on her arm on the desk. She writes a few moments then stands erect to read, "I am going to the New Holland fair." Then she returns to her previous position and writes again. She continues to write this way for twenty minutes and then announces, "Now I'm gonna put the periods in." She proceeds to reread her draft and place periods where she believes they belong.

Traci displayed the same restless behavior that Graves describes in writers as they end one piece of writing and begin another. Other than her somewhat unusual posture, she did not stand out as being different from the other children. Even in her restlessness, Traci was a confident writer, in control of her process, and functioning as an equal among her peers.

Traci selected her topics and wrote about them with ease. Classmates' interest in her pieces about her friends, birthday parties, play, and family activities not only built self-esteem but paved the way for Traci to be a confident and independent learner. The interactions in the writing community developed her problem-solving skills as well as her writing skills and at the same time maintained her integrity as a learner. For example, her writing sometimes rambled from one subject to another. Peer responses enabled her to address this issue.

"When I Saw a Balloon" started out about a hot-air balloon but switched to miniature golf. The other children informed Traci of their confusion when she shared the piece with the group. Traci listened politely to the comments, then stated with finality, "Well, see, it's my writing and I think I'll leave it this way. But thank you for your ideas." During the writing period that followed, Traci inserted chapter heads in her draft to take care of this difficulty, as she had seen other children do. On her very next piece, which was about the library, she told me during a conference, "See, I don't want to put in all this about when we come back to the room, then we got TB shots, and all that because this is just about the *library*." Traci maintained her integrity and self-esteem by maintaining control of her writing. It became a pattern for her to accept suggestions from her peers for improving a piece of writing (sometimes agreeing with them) but not to incorporate these suggestions until a later piece.

Traci developed skills because she learned them in a meaningful context and practiced them daily. Like all the children she wanted her writing to be technically correct and so was receptive to instruction in the needed skills. She also recalled correct spellings and punctuation in her published writing as well as other print materials she read, and transferred this knowledge to her writing. Later she began to implement phonics rules in her spelling strategies. Her speech difficulties interfered, however. Traci spelled words exactly as she pronounced them. Talking with classmates provided many opportunities for speaking, which helped to refine her speech. As Traci began to speak more clearly, her spelling as well as her grammar improved. One day she looked up from her writing and said, "Oh, Mrs. Avery, I thought *the* was t-e-h but it's t-h-e!" and she giggled. That giggle was to reappear frequently from Traci as a reflection of the delight and amusement she felt with the dawn of a new awareness.

Fantasy also became incorporated into Traci's pieces of writing. Traci was so expert at this that I was unaware of it until her mother said, "You know, she makes a lot of it up." The fantasy and reality were so intertwined that Traci herself had difficulty separating the two when asked about it. One day she told me, "Well, see I *forgot* what happened next, so I thought about it, I tried to remember, and this is what I thought." All of Traci's writing was focused on herself and her activities or fantasies of those activities. This appeared reflective of the developmental level of this child. Her peers enjoyed Traci's fantasy adventures and gave her positive feedback. The fantasy enabled Traci to maintain ownership of her writing because she was creating her own meaning in the material. It was quite apparent that she functioned best as a learner when the material was relevant. For Traci, relevant material was that which came from within her, be it fantasy or reality.

Traci put her writing to practical use. She exchanged notes with friends in classroom mailboxes and initiated the creation of a telephone book to list all the children in the room. When it was time to sell Girl Scout cookies, Traci wrote out what she planned to say when people opened the door. She carried her message with her and read it to prospective customers. After the first few houses she struck her message in her pocket and was able to make her request without it.

Traci learned from models provided by other children in the writing community. When she observed others writing factual informational pieces, she attempted one herself: "All Aubunt Jet Planes."

Jet plane's are a nother woRde for arePlane's. But Jet plane's are Samaller then areplane's. They let pepole ride in them. ho [oh] I forgot to tell you Jet Planes has smoke at the end of them. I like jet Planes because once I saw one. Now I will tel you want clor's Jet plane's can be. The one Kind of cloro is Black the other clorl is pink I don't no want other colors thay has. Inside Jet plane's has red carpet. Most jet planes has red carpet. And planes to. Jet planes has window's on eanch side. Jet planes have lot's of seant's in them. I thick jet planes are good. Because they ave peragoubs [parachutes] I like this story because this is stressing [interesting].

Author's Pange hi my name is Traci. I am egnt year's old. I had to be in first grade agin. I thick school is nice because I get lot's of help from Mrs. Avery. I have one dog we had five dog's The one of dog is Kingeey The other name was Bengi I don no want other name's we had.

When children questioned the information about pink jets, Traci had no response. But once again the responses stimulated Traci's thinking. When she read the published piece to the group, she announced, "This is part fiction and part non-fiction, in case you don't understand some parts. The part about what color is fiction."

In mid-April I interviewed Traci. Accurately perceiving herself as an independent learner integrated into a learning community, she said:

> First off, I don't have no questions about writing. I *love* writing! Sometimes I get lots of words out of my mind and I just keep on writing, writing, writing, writing. Sometimes I have to take a break because my hand is so sore. I think I'm old enough to sound out words by myself. I use the periods. Sometimes I just have to read my piece to somebody and see if they have any questions about my story. Sometimes when I read I say, "What's that word? That word doesn't fit in the story." I remember things to put in. Sometimes I think a little while . . . I think of ideas at recess or at home . . . sometimes when I go to bed. I can spell the words. I think the kids here sometimes need some help. I hope they will ask if I can help. I always be *glad* to help some people.

## Physical Education

Activities requiring physical dexterity and stamina will always be difficult for Traci. The physical-education teacher described her as having "weak muscle tone," being "wobbly" on her feet, and exhibiting "developmental slowness." She added, "Traci is a weak student but not a problem student. She always tries." In September, when children participated in the Nabisco AAU Individual Physical Fitness Report, Traci was unable to perform a bent-knee sit-up, a modified push-up, or mark a competitive time in a running event. Poor vision undoubtedly accounted for some of Traci's difficulties; surely she must approach physical activity with an apprehension that is understandable in one who cannot clearly view the world.

In gym-class activities she had difficulty processing stated directions; she watched closely, however, and attempted to imitate activities of other children and the teacher. This strategy was not always successful for Traci, and she was easily confused. In December the class followed an obstacle course with activities such as maintaining balloons in the air while staying within a circle, crawling through a large tunnel formed with tumbling mats, following a pathway around cones while seated on a scooter, and crawling under a hoop suspended on cones. Traci was baffled; she was unable to move from one event to another despite arrows painted on the floor. Her defeat was compounded by the ease with which the other children moved through the course. "Today, this was not a good place for her," was the empathetic comment of the physical-education teacher. "Traci needs to go through activities many times in order to understand what she is expected to do." The single half-hour period a week did not provide this luxury.

Nonetheless, Traci put effort into mastering physical skills. She was unable to manage a jump rope when I first knew her, but her determination to jump with the girls at recess motivated her to practice. It took several months, but Traci became proficient at jumping forward and backward with amazing speed. Roller-skating parties are part of the social life of the school, and Traci learned to roller-skate on the sidewalks outside her home. When Traci was four, her parents were told that she would probably never learn to ride a bike, but Traci amazed them by accomplishing this as well.

The significance of these achievements for Traci was evidenced by the frequency with which they appeared in her daily writing. Bike riding, jumping rope, and roller-skating were all topics which she addressed during both years in the classroom. When she began swimming lessons, this too was a topic. In addition, she sometimes left notes on my desk telling me of her successes. One day she wrote, "dear Mrs. avery I roller skate good love traci." Another time her note read, "I love swimming I can go in the deep end love you'r friend. traci."

## Reading

Traci's parents reported that she had read all summer. "She always has her nose in a book," her mother said, "She just loves to read." Traci affirmed this in an interview the first week of school, telling me in a confident tone, "Next to writing, the thing I do best is reading." The first days of school Traci read voraciously during the time established for the children to browse in books independently. A few days later, this pattern changed. Traci began picking up simple, beginning reading stories such as *The Bus Ride*, a book with a repetitious story line, and asked Megan or Christy or Tiffy to read with her. She appeared to be denying her strong reading skills to her classmates. Don Holdaway discusses "strategies used by young children learning in natural ways." One of these is "enjoying the sense of community in learning. They seem to prefer those activities which make them feel that they are becoming more like other people" (Holdaway 1984). It was clear that Traci was developing a sense of community and that her new priority was to belong. She was quite willing to sacrifice her enjoyment and accomplishment of reading in order to be on the same learning level as the peer community.

Although Traci was a good reader, her comprehension skills were limited to literal interpretation. In a discussion of "The Princess and the Pea" in mid-October, she related to me the exact details of the pea and the twenty mattresses and told me that the prince married the girl because "he did what his mother wanted him to do." Traci brought to the reading her own life experiences, which include a strong relationship with her mother. My questions and discussion of the story with Traci did not lead her any further. This was the developmental stage of Traci's reading and thinking in the fall. The community of learners in a literate environment provided an opportunity for her to grow.

The responses by classmates in group discussions of stories I read to them provided models for Traci which she gradually assimilated. She not only listened to the stories I read but also paid close attention to the comments her peers made. In the fall she often repeated comments others had just made or made statements such as, "I agree with you, Billy," without further elaboration. During the reading of *Warton's Christmas Surprise* by Russell E. Erickson, I asked what was it that Warton felt was cold and wet on the end of his nose. Traci's hand flew up and she answered, "Snow!" She then extended her answer with "because it might snow or rain tonight," and other remarks concerning her enjoyment of snow. When I asked her if all of this was connected with the story we were reading, she giggled and said, "No." Traci's response was indicative of her reading comprehension and thinking skills. She had the correct answer to the initial question then added other information which had been stimulated in her mind. But when questioned, she was able to separate her own experience from that in the story. That certainly was different from the typical response she had given a year before. In the same situation Traci then had said, "He's drinking his cocoa and got it on his nose because when I was drinking cocoa for breakfast I got it on my nose."

Traci loved to read books with her friends, and this too became an important ingredient in her developing comprehension skills. During the class reading time, Traci and a classmate would push their desks together, sprawl on the rug, or snuggle in a corner of the coat cubby with a book between them. Sometimes they alternated reading pages; sometimes they read aloud simultaneously. Traci's superior decoding strategies were an asset to this process. She could be heard to make matter-of-fact comments such as, "No, see that word's *flower*. It can't be *farmer* because there's no *l* in *farmer*." The partner child, meanwhile, would stimulate Traci's thinking with discussions of the pictures and by raising questions and commenting on the content.

The give and take with which these learners taught each other contributed to powerful learning. Traci was not a weak member of a team but a participant in a balanced interaction. Her contributions were valued by her peers, enhancing her self-esteem and confidence and establishing important peer relationships. At the same time, her classmates helped Traci develop her thinking processes and refine her understanding of the communicative aspects of written language.

Traci read aloud at an amazing speed. Words rolled from her lips at such a continuous and remarkable rate that I wondered how she could possibly process them so rapidly. Undoubtedly her comprehension was affected when she read aloud. In fact, when I questioned her on what she had just read, she would reread silently before answering. All my imploring suggestions to slow down were unheeded. It took a comment from a classmate, when Traci read a story to the group in January, to bring this problem to Traci's awareness. "I couldn't understand because your words all ran together and you didn't put your periods in," said Megan.

After two more students concurred, Traci nodded and responded in her typical polite manner, "Okay, I'll try to work on that. Thank you, Megan. Anyway, I know that you're just trying to help me." It was not easy for her, but Traci made the effort. She gradually began reading more slowly, and when she did she also acquired inflection in her reading voice and improved her comprehension.

In late March, Traci read me a story entitled "Big Boss" by Anne Rockwell and correctly answered inferential comprehension questions that I interjected as she read. She accurately predicted early in the story what was likely to happen and interpreted implied meanings. About this time she began responding to the literature read aloud to the class with perceptive comments. Traci improved her reading during the year by emulating others and by interacting in the supportive community of peer learners. Through it all, she maintained her positive stance toward the reading process. After she read a peer-authored book one day, I overheard her say to her classmate, "I just love to read, don't you?"

## Math

Math was a different story. "I can't do math so good," Traci remarked when I passed out the math books in September. It was true; math was difficult for her. The previous year she had not even been successful in tearing pages from the workbook by herself, and the formats and concepts on the pages were far beyond her abilities. Now she was tense and anxious, but determined to try. When I approached to assist her in removing the first page she said, "I can do it myself." She did and looked at me and giggled with as much surprise as delight at her accomplishment. She was also successful in understanding the concepts of numbers and counting and completing the accompanying math pages during the first month of school.

In October, when the concept of addition was introduced, math went poorly for Traci for the first time this year. She had trouble manipulating counters on her desk during the presentation of the lesson. When it came to the workbook page, she worked extremely slowly, arriving at the sums by counting her fingers on her nose. I interrupted her to explain that counting the cubes drawn beside the problems on the paper would give her the answers. Counting these three-dimensional objects and changing strategies further frustrated her. Traci's mother later reported that her daughter arrived home that afternoon in a "terrible mood ... yelling at me ... she was wild!"

The next morning Traci and I did addition problems together. I showed her how to manipulate counters to join sets and arrive at a sum. After two or three successes she said, "I'm proud of myself." She looked at $0 + 5$ and responded, "Oh easy! Just put 5." She had recalled the concept of addition with zero that she had learned the previous year. She handled $2 + 3$ by manipulating the red chips and counting, "One, two, plus one, two, three, equals one, two, three, four, five." She wrote 5, looked up, and added, "And I'm not kidding you either!"

"You remember how I did math last year?" she asked.

"Tell me about that," I responded.

Traci looked me squarely in the eye and emphatically replied, "Difficult!" She paused, then added matter-of-factly, "I think last year I couldn't do math good, but I think this year I can do better." She whizzed through the last two rows of six problems then looked up and giggled with immense satisfaction.

Traci's confidence enabled her to keep pace with her peers in math class, and she did not move to the resource room as she had a year earlier for this subject area. Some days she used counters, other times she switched to using her fingers. Counters were more reliable for her in the fall months because she had difficulty manipulating her fingers. Gradually she became more efficient and eventually abandoned the counters. By January she was counting her fingers without tapping her nose. Since other children in the class used concrete aids to add and subtract, Traci did not stand out as being different. She was very aware that she was functioning well within the group. Traci felt her success. In November she told me that math was her best area in school! In a December interview she said, "I think I'm getting good on math 'cause I'm getting the hang of it. I like it."

The children recognized that math was a problem area for Traci and became supportive and encouraging. Counting money was particularly difficult for her. One day when she had correctly counted out a collection of coins, I asked her how she had accomplished this. "Audrey taught me," she replied. When the class played a drill game of math facts, and Traci answered correctly, the group spontaneously applauded, and Prentice cheered, "Yay, Traci!" Traci beamed and responded, "Thanks everybody. I needed that."

There were days when Traci's math performance faltered and she appeared overwhelmed. Giving Traci reassurance during these low ebbs that she was doing fine enabled her to persist at math. She made progress. By midyear, if given a number of counters, Traci could correctly discover all of the combinations of numbers that added up to this total. When addition facts for eleven and twelve were introduced in March, she independently accomplished this process.

When it came to solving individual math problems for eleven and twelve, however, she was at a loss. Going beyond ten seemed very difficult for her, and she had trouble maintaining pace with the class. Suddenly Traci slipped into old behaviors: she could not tear pages from the math book, could not locate a pencil, and presented a demeanor of helplessness. She wrote random answers without attempting to use counters to determine the correct sums. When I worked with her with counters, she reverted to procedures that she had not used since the year before. She added $3 + 6$ by counting out three counters then moving to the second group and forming it by counting aloud, "four, five, six" rather than starting with one again, and then wrote 6 as the correct sum. Traci's confidence had been eroded by the new material and by her perceived separation from the group. Her thinking processes were blocked, and she regressed to old, useless procedures. Holdaway, in a discussion of the learning environment, notes, "A sense of community sustains complex learning. Nothing destroys or perverts so rapidly as a sense of isolation" (19).

Traci discussed math in an interview on March 14:

> I think I'm not doing really good in math. Sometimes when you teach us I can't catch up with you because you teach too fast and I lose my concentration when everybody's talking. Math is fun sometimes for me. I try to concentrate but I can't. Sometimes I get things in my head and it makes me dizzy sometimes. It feels like the whole world is turning around. Just math. Somedays my mind is somewhere else, like still sleeping. This is one of the days.

When we moved on to double-digit addition, Traci's confidence was restored. The material was more familiar to her because it used only math facts totaling nine or less. In mid-April, when I concluded my study of Traci, she spoke of math: "I'm doing a little bit good."

The many experiences with math throughout the year brought a great deal of improvement over her performance of the previous year but did not bring mastery. Although she had a solid understanding of math concepts by the end of the year, Traci still required concrete aids to calculate math problems.

## TRACI AS A LEARNER

Traci had a successful year. She matured in emotional and cognitive processes in the context of a supportive environment. Her confidence and self-esteem were fostered first by her own writing, nurtured by the interaction with her peers, and thus established a solid foundation for other aspects of her learning.

Traci's learning process is continually evolving, integrating her natural abilities, coping techniques, and personality traits with environmental influences as she strives to make sense of the world. Traci undoubtedly begins with handicaps that the majority of children do not have: weak vision, impaired speech, immature language patterns, poor physical coordination, and weak cognitive processing. Like all children she displays personality traits and behaviors that can be appealing or alienating. Traci is warm and loving; she treasures her friends and exhibits profound concern for their welfare. She is perceptive, sensitive, and easily injured by indifferent or unintentional actions or comments by others. Yet Traci has often wielded her charm to manipulate people and to avoid tasks that overwhelm her. For persons working with Traci, knowing when she truly can manage a task is difficult. Traci continues to be an enigma, but she continues to learn!

## WHY WRITING PROCESS
## WORKED FOR TRACI

The environment of a writing-process classroom has several enabling characteristics that appear to be especially helpful for a learning-disabled child such as Traci. I have identified some aspects that were significant in Traci's case.

*The writing-process approach promotes positive self-concepts and increases self-confidence.* Traci's progress was due largely to her self-confidence, which grew out of peer relationships and from the positive responses of everyone with whom she shared her work. When her thoughts and feelings were received with enthusiasm and interest by parents, teachers, and, most important, peers, Traci discovered herself as a valued and trusted individual. Kronick states that a learning-disabled child "acquires a concept of what he is all about and what he can expect of himself . . . from feedback from adults and peers, . . . and from attempting tasks and learning what he is and is not able to do" (Kronick 1981). Traci invested herself through her writing and received encouraging feedback not only for her efforts but also for her personhood.

*The writing-process classroom incorporates the learning-disabled child as a full and equal member.* Learning-disabled children are often isolated from their peers and have few opportunities to discover and explore their own powers as learners in relationship to other children. The writing-process community offers an alternative. Traci matured in emotional and cognitive processes in the context of a supportive peer environment: the writing community. This atmosphere enabled Traci not only to remain in the classroom but also to function successfully and to learn. She was an active, integrated member of her peer group, and her ideas and responses were valued. In the writing-community setting, Traci was able to learn from others.

*The predictable structure of the writing time provides a secure environment.* The carefully established and predictable structure provided a familiarity that became comfortable for the children. Everybody understood the procedures for composing, revising, sharing, and responding. The regularity of the writing time permitted Traci and the other children to practice their skills every day. Once Traci incorporated the procedures as her own, she thrived on the consistency and continuity.

*The writing allows children a sense of control over their learning.* From the first, writing gave Traci an element of control over her environment. She had ownership of her writing process and resisted any attempt to diminish her power over her work. The control she experienced contributed to her confidence and success as a learner. Because Traci selected her own topics, the first focus was on the *meaning* of her communication. She was not yet able to control the mechanics of her writing, but she was most definitely in control of the content. Students who choose their own topics discover not only what they know but that what they know is important to others. For the learning-disabled child, this is a real boost to the self-concept.

*The emphasis of the responses to the child's writing is on meaning rather than on mechanics.* Often teacher responses to writing in traditional settings are on the mechanics of the communication—that area with which a learning-disabled child has the most difficulty. Through response to the child's meaning, the individual is affirmed, and the child can understand a purpose for correct spelling, legible handwriting, and so on. Skill learning is placed in a meaningful context.

*The writing-process classroom provides a rich language environment which helps children of all abilities learn communication skills.* In addition to writing and reading their own writing, the children read each other's pieces, in which content was always meaningful. They heard books read by the teacher and read trade books. Each day they expressed verbally their ideas and responses during the sharing time. Kronick states that "preschool children use language to structure the world around them. The child with deficient verbal skills is thus less able to make sense of his incredibly complex environment" (Kronick 1981). The writing of Traci and her classmates and the interaction during this process provided an enriched language environment that enabled Traci to construct relevant learning experiences and make sense of her world. She developed communication skills because the implementation of these skills was carried out in contexts that were meaningful to Traci.

*The writing-process approach accommodates to the individual pace of each child.* Allowing adequate daily writing time provides an unhurried atmosphere in which each child is free to accomplish according to his or her ability and at a performance level that varies from day to day. The children are aware that they will continue tomorrow, but rather than procrastinating, they tend to anticipate the next writing period and think about writing outside of school. In a more traditional classroom, Traci's erratic learning pace would have made it impossible for her to continue working alongside her peers.

*A positive attitude growing out of success as a writer is transferable to other tasks.* The success Traci experienced in writing carried to other areas of her learning. While math remained her weakest area, she made definite progress in mastery of math concepts and computation skills. Traci also made astounding progress in physical education skills. She learned to ride a bike and to jump rope, activities that had been predicted as ones she might never accomplish. In these areas of school life, Traci's classmates continued the supportive encouragement they had learned to offer during their writing time together.

In summary, Traci's achievements in acquiring language skills can be credited in large part to her participation in a writing-process environment where she functioned as a successful member of a learning community. In that community she was able to learn in a give and take that allowed for individual differences, including learning disabilities. While we cannot predict success for all learners, we can acknowledge that a process environment permits differences among young learners and encourages individualized learning in a group situation. These factors offer an exciting prospect for future teaching of all children, perhaps especially those classified as learning disabled.

## REFERENCES AND RELATED SOURCES

Atwell, Nancie. "Class-Based Writing Research: Teachers Learn from Students." *English Journal*, January 1982.

Atwell, Nancie. "Writing and Reading Literature from the Inside Out." *Language Arts*, March 1984.

Briggs, Dorothy Corkille. *Your Child's Self Esteem*. Garden City, N.Y.: Doubleday, 1975.

Clarke, Louise. *Can't Read, Can't Write, Can't Talk Too Good Either*. New York: Penguin, 1973.

Clay, Marie M. "Looking and Seeing in the Classroom." *English Journal*, February 1982.

Clay, Marie M. *What Did I Write? Beginning Writing Behaviour*. Portsmouth, N.H.: Heinemann Educational Books, 1975.

Freeman, Stephen W. *Does Your Child Have a Learning Disability?* Springfield, Ill.: Charles C. Thomas, 1974.

Graves, Donald. "Writing Research for the Eighties: What Is Needed." *Language Arts*, February 1981.

————. *Writing: Teachers & Children at Work*. Portsmouth, N.H.: Heinemann Educational Books, 1983.

Hansen, Jane; Thomas Newkirk; and Donald Graves. *Breaking Ground: Teachers Relate Reading and Writing in the Elementary School*. Portsmouth, N.H.: Heinemann Educational Books, 1985.

Harste, Jerome C.; Virginia A. Woodward; and Carolyn L. Burke. *Language Stories and Literacy Lessons*. Portsmouth, N.H.: Heinemann Educational Books, 1984.

Hart, Leslie A. *Human Brain and Human Learning*. New York: Longman, 1983.

Holdaway, Don. *Stability and Change in Literacy Learning*. Portsmouth, N.H.: Heinemann Educational Books, 1984.

Kronick, Doreen. *Social Development of Learning Disabled Persons*. San Francisco: Jossey-Bass, 1981.

Levy, Harold B. *Square Pegs, Round Holes: The Learning Disabled Child in the Classroom and at Home*. Boston: Little, Brown, 1973.

Newkirk, Thomas, and Nancie Atwell. *Understanding Writing: Ways of Observing, Learning, and Teaching*. Portsmouth, N.H.: Heinemann Educational Books, 1986.

Osman, Betty B. *No One to Play With: The Social Side of Learning Disabilities*. New York: Random House, 1982.

Silver, Larry B., M.D. *The Misunderstood Child: A Guide for Parents of Learning Disabled Children*. New York: McGraw-Hill, 1984.

Vitale, Barbara Meister. *Unicorns Are Real: A Right-Brained Approach to Learning*. Rolling Hills Estates, Calif.: Jalmar Press, 1982.

# CHAPTER 6

# Roles and Strategies in College Writing Conferences

*Ferguson McKay*

From case studies of single individuals we move to a study that looks at a teacher's interactions through writing conferences with each of six students. As he looks at the individual responses of the students, McKay also looks critically at his role as teacher. "For some time I had been curious about what makes conferences effective in teaching writing, and it was natural for me to focus my research on conference exchanges. As I listened to and evaluated tape-recorded conferences, I began to suspect that the key element was not the 'instructional' content of a conference but the roles I adopted in various situations with student writers. Roles and strategies then became the focus of my study." As a result of his research, McKay says, "I know better who I am and what I want to do professionally. I see my students more clearly as people needing help with escaping binds that have developed in their earlier education and with expanding their creativity and their ability to control and direct their learning. That means, too, that I need to find more new, good ways to provide this help through classroom work. Conferences are not enough—classroom support is vital."

Ferguson McKay has taught English since 1959, for the past nineteen years at Lyndon State College in Vermont, with breaks to do further graduate study and to be dean at Lyndon for six years. He was educated at Phillips Exeter Academy, Harvard, and Amherst, and earned an A.M. in English at Yale. He and his wife, who is a Chapter I teacher in local schools, live in St. Johnsbury, Vermont. Their two daughters recently graduated from Amherst.

## THE INITIAL RESEARCH PROPOSAL

The original proposal for this study, formulated in August 1984, focused on a single problem: the difficulty that some of the students in my upper-level college writing class have in generating sufficient detail for effective writing. I wanted to study the effects on this problem of different ways of conducting individual writing conferences in my private office. I was also interested in what types of classroom activities would assist students in seeing the need for detail and then generating it. I hoped that a combination of well-conducted conferences and stimulating classroom work would help these writers achieve breakthroughs into longer, better-developed pieces of writing.

## THE WRITING COURSE FOR THE STUDY

The writing course in which I conducted my study is open to students who have passed freshman English (a semester of composition followed by a semester of reading and writing about literature). I teach it by the "process-conference" method described by Donald M. Murray and Donald H. Graves. That is, I give no specific assignments of topics or modes; writing proceeds through several drafts, with conferences each week; students are encouraged to use many prewriting techniques, such as interest inventories, brainstorming, freewriting, mapping or clustering, free-form planning or outlining, and writing leads; and editing is delayed until content and organization are satisfactory. I require no specific pattern of progress through "stages"; each student is encouraged to discover what process works best for him or her in each writing task. Freewriting is required on each weekday, and there is a substantial emphasis on developing creativity. I regularly search out or develop exercises designed to stimulate creative responses. One text for the course is Gabriele Rico's *Writing the Natural Way*. It is, obviously, not a typical college writing course, but it is, to a significant degree, an experimental one.

My philosophy of teaching in this course had an important impact on my research. Since it was not my objective to teach specific kinds of writing for specific audiences, but rather to encourage exploration and development of a writer's abilities and interests, I did not teach rhetorical patterns or theory (though I did sometimes give rhetorical advice in conference). I also did not teach grammar, punctuation, mechanics, and spelling in class, believing that improvement is more likely if these topics are discussed during conference in relation to a student's writing. And I gave little direct instruction about how to improve papers, since I wanted writers to retain control of their writing.

## THE RESEARCH PROJECT

My research was divided into two sections. The first, conducted in the fall of 1984, was a pilot study designed to test and evaluate my original research proposal. Focusing on six students, I tape-recorded a number of conferences with them, kept notes on each conference and their drafts, listened to the tapes, and wrote comments about what I observed. I learned that my six writers were failing to produce more detailed compositions because of problems that went beyond educational deficiencies and lack of writing experience. Psychodynamic problems seemed especially significant: problems that influenced, and were influenced by, the students' relationship with me and the class. There was a variety of defenses against involvement in the course and its demands—mainly efforts to ward off comments or criticism, particularly of the kind that either confused the students or was not useful to them at the time. In an extreme case one student repeatedly asked for my evaluation of her writing and my specific instructions for correcting it so that she could "improve." I conjectured that she had learned to invite criticism as a way of avoiding the effects of it—an odd but workable ploy. I sensed that, underneath these problems of avoidance, my study group had little confidence in themselves as writers.

In the second part of my research, carried out in the spring of 1985, I focused on the interactions in conferences between me and my students. My pilot study had suggested that there are major difficulties in trying to relate many activities and behaviors to one feature of writing: adequate detail. I decided to drop my concern for increased detail in favor of any observable improvement in subsequent drafts or in the writer's understanding or use of process. Working again with six students, I tape-recorded five to seven conferences with each student, promptly made hand-written transcripts of these conferences and added comments of my own, and at the end of the semester typed these transcripts and made further comments. I also distributed two questionnaires to the class, asked them to submit a short paper on "How I Write" at the final meeting, and collected and photocopied the final papers and drafts from the six students.

These six students (along with a good many others) began the course by struggling with a familiar set of problems: finding topics and getting started writing; completing a first draft; revising; and communicating with me in conferences. They were not confident that they had something to say to others, were uncomfortable about writing several pages on a topic of their choice, did not communicate easily with others about their writing. Having an audience—teacher or classmates—could make them anxious enough to block their writing. They did not look forward to conferences. But all of them also showed one other important trait: I sensed that, under the right conditions, all of them could find a self-chosen direction in a piece of writing and follow it.

As I sought to help these students write, I found three broad concepts useful in analyzing conference strategies and student responses. The first concept combined *confidence* and a positive *self-image* as a writer: Could my students think of themselves as people who can and do write? The second focused on who had *control* and *authority* in the course: Could my students see themselves as authors in command of their writing? The third involved the *use of audience responses*: When did my students accept these, find them useful? reject them, find them useless? When were "good" responses not useful? When were "poor" responses not harmful? These three concepts provided avenues for exploring the new focus for the study: In conferences, what types of interaction are most helpful to students having more than average difficulty with finding topics, writing, revising, and talking about their writing?

At the same time, I began to explore this question through a distinction between *direct instruction* and *encouragement*, which I saw as broadly opposed categories of teacher responses in conferences. At first I represented this distinction by these lists:

| Direct Instruction | Encouragement |
|---|---|
| Teaching (directive, explicit) | Receiving, affirming |
| | Supporting, confirming |
| Explaining | Listening |
| Modeling (implicit or explicit) | Suggesting changes |
| Persuading | Expressing enthusiasm (sincere) |
| Evaluating | Responding |
| Being an authority | An equal or partner |
| Correcting | Overlooking some problems |
| Often written—indirect | Conversational—direct |
| Manipulation—intentional or unintentional | Avoiding manipulation (i.e., manipulative praising) |
| Attention to the paper | Attention to the student |
| Criticizing | Clarifying |
| Extensive, detailed comments | Few, broad comments |

Later I decided that possible teacher responses fall along a spectrum ranging from precise, detailed instruction on specific points to a purely supportive stance (depending on the instructor's sense of the writer's needs at the moment). In the large middle range of this spectrum lie many "combination" responses: mixtures of encouragement and suggestions; emotional support mingled with modest doses of specific instruction. This middle range is difficult to describe; its character can vary widely with the atmosphere the teacher has created and the way students respond. It will probably be different for each instructor, just as no two families are alike. But I believe that general behavioral and pedagogical principles can be defined for the whole spectrum (an important future task for research in composition).

This spectrum is closely related to the three concepts, *confidence*, *control*, and *use of responses*. *Direct instruction*, I believe, often reduces confidence and removes control from the student, leading to poor use, or no use, of responses. *Encouragement*, properly employed by the teacher (and by classmates), increases confidence and control and improves the chance that responses will be used effectively. My research, therefore, examined the choices I made during conferences between explaining specific ways to change writing and supporting a student's own (often slow) discoveries of the changes needed. I was, of course, aware of the risk that if I did not "teach," the student would not "learn," but I was also aware of what I believe are greater risks: that the student would not become an independent writer, would not discover what he or she wanted to say, would not explore the writing process, would not learn what communicating in writing involves.

## THE RELATION OF THIS STUDY
## TO PREVIOUS RESEARCH

As I explored through this study the question, What kind of help does a writer need from a teacher and at what times? I searched for answers in the substantial research that has been done on how writers write and how writers learn to write. I found a good deal that was suggestive. Sondra Perl describes the "felt sense" that is the writer's first awareness that she or he has something to express: paying "very careful attention to one's inner reflections . . . often accompanied by bodily sensations" is an essential element in writing (and one Perl believes can be taught, though she does not say how). As this "felt sense" becomes writing, it influences the text by a process Perl calls "retrospective structuring," a continual comparing of the evolving text with this "sense" (which might be called the writer's "intention" or "pre-vision") (Perl 1980). In most cases a writer needs to consult this "felt sense" at least as much as he or she needs instruction or suggestions from a teacher or another writer.

Donald Murray's work is filled with evidence of the writer's need to be self-directing, especially in the early stages of composing. Murray agrees with Perl about respecting the writer's sense of his or her intentions (see especially "The

Listening Eye," 1982), and in "Teaching the Other Self" (1982) adds that the writer listens to an internal "other self" in order to monitor "the multiple complex relationships between all the elements in writing." This "other self" does more than anticipate audience responses by being a critical, experienced reader; it is active even before words go down on paper, and it remains aware of the writer's entire process. Murray acknowledges that students may lack an "other self" but feels that the teacher can both "teach the other self" and "recruit the other self to assist in the teaching of writing." How can a teacher accomplish this dual task? Murray's answer is, "To make effective use of the other self the teacher and the student must listen together" (143). He says the teacher must not "tell" while "they listen." "I will always attempt to underteach so that they can overlearn" (144).

The importance of an affective base for writing has been stressed by a number of writers. Murray, in "Teaching the Other Self," states: "The deeper we get into the writing process the more we may discover how affective concerns govern the cognitive, for writing is an intellectual activity carried on in an emotional environment" (142). Donald Graves (1983) emphasizes that an elementary writing classroom must be structured and predictable before necessary risks with writing can or will be taken by teacher or pupils. He also stresses that teachers should write with their classes to create a sense of a community of writers. Geraldine Susi (1984) similarly emphasizes that to be an encouraging reader and listener, a teacher must be a fellow writer and a human being who can be trusted and empathized with. Murray, Graves, and Susi are all pointing to a role for the writing teacher that is not authoritarian, paternalistic, or purely instructional but has significant elements of a friendly, conversational relationship, as between social equals, family members, or fellow writers.

Much recent research into learning to write and to read has stressed the diversity of ways in which children learn and the multiple strategies adopted or developed by the learner as he or she struggles with code and meaning (see, for example, Bissex 1980). This research makes clear both the interconnection of reading and writing throughout the writing process and the complexity of the teacher's task in deciding when and how to intervene in the student's writing. Such research also reveals that "discovery learning" carried out independently by learners is essential to progress; the teacher cannot teach everything, even everything necessary for minimal performance. The teacher must rely on the student's capacities and previously developed strategies, even as the teacher attempts to convey new information and new strategies. And the student is as likely to develop new strategies on his or her own as learn them from someone else. These conclusions echo Murray's analysis of the "other self," which may be considered a collection of composing strategies the writer is able to apply at the moment.

Research into the roles teachers adopt and the responses teachers make in conferences has produced worthwhile if mixed results. Jacobs and Karliner (1977) contrast the "conversational" mode of responding with the traditional "classroom" mode (teacher authoritatively instructs the writer) and conclude that the first is preferable when the writer needs to develop his or her ideas or sense of what the paper is about. In a "conversation" the teacher listens as the student explores his or her thoughts, and responds as one would in everyday social discourse. Jacobs and Karliner believe that teachers need a repertoire of conference roles ranging "from friendly authoritarian to fellow conversant to recorder" (in the last the teacher writes notes and barely speaks). The teacher needs to "develop a sensitivity" about which role is appropriate when. In these conclusions Jacobs and Karliner echo Murray's concept of alternately listening to and teaching the "other self."

In a later study (University of California at San Diego, 1979) Karliner identifies two teachers roles, "collaborator" and "evaluator," and two student roles, "initiator" and "respondent." The instructor roles resemble her earlier "conversational" and "classroom" modes of response. Karliner observes that the "evaluator" speaks as an authority, employing the "specialized terminology of the English teacher" to tell the student what is wrong with the paper. The "collaborator" speaks "primarily as an interested reader" in "descriptive layman's language," and tries to "elicit student ideas for changing the paper." The collaborator acts as a partner rather than an expert, and employs various strategies to stimulate student initiative in seeing problems and suggesting improvements. These strategies include waiting, puzzling out, suggesting "lots of alternatives," being imprecise and colloquial, not preparing for conferences in advance, and using "I" in preference to "you" in responding. Not surprisingly, the study found that students usually reacted defensively to evaluators, often not understanding the instructors' analyses of problems (the "respondent" role), whereas students were much more likely to discover problems and make important revisions on their own (the "initiator" role) when the teacher was a collaborator. This study suggests that traditional classroom modes of instruction can hinder improvement in writing.

Nancy Sommers, in a study (1980) of both student and experienced adult writers, found that students displayed limited revision skills (they saw revision only as rewording), whereas adult writers revised for meaning as well. She blamed the students' previous education for their "narrow" sense of revision. (Interestingly, Graves, 1983, and Avery, 1983, found, as others have, that first graders can revise for meaning.) In a later study (1982) Sommers examined teachers' comments on student papers and determined that the teachers tended to take control of the paper away from the student, and that their comments tended to be "vague." As a result, students' attention shifted from their own intentions in writing to puzzling out the teacher's purposes in evaluating, leading to an effective "appropriation of the text" by the teacher. Sommers recommends, but does not describe, a change in "styles of commenting," holding that teachers should read student writing as they read literature, and that teachers need "levels" of commenting for different drafts of a piece. These research results support my contention that direct instruction can be harmful, and that other teacher roles often lead to more learning for students.

A stronger attack on traditional direct instruction comes from Brannon and

Knoblauch (1982), who hold that "control of student writing" should be returned to students so that they will not lose "the incentive to write." These researchers begin by pointing out that readers normally grant "authority" to the authors of texts, but teachers deny "authority" (and therefore "control" over their writing) to students. This article recommends that student writing should at least "be read earnestly," if full authority cannot be granted to inexperienced writers. Brannon and Knoblauch advise teachers to evaluate final drafts only, and only on the basis of "communicative effectiveness . . . in a particular writing situation" (a method resembling Primary Trait scoring). This study also describes a teaching method involving multiple drafts and a "process of negotiation" between student and teacher to decide on revisions. In this process teachers attend to the writer's own "purposes" rather than to an imagined "Ideal Text."

But if the teacher moves away from the direct instruction role in college-level writing conferences (and probably in class as well), will other roles, or combinations of roles, turn out to be effective? This question has received little attention. Carol Berkenkotter (1984) studied ten college freshmen writers and found a high degree of variability in the way in which different students responded to both teacher and classmate comments. In two extreme cases students rejected all responses outright: one student could not accept any comment at all, and a second student preferred his own intentions for his piece. In a third case a student over-eagerly accepted comments, temporarily losing control over her writing. This study provides evidence that in some instances no helpful role is available, and in others any attempt to help may be damaging; simply letting the writer continue without a conference may be best.

I found no other studies of variable student responses to conferences, but Nina D. Ziv (1984) studied responses to comments she wrote on the papers of four college freshmen (on second drafts; first drafts received peer conferences, the only oral conferences in this study). She came to a variety of conclusions: "inexperienced revisers need specific directions from their teachers about how to revise their papers," while more experienced writers respond effectively to questions and suggestions; comments are "helpful," but only if teachers respond "to student writing not as evaluators and judges but as interested adults"; an "ongoing dialogue" between teacher and students is desirable; in some cases a teacher "might comment in an encouraging and supportive manner instead of reinforcing the student's poor self-perception"; teachers should "become more sensitive to the intentions of student writers." This study recognizes the breadth of concerns researchers must address in examining one-on-one student-teacher interactions. Ziv's belief that "better styles of commenting" are possible provides a starting point for further studies.

The central issue raised by these research studies and articles may well be this: in conference exchanges between teachers and students, where should the locus, or location, of learning be? Should the teacher "appropriate" the learning (by asserting control over the text) and then "tell" the student what she or he "needs" to know? Or should learning be located in an "other self" that the student already possesses to some degree and the teacher is helping the student to develop? Berkenkotter's study extends this question to ask not simply *where* the locus should be but *when* it should be *where*, because as several researchers indicate, teachers need to adopt different roles for different drafts and different students at different times. In the research results that I discuss below, the primary conclusion is that teachers need Jacobs and Karliner's repertoire of roles and the sensitivity to know which role is appropriate in each situation.

## ANALYSIS OF RESEARCH DATA

The results reported here, for the six students in the second part of my case study, are based on the transcribed exchanges in conferences and my interpretations of these exchanges, supplemented by two questionnaires, the papers students wrote on their writing methods, and the students' drafts. My interpretive comments were written shortly after the conference (usually the same day, as I was transcribing) and at two later times: first, when I typed the transcripts, and second, when I reviewed the transcripts while composing the first draft of this report. Names have been changed. The order in which the students appear below is not significant.

### Fran

Fran reported that early in the semester she felt detached from the course and was waiting to see what would happen. I sensed that she liked to listen to others and cared about their opinions of her, but also that she found the usual academic evaluation of her work unpleasant. Evaluation shook her confidence, made her doubt that she could judge her own successes and failures, and put pressure on her. She was, however, easy to work with in conferences because she reacted quickly and positively to encouragement.

In her first and second (recorded) conferences we discussed the first piece of her writing she felt enthusiasm for. In it the voice and detail were so strong that I decided simply to "receive" the writing (Donald Graves's term) and confirm its quality, in a conversational mode. She expressed uncertainty about her accomplishment several times in both conferences ("Do you think so?" was a typical response), but also readily accepted my confirmations and soon acknowledged that she felt "confident about this paper." She needed two conferences to be sure that I thought well of her paper, but then she moved abruptly and easily to the topic for her next piece.

Along with this uncertainty, Fran displayed a sophisticated awareness of writing techniques. She was freewriting to discover what she wanted to say, then revising first to add and exclude material and second "to find just the right words and phrases to get across the meaning that I want." I noticed her assertiveness when she continued to talk after two attempts on my part to end the first conference (I simply wanted to support her, not to discuss any issues or problems). She wanted me to know that she was beginning to like writing and that the conference had helped her (yet I had not made any suggestion except that she continue writing).

I began the second conference with mild praise of her paper, but she didn't want praise (she reacted blandly: "Yeah, it's that"), so I asked for her judgment about content ("Do you feel you covered what you wanted to?"). To this question, which can be threatening if a writer is fearful of being asked to revise, Fran answered positively: "I think so." I responded by suggesting that the paper was finished except for "tinkering" (editing for fine details, a task she could perform well). But she objected by asking two questions ("What do you think of the dialogue?" "Is it bad to have a parenthetical reference?"), which I interpreted as requests for further confirmation. I judged that she wanted support rather than instruction or evaluation, even though her questions were specific. Her confidence grew noticeably, and she shifted the discussion abruptly to her next paper topic. I got her talking about the new topic, listened, and confirmed again. In both conferences Fran reacted positively to my supportive role: "You've given me a good push. Thank you."

In her third conference Fran sounded pleased and confident about her progress on papers three and four. I continued listening and confirming the quality of her writing, without suggestions or comments about possible weaknesses. She did most of the talking, interrupting me frequently, and I felt that she had learned how to use a conference to motivate further writing. She didn't want my criticisms or comments—just the sense that I agreed with her that she was a writer successfully at work. Interestingly, a good part of this conference dealt with "housekeeping": What was in her folder? Should she type her papers? The only substantive question about her writing she raised herself: was her dialogue "strong enough"?

Fran's fifth piece, brought in for her fourth conference, was her most ambitious work to date. It was stimulated by a class exercise in writing stories. Again, Fran dominated the talk in the conference, and I made no comment except to say that I liked her story. She opened the conference with happy remarks about the value and pleasure for her of writing ("It's therapy"; "Whatever hits me in the head, I actually write it down"). I saw this happy spontaneity as a major gain over her initial struggles to write a piece she liked. She also mentioned several concerns: about being a "one-draft" writer (I reassured her that anything that works for a writer is fine); about classes she had missed (she was surprised that it was as many as five); and about missed conferences. She was worried about her course grade (which depended partly on attendance) and about receiving credit for her successes (which were a growing surprise to her). I felt that she was making progress in overcoming her earlier uncertainties and worries, and so I continued to "confirm." I did not want to upset her new perception that she was in control of her writing even if I was in control of the course and grading. She was beginning to recognize that her evaluation of her writing was more important to her than mine, but she also wanted a good grade as recognition that her evaluation was sound.

Then I tried a change in tactics. Fran said early in her fifth conference that she was in trouble with her fourth paper (she diagnosed the problem correctly: "too neat," too quickly "resolved"), and I switched from confirming to making a suggestion. I wanted to discover if her confidence was strong enough for that. Unfortunately my suggestion was to make the dialogue more realistic, an area she had fretted about in two earlier conferences. Even worse, I explained the problem in detail. She seemed abashed for a minute or two, even though she understood me quickly. Since the conference ended a few moments later, I was not sure if her confidence was intact.

Her solution to the dialogue problem became clear in the sixth conference. She had cut the entire dialogue and written a much shorter ending that avoided the too-quick resolution. This was a successful revision, but I wondered if she had removed the dialogue because she felt that she couldn't make it more realistic. Had a previous teacher criticized her dialogue? She was eager to do well in the course, and I guessed that my abrupt role change had indeed shaken her confidence. But a decision to resume my confirming role was made easy by the success of Fran's revision, followed by the even greater success of her sixth paper (which she presented in this conference). I was also prompted by the reappearance of her earlier uncertainty ("Do you think it's going to be all right?" (she asked about her fifth paper). It now appeared to me that I had chosen my role correctly at the start; instruction in any form—even a single suggestion—was unlikely to help her.

This conclusion was strengthened for me in the sixth conference when Fran asked me to read a new paper, "because then I could know if it's going to be accepted." It was a powerful, moving story about death in a grim accident, and she knew it was good. She had even asked a friend's opinion, but mine might still contradict hers; I was still the "controlling decider." She displayed no brash, assertive confidence even when she knew that she had written well. I responded by simply confirming her story's success. Then she said something fascinating. Earlier she had mentioned her search for the "right words" (first conference); now she said, "That's what I wanted. If I only did one this semester, I wanted to do one like that" (a paper the reader couldn't put down). I believe she wanted to feel in full control of her writing, to have the important revising done before I saw the paper. She wanted to hear unqualified enthusiasm from me on my first reading. That would mean she had really succeeded. Her goal had become independence as a writer—the thrill of doing it all on her own.

In the seventh conference this conclusion was further supported when Fran extended our conversation in order to tell me how much I had helped her with her writing. She liked my "attitude" ("You're so low-key it takes the pressure off"). What she called my "help" had been support and encouragement; she had ducked my one suggestion of the semester! She was oscillating between assertiveness and self-doubt, with the latter very much dependent on my responses. If I had intensified her doubts, I believe she would not have developed the enthusiasm that led to her successes. In her end-of-the-semester questionnaire she described the course as "perfect" for her: "My Friday conferences were always a good ending to my week because you made me feel so good about my writing—and about myself because of that."

### Andy

Andy seemed a quiet, self-contained person at first, with a respectful and gentle attitude toward other people, especially older ones. A large area of his life was what he called "personal"; he was reticent about exposing himself to others beyond certain boundaries. During the course he learned to open up some of these private places and make them subjects for writing. And he learned to enjoy sharing his writing. He did not seek out responses to his writing, but he was not afraid of them either, and his confidence was not shaken when they pointed to possible shortcomings. He could make up his own mind about what he wanted to do, and he could respect his own decisions. It was usually easy to explain problems or make suggestions to him, and he accepted encouragement.

His first conference had a typical opening; he said that he had started his paper but "might want to change it. I don't know yet." He meant not that he was stuck or low on confidence or suffering from doubts but only that he hadn't discovered how to make the paper work. I could always ask him for his evaluation of his progress ("How's it going?"), and he would answer with something like, "Pretty good." Then he would analyze his problem and sometimes make a suggestion himself for change. This time he recognized quickly that his suggestion wouldn't work, in response to two questions from me: "Have you got a lot of stories (anecdotes) you haven't told yet?" and "So you probably don't have enough variety of stories to make that the center of your paper?" So I told him directly what he could do. For a moment he was uncertain and questioned me, but when I reaffirmed my comment, he accepted it. We talked a minute longer, with my saying a bit more than he needed to hear, but the conference ended with his having a clear idea about what he would try next in his paper.

In this conference he revealed that he had been blocked by fear that the first section of his story was boring, but I assured him it had potential. He was looking not for assurances that I liked his writing but only for a solution to his problem. Confidence was not the central issue; success at doing something was. He didn't want to be derailed. So I chose to make a single comment that would deal with his self-diagnosed difficulty. This instance of instruction was embedded in a conversational conference that focused on his need and was not critical or condescending. I found that, because of the noninstructional atmosphere in the conference, and because of his reasonable level of confidence, I could "tell" him something without stirring a defensive response. It was a "collaborative" conference (Karliner's term).

His second conference gave me an easy chance to confirm his success in revising his story. Partly in response to comments from classmates, he had made changes beyond the one I had suggested in the previous conference. He was learning to use audience response in revision. After confirming, I moved the discussion on to his next paper topics. He briefly described his fifth paper while I listened. Then I turned to his fourth paper, which was a story developed from our class exercise on short-story writing. When, as usual, he described his uncertainties about the content of this story, I made no comment, only a hazy suggestion: "If you want to tack an ending on, you can." A long pause developed when I did not say any more (I wanted him to depend on himself, to work out his own solutions). He seemed surprised, asking, "Does that sound good?"—not a usual question for him. I was holding back because I sensed his confidence building as the conference progressed and because I saw that he was revising well. I hoped that he would understand after this conference that he could be on his own and do well.

I did not handle the third conference well. To begin with, I was confused by a repeated phrase and by the similarity of two names in a new paper, and it was a bad day for me for personal reasons. A pointless dispute developed in which I tried to prove several doubtful points and one sound one (that a major action in his story was hard to believe). The interesting fact was that Andy held his own in the dispute, not giving in to me or becoming doubtful about his position or intentions in his story, even when I tried to rewrite one of his sentences. Afterward, I felt that I had given too much direct instruction but this conference did Andy no apparent harm.

He returned three days later for his fourth conference with a much-improved version of his story, and with most of the changes his own (he did correct the plausibility problem). This conference was very short; I simply confirmed his success with his story. I concluded that his ability to assert himself and his confidence in his decisions had not only prevented a defensive reaction to the third conference but had also allowed him to make substantial revisions in his story "to make it clearer to the reader." My decision in the second conference to encourage his independence now seemed to be correct.

In his fifth conference Andy presented a new paper (describing the feeling of autumn in Vermont), checked with me to see if it worked ("You never know when someone else reads it if they get the idea or not"), and accepted my judgment that it did. My object was to confirm and encourage only. The paper was just average for Andy; he didn't have a "hot topic." I doubted that revision would have much effect on it. Since he had a sixth paper to write and the topic for it sounded promising, I decided to direct his attention to it.

This strategy appeared sound when, in his last conference, he showed me an amusing paper based on a far-fetched analogy (another of my class exercises). Except for the ending it was good, and it was his liveliest piece to date. It was one of the most popular papers in our final class reading (each student chose his or her favorite piece, and we passed them around in a large circle). I felt that my decision to encourage him in the fourth and fifth conferences (following the decision to leave him on his own) had paid off in his feeling free and able to explore new options in writing. Few students write analogy papers (since, for instance, comparing falling in love to the AT&T long-distance telephone network is challenging), but Andy had the confidence and the independence now to do such a paper.

With Andy I noticed that writers who are making progress through using conferences well often speak in a hesitant, broken syntax, with a number of repeated "speech tags" (Andy's were "kind of" and "and stuff"). Clear, correct speech is associated in my experience with more defensive writers. Another group of writers—those having major problems getting started—often show confusion in their speech, as well as many stops and starts. Andy's speech was not confused; he was simply searching for answers by trying different ways of wording his statements. I suspect that future research will find confidence more often associated with broken syntax than with clear assertion.

I felt that Andy presented me with a choice. I could try to show him how to be a more sophisticated writer with a better style, or I could help him find his own way to his own kind of development as a writer. I chose the latter, partly because I don't believe that there is an "Ideal Text" students should be imitating, and partly because I believe that development in writers should not be forced into preconceived patterns or directions. At the end of the semester Andy wrote these comments on the course: at the start he had been a writer who organized his topic into paragraphs in his head before he put anything on paper (but he did learn early in my class how to use freewriting as an exploratory technique). This basic habit of preorganizing did not change during the semester, nor did his need to wait to begin writing drafts until late at night or until his deadline was near (so the writing would come fast and without much editing). What changed was his attitude toward writing and the amount he could produce: "I really enjoyed some of the papers that I worked on, and I didn't think that I would ever enjoy a writing assignment." "To sum up what this class has done for me as a writer—at the beginning of the semester I would have filled half of the front page of this questionnaire, but now I feel that I could go on for pages."

A major reason for this change in Andy was, I feel, my alternation between direct instruction and encouragement within conferences conducted in a conversational mode. As he became more confident and more self-directed, I pulled back from instructing into a predominantly encouraging mode (the last three conferences). That gave him the chance to discover what he could do on his own.

### Barry

Barry's main effort all semester was to get started, then keep going, on a piece. He was visibly struggling to write. As he said at the end, "I've never really liked writing at all." My objective was simple: to help him get six papers written from beginning to end. Variety of topics, genres, or modes didn't matter; this writer needed to discover that he could complete the course and enjoy at least some of it.

Barry selected one idea from the course to repeat and emphasize: "lower your standards"—get a flow of words going. He described his preference for a "crummy" piece of paper "because then my ideas can be as bad as the paper—it's easy to lower my standards this way." It also helped him to be tired, and to think about his topics as he drove home and back to college on weekends. He mentioned, "I'm very uncomfortable when writing a letter to an important person." I suspected that his low self-esteem as a writer was traceable to high standards demanded by previous English teachers on assignments he could not handle well. He needed, I believed, to become free from his preoccupation with meeting standards and to discover how to "get black on white" (de Maupassant) in substantial quantities.

The two most noticeable of Barry's behaviors in conference were a very quiet voice (I sometimes couldn't hear him at all) and a barrage of nervous "y'know's" (his only speech tag). He had no trouble talking; he liked conversation, and it helped him to talk. His speech was full of broken syntax, and it wasn't easy for him to say exactly what he meant, but he kept trying until he had figured out an answer to a problem with a paper. He seemed to be fighting against confusion in his head as he sought answers. His mild assertiveness focused on getting answers; he had no difficulty accepting suggestions from me once he discovered that I wouldn't criticize his efforts to write. He was a somewhat shy, but not a defensive, self-protective person.

At the start of his first conference he identified the major problem with his draft: the ending didn't fit the story. I responded by confirming that the story was good. Then I asked for his judgment of the whole thing, throwing him off for a moment (he became apologetic about "weak spots" in the story). But he wanted to talk about the ending, so I let him, and responded as a reader with questions. Next I began to tell him what he might do, but in the manner of a reader saying what he might like to see happen next. It was apparent that the ending (a suicide) was too drastic and wouldn't work, but I didn't say so. I was waiting for Barry to come to that conclusion on his own. He did ("I guess I can figure out how to do that"), and by the next day he had a new ending. The key here, I think, was leaving control of his story in his hands by not acting as a teacher who has the answers.

Barry opened the second conference with an explanation of his efforts to keep his first ending, followed by his yielding to another reader's suggestion that the story should have a happy ending (someone had told him what I wouldn't). I let him talk, and he revealed how hard it was for him to assemble parts of a story into a successful whole. In the rest of the conference I did a little of everything, so to speak: some affirming that he had done the right thing, some confirming of his opinions and his success, some questioning, and some reminding that he had done what I had said he should in the previous conference. Then he shifted the discussion to his concern that "it doesn't flow easily" or "seem smooth reading" (ideas he had heard in class). This kind of focus shift I found a common event in conferences when I retained the conversational approach with an at least moderately assertive writer. My holding back seemed to encourage the introduction of new concerns of the writer. Barry continued by mentioning an aspect of his writing process: when he found a topic that worked for him, "it feels like a click," but then came the struggle "to get it on paper." He also needed to be interested in the topic or "you get kinda stuck." Expressing these self-observations to me seemed to help him and please him. He was getting some control over the first steps in his writing process: finding a topic and writing a workable draft. And he had the confidence now to say so.

I did not manage the third conference intelligently. When Barry said that he didn't like "the way I've worded" the new ending to his story ("It's kind of blah"), I jumped into a long instructional speech on vivid description. He understood what I was saying fairly soon, but I kept talking because his reserved manner gave no sign that he understood. I was annoyed by his quietness, when I should have realized that I was encouraging him to see me in a controlling, deciding role requiring respect from him. I could tell that I had "overtaught" when, after I stopped, he abruptly shifted the discussion to his next paper. Then he spoke again about his writing process ("I think it kind of helped me going piece by piece," "I don't know too much about it yet, but it's coming along") and about his freewriting ("When I'm in a bad mood . . . I can just rattle it off without even really thinking about it. Just let it flow"). This conference gave clear evidence that he preferred his own discoveries about his papers and way of writing over any instruction I gave, though he listened politely to me. I couldn't offer him the excitement he was finding in writing, the satisfaction and confidence that were helping him "tune out" my talking.

Beginning with the fourth conference Barry and I had writer-to-writer conversations concerning what he might do about the various places where he was "stuck" in his stories (he stayed with the story form once he found his "piece-by-piece" method of writing). My goals were to confirm his successes and express my enthusiasm for them, and to continue as a reader who speculates about what he might like to see happen. Barry was sometimes wedded to an idea and had trouble seeing that the story wouldn't work with that element in it. I could sense his confusion and bafflement at times when his plan for a story seemed to be collapsing (a threatening situation for him). The struggle to make the pieces fit consumed most of his attention. He accepted my ideas sometimes, and at others he came up with new solutions either from other readers or on his own. His talks with me seemed to be increasingly helpful to him as he became more confident and understood how to use our conversations to figure out answers to his problems. I saw in Barry a writer really struggling with the basic issues of content and organization, probably for the first time. I wanted to support that effort.

In his seventh conference I encouraged him to be satisfied with a story he felt was still "boring," because he had found a new topic that strongly interested him (and because he still had a sixth paper to write within three days). I didn't want to undermine his new enthusiasm and confidence with anxieties about having left too much writing until the last moment. His final paper was perfunctory, but since I was going to grade only three or four of the six, he had an "out." I didn't tell him he would lose some credit for lateness; he probably knew that without my help. I invited him to have an eighth conference, but he didn't come. I think his judgment on that was right; he had already gotten what he needed and what he could get from the course. As he wrote in his final questionnaire: "Overall I think I could say that through this course I can express myself through writing and feel more confident. I guess you could say I also enjoy writing a little more."

### Ellen

Ellen liked to revise her papers until she felt that they were done, before she showed them to anyone. She wrote at the end of the semester, "I still have the feeling that I want to be perfect (or close to it) before anyone else reads it." She also liked to plan her papers in her head first, so that revision would be mainly minor rewording, correcting grammar, and changing punctuation. This planning seemed to follow definite concepts about how a paper should be constructed. In conference she did not want to discuss revising for meaning or for impact on a reader; she was clearly uncomfortable with any suggestions about such changes. She spoke very quietly and, at least at first, in correct, formal English (no "yeah's," no speech tags, no stops and starts, no broken syntax). She never became really comfortable even with friendly conversation, and she avoided conferences (she missed six of them). She was noticeably reserved with me. I guessed that she was afraid of teachers because of their specific and often idiosyncratic demands, and that she took those demands very seriously. Her writing process (a rapid and safe path to "perfection") appeared to be a protection against criticism and poor grades.

She was a challenging writer to work with because of her nervousness about communicating. The quality of her writing added to the challenge; her papers were always at least competent, if not above average, so I could simply have confirmed their quality and accepted them as finished. That, however, would have made conferences pointless; and since one purpose of a series of conferences can be to extend a good writer's experience with process and with options in writing, I wanted to see her make some progress in those directions.

The first conference was a failure on both sides. Ellen didn't want to discuss specific possible changes, so she simply described her writing process in vague terms. When I "confirmed" her process, she said nothing, leaving the conference dead in the water. Then I launched into a long spiel about adding detail and shifting emphasis to "help the reader"; she continued to say nothing except "un-hunh." My effort at instructing (which I tried to make sound like a suggestion) only caused her to withdraw into herself. I was pushing her, to no avail.

My tactic in the second conference (which was a month later—she had been avoiding me) was to "receive" by casually conversing with her about her topic, then to try asking for her judgment. This tactic failed; she responded by parroting me about adding detail. So I returned to the "receiving" conversation, and finally made a suggestion: "It would be interesting to have that at the end of the paper." This conference seemed to work better; the topic was a familiar one she could talk about easily, and I was able to pay attention to her instead of her writing. I avoided sounding like a teacher (giving specific instruction), and I could feel her confidence and comfort grow during the conference.

By the time of her third conference I had resolved to avoid any direct instruction in favor of helping her find her voice and greater confidence with me. I assumed she was blocked from learning because of her tenseness with teachers (at mid-semester she wrote that what had helped her most in the first half of the course was "the lack of pressure for a perfect paper"). So in the third conference I encouraged her to talk; she did, and I "confirmed." When I spotted a weakness in the paper I would normally have mentioned, I dropped a hint; she didn't respond, and I overlooked it. By the end she was saying "you know," "yeah," and "yup," and seemed more comfortable.

Her fourth conference was a casual "conversation over the back fence" about her topic, with one suggestion from me at the end, which I embedded in a set of "confirming" remarks. The conference seemed to go well, but I was left with nagging doubts about whether I was really helping her. My notes made imme-diately after the conference focused on her self-protectiveness, which seemed to narrow her range of choices as a writer (topics, styles, voice). I believe now that I was temporarily troubled by the sense that she saw me as a teacher making puzzling and perhaps unreasonable demands on her (Why couldn't she write without all this hassle of talking about it?). I had, no doubt, expected too much of us both.

In her last conference I decided not to discuss her paper at all but only to ask about her process in writing it. She replied that it had taken about a half-hour and had needed only a few minor revisions. Since it was a competent paper, I agreed with Ellen that lack of pressure had helped her fluency as a writer. She seemed happy about writing it with less effort than usual.

In retrospect I think that conferences helped Ellen more than I thought at the time. Her writing process did not change much (the "perfect" papers were coming faster now), but she was beginning to relax. I feel that before she can accept fault in her work enough to begin "messing up the page" with extended revisions, especially for meaning and effect on an audience, she will need a good deal more contact with a supportive, encouraging writing instructor. She made clear to me how important the student-teacher relationship can be in stimulating a particular writer's development.

## Donna

Each of my students brings an agenda to my course—a set of habits, an established way of attacking a writing assignment. With most students my effort is to change this agenda into a more productive, more personally satisfying writing process (a few have already found what works well for them). The amount of change possible in one semester ranges widely from one student to another, but is usually quite limited, often focusing on one problem or aspect of writing. And interestingly, most of the change does not become visible until after midsemester. I have to wait for it.

Donna's agenda contained two strong preoccupations. One was a need or desire to write about cases in the news that had attracted considerable attention. She dropped this concern in mid-April and then wrote with more fluency and pleasure. The second was her belief that she would always have great trouble ending any paper she had started. Both of these preoccupations I felt had been established in previous writing classes; I set out to reduce her anxiety in hopes that she would become free of them. She was an anxiety-driven writer, and she remained "nervous" (her word) throughout the semester. She missed six conferences out of a possible thirteen, and she was absent from class nine times (both were high figures for my study group).

In her first questionnaire she stated that freewriting was the most helpful part of the first half of the course for her, and in her second questionnaire and her "How I Write" piece she focused on the usefulness to her of a free flow of ideas. I think that the feeling of being "freed up" was a major contribution of the class to her writing. She was, however, not fully aware of what was happening. In her end-of-the-semester questionnaire she wrote: "I feel that I'm a better writer because of this class. I can't really pinpoint why though. I'm not really sure. I believe it's easier for me to sit down and write a paper than it was before. I feel I use more detail in my stories than I would have before. I also feel that I can tie a story together easier and end it faster." She did not see any connection between her difficulty in ending a paper and her earlier focus on ideas taken from the news. Naturally she would have trouble believing that her problem could be traced to teachers' demands that she write about news topics she was "interested in." Her "ending" problem vanished when she began to find her own ideas. In "How I Write" she said:

> It's really hard for me to pinpoint how I write. At first I would have an idea and write a paragraph from that. Then I would be stuck, I couldn't come up with anything. Then, I started getting ideas in all these weird places. I would be in philosophy class and out of nowhere an idea would come to me about my story. It was like a newsflash inside my head. So I would jot down some ideas.
>
> Now when I have to write a paper I usually write a paragraph, and sit there and stare at it. Soon after, ideas usually come to me right off. If this is not the case I usually file the idea for another time. Then I'll write another paragraph and do the same thing.

> If ideas come readily I usually stay with this idea. I find it easier to write this way and the ending comes quicker.

She had become her own source of "newsflashes"! Meanwhile it had taken her so long to reach this new "freer" condition that the end of the semester was close, and she still had three papers to write. That created a new anxiety, which she handled by writing rapidly and avoiding conferences. She felt that she might slip back into her "ending" problem and fail the course. Talking with me presented the threat of new teacher demands that might confuse her and block her writing. Here was a situation in which a student could do better on her own than with my responses in conference. I had already given her the help she needed by introducing her to freewriting in class and requiring it on a regular basis.

In Donna's first conference she began: "I wanted to know exactly where I was going because I missed my first one [didn't discover an ending for my first paper]. I started to finish it, but I did four drafts and I still can't end it . . . I wanted to take something that would have an ending." In this case the ending was to be death (a sure way to stop a paper!). She meant that she could not exercise control over her writing; something outside her would have to do that. Since she wrote capably, I decided to respond by playing the interested, questioning, and impressed reader. My approval of her paper excited her ("Do you really? Wow!"), but then she had to ask, "Do you think I should keep going?" I was emphatic that she should, but I gave no suggestions. I thought she needed to discover that she could write her own papers well without checking with a teacher.

Donna opened her second conference by repeating her worry that her paper wouldn't end. I offered a few suggestions for endings, but decided to drop that in favor of confirming her successes and discussing in general terms her concern about finding endings. Next she described her start on a new paper, with special attention to her use of freewriting as a way of finding ideas. I let her talk without interrupting because I sensed her desire to control the direction of the conversation, and having control in the presence of a teacher was what she needed. I have found that when students assert themselves in conferences, something good is usually happening.

By the beginning of Donna's third conference she had decided on an ending for her paper (this was one week after the first conference), but she was also very much concerned that she hadn't finished even one paper by midsemester. I noticed that her assertiveness in conference was growing. She was telling me now as much as asking me ("I'm almost there. I'm just going to make some comment about how a situation like this could arise," as opposed to, "You think that'd be okay?"). I attempted to change the direction of the conference, away from anxious talk to a simple suggestion about a way to make her paper work better (insert asterisks or a line to break the page), but I failed. She ended: "I've got to straighten things out. . . . I'm getting nervous." In so tense a situation a teacher has a hard time knowing what might help.

The paper Donna brought to her fourth conference was a breakthrough for her. It had been stimulated by a class exercise and had almost poured out of her. Clearly it was a "hot topic," and it was well written. The ending had not been a problem. In the conference she again alternated between asserting her enthusiasm for her accomplishment and expressing her doubts that I would approve it. I gave her several suggestions for editing (pronoun reference and punctuation), assuring her that otherwise the paper was fine. She was so excited that twice in the conference her words came tumbling out in near total confusion. She was most impressed because "this is the easiest one," "this came out so easy," without recopying or "anything." A great discovery—she didn't have to be blocked! Unfortunately she still had three papers to write in the last three weeks: "I'm getting so nervous. I only have three done."

Three weeks later, on May 7, Donna breezed in to her fifth conference with about half of a fourth paper for me to read but refused to discuss the rest of it or let me see a draft she said she had done. I felt again that she didn't want any interference from me. She had six days left to complete half the writing for the course (and she was graduating). Again she mentioned that she had freewritten the paper ("I don't believe it!"), with the implication that I might disapprove. I said nothing about her writing, I had the sense that I might confuse or upset her. (I could have reassured her about freewriting her papers, but she was taking charge of the conference by talking fast and asserting herself. I was sure she didn't want to listen.)

I did not see Donna again in my office. She sent a friend to pick up her papers. On May 7 I was afraid that she had given up the course, but she completed the required papers and passed. In retrospect, I think she was so seriously blocked that she could not have avoided the end-of-the-semester bind she was in. Her behavior at the end was consistent with what I had learned about her anxieties as a writer. The gains she reported in her final evaluation I think represented important advances for her in writing.

### Carol

Carol's writing included a noticeable number of mistakes in spelling, punctuation, and grammar, and in our first meeting I sensed that she had frequently been reminded of them. In the past, when I have asked students like Carol about their "errors," they have usually commented that their problems have persisted despite years of special attention (even private tutoring). As a result I prefer to try a different approach: I assume that too much direct instruction is to blame. Of course in this I run from one extreme to the other, but that is intentional. I feel that an opposite dose may be a successful antidote to previous experience. I want to know if supportive, "benign" neglect of students' errors will help.

To carry out this plan I overlook errors as much as I can. For instance, I suspected that another instructor had advised Carol to take my course "to help you with your writing" (or some such euphemism, if any was used), but I did not ask her if that was the case. I even avoided inquiring how she felt about the errors on her pages, because I didn't want to suggest that I was concerned. I relied instead on my experience that errors tend to disappear through a series of revisions if the student's attention is primarily on meaning and word choice. Of course this happens partly because students ask their friends for help with proofreading, a situation I encourage by pointing out that published writers need and have editors. I suspect that students learn more that sticks with them when they consult peers. Asking me should be a last resort (and my students seldom do, yet very few errors appear in most final drafts). Carol's conference transcripts show that I kept postponing editing while I waited for encouragement to show its effects, until I finally decided not to edit with her at all.

Did my approach produce the effects I had hoped for? My research materials aren't appropriate for a firm answer, but there are some indications. Carol's final drafts were almost entirely free from mechanical errors (something had happened, but I did not learn what), and her end-of-the-semester questionnaire stated:

> After this course I look at writing [as] more enjoyable. I used to think of writing as an unpleasant task. I feel more comfortable with my writing.
> The best part of this course was the positive comments. No one is perfect and I needed a lot of help and I felt very comfortable talking to you about my writing.
> I feel that this course was beneficial and would recommend it to anyone. It is a different way to look at writing—something we all could use.

Throughout the semester Carol was concerned about needing "a lot of help" and not being "perfect." In her self-evaluation she described her day-long struggle to get her papers started (ending up alone in a bathroom full of steam!). She had not become a fluent writer. At midsemester she wrote that freewriting was pleasant but no help with her papers (the opposite of Donna's experience in this respect). Yet she emphasized an increase in enjoyment and comfort and thought that the course was "beneficial." If "the best part of this course was the positive comments," I am encouraged to think that my almost exclusive attention to her achievements paid off for her. But I have no clear evidence that the number of her errors in final drafts decreased as a direct result of my conference strategies.

In her first conference Carol described her frustration with finding workable topics. I decided to have a simple sociable conversation with her on this subject. When the chance to edit a draft came up later, I said that I would postpone "going over" her writing until Friday, two days later (she didn't show up again for two weeks). At this point I was uncertain what role to adopt in conferences, so I decided to wait until she had done several drafts of three papers. I needed more information.

The two-week delay was a clue. She liked the paper she brought to her second conference, making it easy for me to have a writer-to-writer conversation and ask her, "What's next?" (in her draft). At the end I felt free to make a suggestion about restructuring the story, which she accepted easily: "No, I don't think once I get back into it I'll have any problem." Since she had waited for her second conference until she felt good about her new paper, I decided not to proceed to editing any of her papers (there were several in her folder). I didn't want to hurt her comfort or confidence, which seemed not very secure. I decided once again to wait and see.

In her third conference Carol talked easily and well about her problems with the paper we had discussed in our second meeting. I confirmed her successes so far and encouraged her desire to continue working on it. Next I lapsed into a largely unnecessary monologue that included a suggestion, but she didn't seem troubled by my taking over the conversation briefly; I didn't distract her from her intentions. I was still trying to decide if the time for instruction had arrived. While I waited, I held back on advice on specific details, trying only general suggestions.

An important moment for decision came in the fourth conference. A new paper was at the final editing stage. After confirming her success with revision, I suggested that she "correct some of the things you put down that you didn't intend to put down that way" (I assumed she had miscopied rather than calling an error an error—a tactic). A sudden increase in the strength of her voice suggested that what she had been afraid of was about to happen. When I said no more about correcting, she was suddenly very happy (she was free to do what she could on her own). My comment on this conference (at the time I transcribed) pointed to her still shaky confidence and low self-esteem as a writer. I had decided to encourage her independence in writing as much as I could.

I used the fifth conference as a confidence-builder. I started with sociable conversation, then asked for her judgment of her paper. Next I gave a few reader responses while also confirming her success with writing a travel piece. She accepted my various approaches calmly, and I was satisfied that I had done what I wanted for her confidence.

I was less successful in the sixth conference because I tried too hard to move into a more instructional mode. When I attempted to explain ways in which she could change her new story, my advice sounded too complicated. I would have been confused myself by such talk. Her response was to change the subject abruptly. I didn't have another chance; Carol's seventh conference involved only turning in finished papers. She was happy that she was ready to graduate; she had nothing more that she wanted to discuss.

Both Donna and Carol were competent and creative writers who were blocked by specific misconceptions about how to develop an effective personal writing process. Donna's misunderstandings concerned topic sources and conclusions; Carol's focused on the role of correctness. Both benefited from the chance to explore their writing talents in a low-pressure, supportive atmosphere. Both seemed ready at the end of the course to approach future writing tasks more capably. I think, too, that Carol has discovered how to view her errors in a more constructive way, and so will have less difficulty with them.

## CONCLUSIONS

The results of this study support the view that the locus of learning should be primarily within the student writer and that learning should be stimulated and guided by skillfully selected modes of interacting. I found my roles, in each conference, to be more important than any relevant subject matter, so I decided in some situations to forgo discussing obvious problems in the interests of preserving a role. In order to achieve my choice of objectives for each student, I employed a variety of roles. When low confidence appeared to be the predominant problem, a role that supported and confirmed seemed best. When inadequate confidence was combined with other difficulties, such as an active struggle to organize and revise, or a set of constricting writing habits or anxieties, alternating among several roles seemed most effective. In such cases I could choose to supplement the supportive role with various sorts of collaboration, such as sociable conversation, writer-to-writer talk, reader-to-writer comments on possible reactions to a text, attentive listening with a few neutral remarks, or making specific suggestions. These collaborative roles fall in the middle range of the spectrum of possible teacher responses. Interestingly, in all of them a conversational, tentative, exploratory tone worked better than a positive, authoritative one; that is, an atmosphere of encouragement was preferable to an impression of direct instruction, because such an atmosphere placed control over learning in the student's hands.

This study also suggests that an instructor may have to focus his or her efforts on the "agendas" students bring to conferences. Existing writing habits or attitudes can be so disabling that the pedagogical objectives of the writing course should be secondary to the student's immediate needs. I also found it essential to treat each student as a unique individual in conferences. General descriptions of the teacher roles I adopted in conferences obscure the careful tailoring of my responses to the specific person who was writing. Role descriptions, therefore, must be interpreted flexibly, with discretion.

During this study no situation occurred in which direct instruction was the best role choice. There are undoubtedly some such situations, but I think fewer will be found than most teachers expect. My experience, in this research and generally, is that confidence is a writer's central need; conferences in which direct instruction dominates increase confidence for very few students. But this conclusion does not imply an abandonment of specific teaching. Collaborative conferences provide many opportunities to teach particular concepts or strategies within a "low-key" environment. And students who are permitted control over their writing, whether through collaboration or support, learn a good deal on their own and from each other. I have found that the teacher is frequently not the only (nor the best) source of instruction in the writing course.

## REFERENCES

Avery, Carol S. "Young Writers Learning to Read." Northeastern University Summer Institute on Writing, August 1983.

Berkenkotter, Carol. "Student Writers and Their Sense of Authority over Texts." *College Composition and Communication* 35 (October 1984): 312–19.

Bissex, Glenda L. *GNYS AT WRK: A Child Learns to Write and Read*. Cambridge, Mass.: Harvard University Press, 1980.

Brannon, Lil, and C. H. Knoblauch. "On Students' Rights to Their Own Texts: A Model of Teacher Response." *CCC* 33 (May 1982): 157–66.

Graves, Donald H. *Writing: Teachers & Children at Work*. Portsmouth, N.H.: Heinemann Educational Books, 1983.

Jacobs, Suzanne E., and Adela B. Karliner. "Helping Writers to Think." *College English* 38 (January 1977): 489–505.

Karliner, Adela B. "Collaborator or Evaluator? The Role of the Instructor in the Individual Writing Conference." University of California at San Diego, 1979.

Murray, Donald M. "The Listening Eye: Reflections on the Writing Conference." *Learning by Teaching*. Upper Montclair, N.J.: Boynton/Cook, 1982.

———. "Teaching the Other Self: The Writer's First Reader." *CCC* 33 (May 1982): 140–47.

———. *Write to Learn*. New York: Holt, 1984.

Perl, Sondra. "Understanding Composing." *CCC* 31 (December 1980): 363–69.

Rico, Gabriele L. *Writing the Natural Way*. Los Angeles: J. P. Tarcher, 1983.

Sommers, Nancy. "Revision Strategies of Student Writers and Experienced Adult Writers." *CCC* 31 (December 1980): 378–87.

Sommers, Nancy. "Responding to Student Writing." *CCC* 33 (May 1982): 148–56.

Susi, Geraldine L. "The Teacher/Writer: Model, Learner, Human Being." *Language Arts* 61 (November 1984): 712–16.

Ziv, Nina D. "The Effect of Teacher Comments on the Writing of Four College Freshmen." *New Directions in Composition Research*, edited by Richard Beach and Lillian S. Bridwell. New York: Guilford, 1984.

# CHAPTER 7

# The Effect of Poetry in a First-Grade Classroom

*Elizabeth Cornell*

In Liz Cornell's first-grade classroom, as in Ferguson McKay's college office, student writing is encouraged in ways besides direct instruction. Instead of telling the children how to write poetry, Liz provides an atmosphere where poetry is abundant and alive. In her research she sought to examine closely how that poetry affected her students' language, reading, and writing. Her presentation is likewise a showing rather than a telling, as she documents the poetic life of her classroom during one year.

After sending her two daughters off to college, Liz returned herself, earning a degree in education with a minor in art from Muskingum College in Ohio. Having moved then to Lebanon, New Hampshire, with her husband, she began her teaching career as an art teacher with 519 students in four different elementary schools in the Hartford, Vermont, school district. "When I began to feel like 'the old woman in a shoe,' I requested a switch to the self-contained classroom, where I found I could do all the exciting things an art teacher does and at the same time enjoy a closer relationship with a smaller group of children."

Having taught second grade for three years and then first grade for five, Elizabeth Cornell spent the 1985–86 school year on sabbatical, visiting schools in Europe, Canada, and across the United States to gather information for her current research on classroom arrangement and teacher expectations.

## September 5

My room is at the rear of a two-story brick structure built for high school students, located behind the community grocery in the small town of White River Junction, Vermont. Entering the door at the back of the room, you will see nineteen small desks arranged in a block U shape which opens at the chalkboard. Each child is the center of attention, and it is possible for each and every one to make eye contact with the others while reading, writing, discussing, working on art projects, or whatever the class is doing. This year, because of class expansion, the U is larger and there is a nine-by-twelve-foot rug in the center of the desk arrangement, affording relief from sitting in chairs as the children move back and forth, depending on the activity.

Today was the first day of the school year, and I sense already this is the best class I have ever had. I am teased by my husband and colleagues, who have heard this statement before. Each year I seem to feel this, and each year I fear next year will be different. As my children leave, going on to second grade, I know I will never again have a class like this one, and yet each fall, somehow, my class is the best yet. This year is no exception.

As a student teacher I discovered the magic of poetry in the classroom. My master teacher had the habit of writing something on the chalkboard each morning for the children to copy while she was busy with her reading groups. During my solo week, in search of a little fun, I found the poem:

> Jerry Hall
> Is so small
> A rat could eat him
> Hat and all

which I put on the blackboard for the daily copy exercise. I called for a volunteer to read the poem before we started to write. Several hands shot up. Not wanting to discourage their eagerness by selecting only one, I took time for a couple of children to read it. As each child read, other hands came popping up until every last one of them had read the poem. Children who couldn't have read this little poem at first read as well as the best readers; even the tail end of the class succeeded. After twenty repetitions the children had memorized the four lines.

The exercise took only ten minutes and no one was bored; in fact they loved it. Another poem the next mornng, and I was on to something that makes reading easier and encourages expressive and creative language.

I have continued this daily practice with nine classes of children, each child taking a turn reading four lines of poetry. The best readers read first, with the other children raising their hands when they feel confident enough to read.

My first full-time teaching assignment was in a basement with windows at ground level. The children who rode the early buses would peek through the windows to read the new day's poem as they waited on the playground for school to begin. My students who lived close to the school would come back to the grounds to play on the swings in the late afternoon and, seeing a light, would knock on the window, pressing their noses flat against the glass to see the poem printed on the chalkboard for the morrow's reading. Not being able to resist the opportunity, I would open the window and we would have a practice session, children hanging through the window reading poetry.

My children taught me, that first year, that children love poetry. Year after year the children reaffirm that understanding. John Ciardi said as he was being interviewed by Charles Kuralt on the television show "Sunday Morning," "Poetry opens up such wonderful possibilities," and so it has with us.

## THE USE OF POETRY
## FOR BEGINNING READERS

The child is busy having a good time with the poem. The poem pleases and involves him. He responds to it in an immediate muscular way. He recognizes its performance at once and wants to act with it.

*John Ciardi*

Once one has learned to experience the poem as a poem, there inevitably arrives a sense that one is also experiencing himself as a human being.

*John Ciardi*

Researchers of the human brain would have us understand the need to design schooling in such a way that both sides of the brain are stimulated. The selection of early reading material must take into consideration both the left and right hemispheres to guarantee success for the beginning reader.

Short poems with repeating words and repeating lines work well, since they involve the spatial, holistic perception of the right brain as well as the analytical, logical, verbal functioning of the left hemisphere. The rhyme, rhythm, and repetition of a little poem can be sung, clapped, and danced, pulling the whole child into the activity.

The poem works best when it has meaning to the child, although children love nonsense verse as well. The length of the material is also important; children become discouraged when reading material is too long or involved.

On the first day of school the children come expecting to learn to read, and I don't intend to disappoint them. I always start the year with:

> I like shadows.
> I like sun.
> I like you
> More than anyone.

This little poem is a good beginner. It has rhyme and rhythm and is short and easy to memorize. The repetition emphasizes the size and shape of the words "I like." The repeated lines give the child a sense of security and confidence. The children like this poem immediately. They want to know, more than anything else, that I like them.

Each child reads as I point to the words written in bold letters on a chart. One by one, the children raise their hands when they feel confident. By the time they have heard it eighteen times, the little poem is in their heads.

We read it again in unison, just before dismissal, and the children take a copy of it home to read to their parents or anyone who will listen, and, sure enough, they are all readers.

When a child thinks he can do something, he can. When he thinks he can't, he surely will have difficulty.

## September 13

Today we had an intern visiting in the morning, and I guess I am basically a performer. I enjoy showing off my class. We had finished USSR (Uninterrupted Sustained Silent Reading), and were putting our books away and readying for reading the four-line poem. I was pulling the poetry chart to the center of attention when Michael D., on his way back to his seat, caught sight of the words:

> I like shadows.
> I like sun.
> I like you
> More than anyone.

Without waiting for the class to settle, Michael D. began to read as if he were the only one in the room, and before I knew it other voices in the room, not in unison, were doing the same thing. I could sense their fun in recognizing the familiar words. I pulled them together and we read the poem in unison. We also read:

> Come and see,
> Come and see,
> A black hen has laid
> A white egg for me.

These poems I use early in the year. The repetition helps to make the reading easier. We then read the new poem:

> Dog means dog
> And cat means cat
> And there are lots
> Of words like that.

I encourage the children as they read to fill the room with their voices. When the child speaks up, the class's attention is better held, and it's amazing how the children's self-confidence grows when they are able to speak and hold the attention of the group.

Following snack, we had been reading *Brown Bear*, Bill Martin's Big Book. (The Big Books are scaled as large as twenty-four inches square, with bold print large enough to be seen from a distance of four to six feet. In a one-to-one situation, the child sits either on the reader's lap or near enough to be able to see the words as they are read, as well as the pictures in the book. The Big Books are an attempt to satisfy this need for "lap treatment," as I call it, for a whole group of children. The large type can be seen when the text is read in unison, sung, or whatever.) Reading the Big Book in unison had lost its excitement, so I decided to add a new dimension by giving each child a book to hold. I borrowed eight small copies from the adjoining first grade, and together with my eight we had almost enough for everyone. I brought out my guitar and we sang the words, "Brown Bear, Brown Bear, what do you see? I see a redbird looking at me," to the tune of "Baa Baa Black Sheep." It took quite a while to get through the whole book, only to hear the request to "sing it again." We voted and decided to do it again. The performance went well, and our guest was impressed with the capacity of these five- and six-year-olds to stay on task for such a long period of time.

Later in the morning Danny returned from gym class, walked to his seat, and, passing the poetry chart, looked at the words and said, as if a light bulb had just been turned on, "I can read that," and he did.

## October 11

This year, for the first time, a child was spending a second year with me. Mike T. was repeating not because of any lack of intelligence but because of immature behavior. Today we all read:

> If I were as small
> As a little black ant,
> I would do things
> That big people can't.

Mike was familiar with the poem from last year's reading. He could read some of the words and, in so doing, was able to put the other words in their places. After only one reading he could recite it. I could feel the excitement in his voice as he recognized the familiar words. In fact, he read it before school started. I was afraid he would be bored with the same group of little poems used in his last year's first-grade experience; instead, he loved the introduction of each little poem, greeting it as an old friend who conjures up pleasant memories. They are obviously a part of him.

### October 18

Ten minutes before lunch the children gathered for poetry reading, a time scheduled for my reading poetry to them. They sat without moving as I read from the collection *Poems Children Will Sit Still For* (ed. Beatrice Schenk de Regniers, Eva Moore, and Mary Michaels White): first "The Swing" by Robert Louis Stevenson, followed by "Brother" by Mary Ann Hoberman, then "My Favorite Word" by Lucia and James I. Hymes, Jr. I had just finished reading "Someone" by Walter de la Mare, mentioning that I would read "The Old Wife and the Ghost" by James Reeves next time, when Michael D. petitioned me with an urgent "Read it now." I couldn't resist, so we went to lunch a couple of minutes late.

THE OLD WIFE AND THE GHOST

> There was an old wife and she lived all alone
>     In a cottage not far from Hitchin:
> And one bright night, by the full moon light,
>     Comes a ghost right into her kitchen.
>
> About that kitchen neat and clean
>     The ghost goes pottering round.
> But the poor old wife is deaf as a boot
>     And so hears never a sound.
>
> The ghost blows up the kitchen fire,
>     As bold as bold can be;
> He helps himself from the larder shelf,
>     But never a sound hears she.
>
> He blows on his hands to make them warm,
>     And whistles aloud "Whee-hee!"
> But still as a sack the old soul lies
>     And never a sound hears she.

From corner to corner he runs about,
   And into the cupboard he peeps;
He rattles the door and bumps on the floor,
   But still the old wife sleeps.

Jangle and bang go the pots and pans,
   As he throws them all around;
And the plates and mugs and dishes and jugs,
   He flings them all to the ground.

Madly the ghost tears up and down
   And screams like a storm at sea;
And at last the old wife stirs in her bed—
   And it's "Drat those mice," says she.

Then the first cock crows and morning shows
   And the troublesome ghost's away.
But oh! what a pickle the poor wife sees
   When she gets up next day.

"Them's tidy big mice," the old wife thinks,
   And off she goes to Hitchin,
And a tidy big cat she fetches back
   To keep the mice from her kitchen.

As I was reading, a worrying thought occurred to me: perhaps the poem was above their heads. It vanished with five-year-old Jeff's comment, "She should have her ears examined!"

## October 22

Charlie and his father stood at the entrance to the classroom. Both were reluctant to let loose. Charlie kissed his dad good-bye and went with me to the empty seat reserved for him. We expected our new boy last Monday and wondered, through the week, if there really was such a person as Charlie.

After being introduced to the other children, Charlie sat watching to see what was expected of him as we moved through the early-morning business. At 8:40, the scheduled time for reading our four-line poem, eighteen children took their turns:

Old Mother Witch
Fell in a ditch,
Picked out a penny
And thought she was rich.

It was Charlie's turn. He seemed unaware that he, too, would be expected to read. "We didn't learn those words in my other school," was his response when asked if he would like to read it. I said, "Don't worry about the words, just read it." I think he surprised himself as he repeated the words the other children had read.

Reading is the transfer of meaning from one mind to another through the medium of written language. Charlie didn't know this. He had been introduced to reading as a task—saying the words correctly, one after another—and not as a process of "getting meaning."

After snack we gathered on the rug with twenty *Mother Goose* paperbacks, reading several poems, including "The Old Woman in the Shoe," "Three Little Kittens," and "Old Mother Hubbard." Some I read with knowing readers chiming in; with others we took turns or read in unison. We sang "Sing a Song of Sixpence," "Three Blind Mice," and "Yankee Doodle." Michael D. sat by my elbow pestering me, wanting to read "This Little Piggy Went to Market." We spent about twenty minutes going from page to page.

### October 30

Trick or treat,
Trick or treat,
Give us something
Good to eat.

Give us candy,
Give us cake,
Give us something
Good to take.

"I said the poem to my mother," Katie announced to me this morning. "I said it at suppertime." Smiling, I asked the class, "How many of you can say the poem without looking at the words?" The poem was introduced yesterday, and thirteen of the children raised their hands. We then took turns reading the poem, and every child read without an error. This little poem has rhyme, repetition, rhythm, is predictable, and has meaning for children, making reading easy and fun.

### November 8

I'm losing all my teeth
One by one.
Pretty soon, if they keep going,
There'll be none.

At 8:05, before school started, I overheard Katie reading the poem, on the chart, which we had taken turns reading the morning before. Mae heard her reading and joined in.

At 2:10, just before dismissal, Mae went to the shelf for a piece of paper. The shelf was empty. "Mrs. Cornell, can I write the poem down so I can read it to my mom and dad?"

### November 19

> Thank you for the world so sweet.
> Thank you for the food we eat.
> Thank you for the birds that sing.
> Thank you God for everything.

Catherine recognized the poem on the chart as the prayer her family says before each meal. She read it first, with special interest. The reading was easy for most of the children. The repetition helped, but I suspect that many of them have heard it before. The children were unusually quiet, and a sense of reverence settled over the room as each child took a turn.

### November 26

Waiting in the hall before recess and again as we stood in the hall before music, the children read the poem "I'm Losing All My Teeth" on our "teeth" bulletin board. Renee shouted (although we're supposed to be quiet in the hall), "I can read that, Mrs. Cornell!" "So can I!" came from April. Renee read it, followed by April, and I do believe they all would have taken their turns had we had the time. The children reluctantly moved on, pressed by me, but a repeat performance occurred as we waited for our restroom users after music class.

### January 2

Our book for today was *Dan the Flying Man*. "Dan, Dan, the flying man, catch me, catch me if you can," I read aloud. Then we read it twice in unison, and the children were still not ready to stop. Several times during the day—at lunch, in the boys' restroom, and when we were lining up to go home—there were takeoffs on the poem:

> Mike, Mike, the motor bike
>
> Katie, Katie, the pretty lady
>
> Mae, Mae came today

If not for the catchy rhyme and rhythm, the children would not have lingered or toyed with the words so long after the initial reading.

## February 3

Angela brought a children's poetry anthology to school and read several poems to the class. She had obviously practiced reading them. She shared the book with Katie, who came to me all excited when she discovered one of the poems we had on the poetry chart:

> One, two, three, four, five,
> I caught a hare alive.
> Six, seven, eight, nine, ten,
> I let her go again.

"Mrs. Cornell," she said with an accusing look in her eyes, "That's where you get all these poems, from books."

## March 9

Patti told me about climbing into bed with her parents and reciting the poem, "Five Little Squirrels." "I remembered the whole thing, Mrs. Cornell."

## March 10

We are memorizing

> KEEP A POEM IN YOUR
> POCKET
>
> Keep a poem in your pocket
> and a picture in your head
> and you'll never feel lonely
> at night when you're in bed.
>
> The little poem will sing to you,
> the little picture bring to you
> a dozen dreams to dance to you
> at night when you're in bed.
>
> So—
> Keep a picture in your pocket
> and a poem in your head
> and you'll never feel lonely
> at night when you're in bed.
>
> *Beatrice Schenk de Regniers*

Carrie wrote in her journal of feeling lonely and thinking of the poem:

> March 18, 1985
> Last night I felt lonely,
> And then I remembered
> the poem that we learned
> in school. So I thought for
> a minute and then I thought
> of a poem. The poem is, I like school,
> it is fun, at school I can
> play in the sun And
> then I thought of a picture.
> The picture was me playing
> in the sun. I like the sun.

## March 22

Katie rides the late bus and often stays after school for a reading conference. We both enjoy the relaxed atmosphere, the peace and quiet of the empty room. Having finished the story in her reading book, Katie began to read the poems taped to the window shades. She finished those off, walked to the chalkboard to sign out her reading book, and, coming to the flip chart with still more poems, couldn't resist reading the one on top. She flipped it over to the next one and would have gone through all the poems we have read daily since the beginning of the year had I been willing to spend the time. She loved the audience, but most of all she loves the poems. No matter how many times they have been read, good poems still have the power to hold a child's attention.

## April 9

Michael T. was tardy again. He entered the classroom quietly and sat down in his seat. We were in the middle of USSR. As we finished, a hum went up in the room as the children put their books away. Michael walked up to me. "Mrs. Cornell, I was reading when I walked to school this morning. I can read two poems in my new reading book." He wanted to demonstrate his skill right then and there. He hadn't practiced the first story, but he had read both "Mice" by Rose Fyleman and "Song of the Train" by David McCord, poems considered by the publisher to be much more difficult than the story. He knew where every poem in the book was.

## April 15

As Mae finished her story and turned the page, she appealed, "I wanta read this poem. I can go *foofff* right through the whole thing."

THINGS I LIKE

I like a little ladybug
Crawling on my thumb,
I like a little hummingbird,
Hum—hum—hum—

I like a little sea shell,
And dandelion fuzz,
Or a brave little bumble-bee
Buzz—buzz—buzz

I like a little lizard
Hiding in the dark,
But most, I like a puppy,
Bark—bark—bark.

*Patricia Miles Martin*

Mae read so well she had obviously read it many times for her own enjoyment.

Parents often comment, and I've heard teachers say too, "He's not really reading, he has just memorized the words." Memory is often frowned upon, which is hard to understand, because memory is an important step in the reading process. Both my daughters learned to read before they started to school. I didn't teach them. They learned to read as I read and reread their favorite books. How many times I heard, "Read it again, Mommy." They began correcting me when I carelessly substituted a wrong word. They had memorized the words that went with a certain picture on a certain page. But soon they began recognizing the words in a different context, and I realized they had been concentrating on the size and shape of the word as well, making discoveries as I read to them. The same thing happens when a child reads a poem over and over again.

## March 30

The record book showed that Katie was on page 72 in her reading book. She read the next story, and on the following page was her favorite poem, the one she had read to me the first time she came with this particular book for a reading conference.

NIGHT SONG

Out of the window
A yellow balloon
Is caught in the treetop
And looks like the moon.

Into the window
It smiles at me
And asks me to lift it
From out of the tree.

*Myra Cohn Livingston*

"This is my favorite poem," she chirped. "I can sing it, Mrs. Cornell."

Katie had read this poem so many times, she had put the words to music. When a child likes a poem as Katie does this one, it is not difficult to get her to read it several times. When reading the material for the first time, the child spends her energy sounding out the words. When she goes over it, in repeated readings, she is free to make discoveries about how the words are put together, making sense out of phonetic consistencies, syllables, beginning and ending sounds, punctuation, and so on. When children are constantly reading new material, discoveries are less likely.

## THE EFFECT OF POETRY READING ON POETRY WRITING

My children begin to write poetry in the late winter or early spring. I have witnessed the same happening with both first- and second-grade children over the past eight years. The poetry writing occurs after a considerable amount of exposure to poetry in the classroom and also in direct proportion to that exposure.

Whenever poetry writing is mentioned in the company of other teachers, the immediate response is, "Have you read *Wishes, Lies, and Dreams?*" by Kenneth Koch, or they describe some other means of closure to get children to write poetry. Closure is a technique requiring the student to complete something started or instigated by the teacher. The idea is the teacher's, and the task of finishing it is relatively easy; for example, our second-grade teachers use closure to encourage poetry writing for a bulletin-board display. The child's name is written vertically. The first word of each line begins with a letter of the child's name. The words are to tell something about the person whose name is used:

BILL

B   Beautiful
I    Instead of
L   Like a
L   Lizard.

Closure is merely a starter for those timid children needing extra encouragement. It allows for some creativity but at the same time denies the self-initiative embodied within the full creative process.

Closure should be used sparingly and needs to be identified as a technique used by the teacher that, when used extensively, creates and encourages dependency. The child depends on the teacher for initiative, and the teacher, enthralled with the immediate results, becomes dependent on the use of closure. Unless the pitfalls are known by the teacher, there is a likelihood of a dependency developing, and closure will be used again and again.

Last year Adam brought his journal to me, exclaiming, "Mrs. Cornell, I wrote a poem!" He knew he had written a poem; it wasn't an accident, it wasn't set up by a teacher using a form of closure, and it didn't rhyme:

> There is a little club house
> And there are two secret doors
> That only two people know.

Adam came to school that day excited about a new friendship. Christine lived in Adam's neighborhood but usually went to a sitter's house directly after school. Neither of them knew they were neighbors until suddenly they found themselves on the same bus headed for home. Both were pleased with the discovery and were writing in their journals about their new clubhouse when Adam wrote his poem. How did this child know he had written a poem? "We learn what poetry is from reading it" (T. S. Eliot).

I am pleased but not surprised when my children begin to write poetry. The same thing has happened to me. Sometimes just the right poem for the class is hard to find, so I began writing poems here and there to fit in with the curriculum. I found my thinking and expression altered by the poetry we read and by the children's reactions to it. If it was happening to me, why not the children?

One morning last year in early March, our school secretary came to the classroom door with a telephone message. The note read, "Carrie Quinn will not be in." I read it to the class, and the rhyme caught our ears. "That sounds like a poem!" noted a voice from somewhere in the room. I wrote it on the board, changed it around a bit, and ended up with:

> Carrie Quinn
> Will not be in.
> She is home
> And sick in bed.
> Stuffed-up nose
> And fevery head,
> Carrie Quinn
> Is home in bed.

The poem grew before our eyes. "That can be the poem for today," Michael T. blurted out, forgetting to raise his hand.

We took turns reading it, and four girls copied it to take home. I then decided to mimeograph it so each child would have a copy, and sent one home to Carrie. It may have been a coincidence, but two days later Carrie came in disgruntled with an older girl who was giving her a problem on the bus. She busily went to her seat and wrote on a piece of paper,

Being bossed around by girls in third grade isn't any fun.
If you are being bossed around, just run.

Her mood changed as I read the words handed to me. I suggested she share it with the class and hung it in a prominent place, communicating to the other children that first graders can, and do indeed, write poetry.

That same week a little transplanted southerner, who habitually came unprepared for the weather, wrote in her journal,

Snow, snow,
Go away.
I don't got my mittens today.

## POETRY WRITING 1984–85

Because of this research project, I'm sure that there is an even greater concentration on poetry in my classroom. In the past, as I have said, the conscious effort on the part of my children to write poetry has occurred in the early spring. This year it started in late October, supporting my thesis that poetry writing occurs in direct proportion to the amount of exposure to poetry in the classroom.

### October 18

Michael D. came up with two spontaneous little rhymes. We got a note from the office confirming that Michael D. was to take the bus home—his father was home because of illness. Michael shouted, "Hip, hip, horray, I get to take the bus today!" His ears caught the rhyme and his face lit up: "That's a poem!"

Another day, just before lunch, when I requested, "Everyone in your seats," I overheard Michael mumble something to himself, followed by a spark of excitement. "I got a poem!" He had my attention; there was a pause as he stopped to rethink his words and then repeated, "I don't know how, to sit down now." I suggested he write it down, but he never did.

### October 22

Carrie read her first poem to the class. I posted it on a large sheet of paper. We then read it together.

HALLOWEEN

Halloween night
Is such a sight
Owls say hooooo.
People say boooo.

Your name can be Bob.
Your name can be Sue.
Your costume can be
Any color, even blue.

## October 31

Another poem from Carrie:

FALL

Leaves are falling on the ground.
Some are bumpy, some are round.
If you look and look and look,
You can write a big long book.
If you look very carefully
You can see the veins,
To make the leaves fall it rains and rains.

## November 7

And another:

ME AND MY POEMS

I like to make up poems myself.
When I'm done it goes on my shelf.
Poems are a lot of fun.
The real best part is when you are done.
You can make them again and again
And read them to ladies and men.

Angela offered, as we lined up for lunch, "I made up a little poem last night."

Where's the bat?
Where's the bat?
I don't know where he's at.

## November 15

Carrie came in the door with a smile of satisfaction on her face. She handed me a new poem. I ran my eyes over it and then, with pleasure and enthusiasm, read it to the children clustered around us as Carrie hung up her coat.

MY TEETH

I brush my teeth every single day.
When I am done, then I can play.

> I clean them so they won't get rotten,
> But sometimes I forget and they are forgotten.

When she came for her reading conference, I requested that she bring her poem. I had a few questions: "How did this poem grow? How did it come about?" Carrie answered, "I just started to write, then I thought of a word that rhymes and I thought some more." I was interested in the erasures at the bottom of the page. She had revised the last line, from

> I forget to brush them and then they are forgotten

to

> But sometimes I forget and they are forgotten.

When asked about the changes, she replied, "My mother said if I change the words around it would have more rhythm and the poem would sound better." "Did your mother tell you how to fix it?" "No," she said, "I just changed the words around."

I suspect that the poetry writing my children do is related not only to the amount of exposure to poetry but also to the amount of time given to writing in our classroom, which of course is related to the amount of writing the children actually do. We have a forty-five-minute writing period daily. We write for thirty minutes, saving the last fifteen for whole-group sharing.

Carrie is always the last one to finish her writing; forty-five minutes is never long enough. She continues to write as the rest of us get ready for sharing, often petitioning for "just one more minute."

Phillip confided during a reading conference, "I like to write in my journal, that's my favorite thing."

Michael D. tells us what to do when you don't know what to write in your journal: "You sit there and you think of something, you write it down, and that makes you think of something else. Pretty soon you have two whole pages."

## November 26

Yesterday I made a large copy of Carrie's latest poem, "My Teeth." I thought it would be fun to use it as our poem for the day, each reading it. At first I wrote it in four lines.

### MY TEETH

> I brush my teeth every single day.
> When I am done, then I can play.
> I clean them so they won't get rotten,
> But sometimes I forget and they are forgotten.

This I decided the children might be able to read it more easily if I changed it to eight lines:

MY TEETH

I brush my teeth
Every single day.
When I am done,
Then I can play.

I clean them so
They won't get rotten,
But sometimes I forget
And they are forgotten.

Since I had two different forms, I decided to post them both on the chalkboard and ask Carrie and the others which form they preferred. They unanimously chose the first form. I asked Carrie why she preferred that one over the other, and she said she liked the rhyming words at the end of each line, just as Chukovsky's sixth and eighth "commandments for children's poetry" read: "A need for frequent rhyming, at least at the end of every few words. It is much more difficult for the young child to get the sense of the poems when rhyming is not contiguous"; and "Every line of a poem must have a life of its own, it must be a syntactic whole because the child's thinking pulsates in the same rhythm as the verse."

## January 2

Carrie came in with four other children for their early-morning reading conferences. I was listening to David read as she hung up her snowsuit. She walked over and without saying a word handed me a piece of paper, another poem entitled "Winter":

When you come in from the snow,
You always want a cup of hot cocoa.
Hot cocoa is very, very hot,
And I bet you like the snow a lot.
I like snowflakes on my tongue.
I like carols that are sung.
I like snow and I like to slide.
In a sled you can take a ride.

She read her poem to the class at "show and tell." "Almost forgot," she said. "I might make a book of my poems. I could use the paper the same size we use for writing workshop." "How big do you think the book will be?" I asked. "Oh, about ten pages or so. I think I can remember my poems so I can write them down," was her reply.

### January 6

Stocking, stocking,
You will stink
On Christmas day.

Kenny wrote in his journal and labeled it "a poem by Kenny." We share our journals at the end of journal-writing time; he read it in a rhythmic, singing fashion. "I couldn't hear," Catherine complained, leaning forward in her seat. Kenny has trouble with his speech, so I requested that he read it again and this time slow it down a bit. The class laughed and wanted him to read it a third time, which he did.

I commented, "It certainly has the rhythm of a poem." "But it doesn't rhyme," cut in Carrie. I took the opportunity to inform the class that poetry doesn't always rhyme. Rhyme makes the material more predictable and easier to read, so most of the poems we read do rhyme.

### January 8

Kenny excitedly announced, "I got a poem." School was just starting and I was trying to pull things together, which isn't always easy. As we wait for late arrivals, some children just barely get involved in a project and are asked to put it aside to work on later. Kenny, upon getting my attention (which he does by nudging my arm when I am involved with someone else), said excitedly, "I got a poem:

I'm busy, busy,
Everywhere you see me."

### February 3

For the last couple of days we have been working on a winter theme at writing time. Writing workshop had bogged down, and I wanted to use something we were all experiencing to get things moving, so the children would stimulate each other. I made a folder for each child and put the words "Winter Activities" on the bulletin board. We discussed chimney sweeping, sledding, skiing, ice fishing, snow-mobiling, playing on the merry-go-round when it is piled with snow, getting stuck in the snow, and so on.

I encouraged the children to bring in winter poems from home or find them in books in the classroom. Carrie brought in a poem and announced to the class, "I couldn't find a poem so I wrote one:

The month now is February,
I think back in December.
My birthday was then, Oh yes, it was,
And I can still remember.

This poem, like all the others Carrie had written, was related to what was happening in the classroom. When I asked her mother at conference time if Carrie wrote before coming to school, she said, "Only her name and letters." I wanted to know what changes she had noticed since Carrie had been in first grade. Her reply was, "Her written expression, the way she is putting it all together." She thought a minute before she continued, "All this interest in poetry is a new development since she entered first grade."

When Mae's mother was asked the same question, she appreciatively answered, "Poetry, the greatest gift you have given her. She recites them to Jimmy—he's so proud of it. Jimmy's uncle was schooled in Ireland; he's in his late seventies now, but he recites five and ten pages of poetry about Irish heroes. He still remembers them from when he was in school."

### March 20

We celebrated the first day of spring. Since we don't know the birth date of our classroom rabbit, this was as good a day as any to celebrate Inky's birthday. I wanted a poem to fit the occasion, but I found nothing that was quite right.

During an evening walk with my husband, we were talking about the rabbits we have known. My thoughts turned to Peter Rabbit and his disobedience. With a couple of rhyming words in mind, some sense of where I was going, and a rhythm that seemed to be developing, I wrote, revised, and rewrote a poem several times. I never did get the last two lines quite the way I wanted them, but I needed it first thing the next morning, so I decided to settle for what I had:

A SAD TALE

What happened to Peter
On that warm spring day?
Peter learned his lesson,
But he learned the hard way.

He disobeyed his mother
As one should never do,
So he ended that day, in
McGregor's rabbit stew.

A sad tail . . .

The children read it easily, Carrie first. The cadence was good, and the rhyming words seemed to be in the right places. They especially liked the word *disobeyed*, a new reading word for most of them. I told them I had written the poem, describing how it had grown. I overheard Carrie telling our reading specialist, who was reading the poem printed on the chalkboard, "Mrs. Cornell wrote it."

**April 19**

Kenny wrote a poem in his journal:

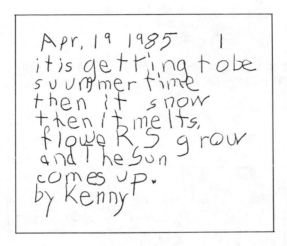

He went on to the next page, numbering the revision "2" at the top of the page, again signing it.

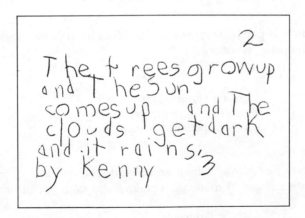

**April 29**

We have been on spring break for the past week, and the children came to school full of vacation happenings, eager for "show and tell" and journal writing. The whole class was excited, wanting to share something they had done during the past week, but Kenny was thinking about poetry. As soon as he had his journal in hand, he placed a big, determined "3" at the bottom of his last journal entry, turned the page, and wrote:

SPRING POEM BY
KENNY

The flowers grow
up. The Sun comes
up and I grow
up too.

When he read it to the class, feeling a further need for revision, he pencilled in "will" between "I" and "grow" and with a look of satisfaction reread the finished poem:

Our collection of poems is growing. Mae brought to "show and tell" a poem she had written during vacation:

SPRING

Trees start growing green leaves,
Flowers are blooming around the trees.
It is very special when everything
                              is alive again.

April came to me with an air of excitement. She and Carrie had exhausted themselves on the swings. "I made up a poem," she said, out of breath:

I'm high!
I'm high!
I'm touching the sky!

**May 23**

Phillip rides an early bus and comes in at 7:30 for an early-morning reading conference. This morning he said, as he entered the door, his white knees obviously exposed, "Can I use the computer? I got a poem to write." (We've had an Apple Macintosh, borrowed from Dartmouth College by a stroke of luck, for the whole month of May.) Phillip typed in "Spring," gave the "return" key a couple of punches, and wrote,

> The flowers are up
> and the green grass is mowed
> and I can wear shorts.

### June 14

On the handy little Macintosh I printed a book of the children's poems. I thought it would make perfect reading for the last day of school. With a touch of sadness, but also joy, I handed copies to the children, sitting at their desks in a U formation. A serious, respectful silence settled over the room as these children read their poems.

Our school's lost and found gives testimony to many things left behind, unclaimed, disowned, to the chagrin of parents and teachers alike; but not a single poetry book was forgotten that day, as the children hurried for the buses waiting to take them home.

Surely I'll never again have a class like this one.

### SUMMARY

Chukovsky would have us remember that children do not limit themselves to playing with objects; they also enjoy playing with sound and words. As I listened to my young students express a love for poetry and sensed their eagerness and willingness to read a poem many times without boredom, often committing the poem to memory, poetry quite naturally became for us ideal early-reading material. Add this realization to Bill Martin's assertion that "literature impresses language on the memory by which a person can recreate the literary experience," and my first graders quite naturally developed into writers, confident that they too could express themselves poetically.

If we want our children to use language creatively, we need to know that children, like adults, do not create in a vacuum. We need to playfully and extensively expose children to creative language, expect them to write, allow time for expression, and give audience and display to their successful efforts. The audience is extremely important. Sharing expression (oral or written) with an interacting group, which is also motivated and attempting to create, serves to provide the feedback needed to improve and continue the effort as well as give that "I can do it, too" attitude to the other members of the group, contributing to a snowballing effect which collects and grows. Children learn from each other as well as from the enthusiasm, emphasis, attention, involvement, and expectation of the teacher.

## REFERENCES AND RELATED SOURCES

Chukovsky, Kornei. *From Two to Five*. Berkeley: University of California Press, 1963.

Ciardi, John. *How Does a Poem Mean?* Cambridge, Mass.: Riverside Press, 1959.

de Regniers, Beatrice Schenk; Eva Moore; and Mary Michaels White, eds. *Poems Children Will Sit Still For: A Selection for the Primary Grades*. New York: Citation Press, 1969.

Eliot, T. S. *The Uses of Poetry and the Uses of Criticism*. Glasgow: The University Press, 1959.

Frost, Robert. *The Figure a Poem Makes*. In *Selected Prose of Robert Frost*, edited by Hyde Cox and Edward Connery Lathem. New York: Collier Books, a division of Macmillan Publishing Co., 1974.

Koch, Kenneth. *Wishes, Lies, and Dreams*. New York: Vintage, 1971.

Martin, Bill. "Teacher's Guide" to *Brown Bear*. Big Book, Holt, Rinehart and Winston of Canada, Limited, 1982.

MacLeish, Archibald. *Poetry and Experience*. Boston: Houghton Mifflin, 1961.

Restak, Richard M., M.D. *The Brain: The Last Frontier*. New York: Warner Books, 1980.

Vygotsky, L. S. *Thought and Language*. Cambridge, Mass.: M.I.T. Press, 1962.

# CHAPTER 8

# Visions of Communication: The Use of Commonplace Books in the English Class

*Judith Boyce*

Rather than presenting complete case studies, this chapter and the following one present brief articles based on those studies. Judith Boyce examined the commonplace books produced by four of her sixth graders. The books contained weekly entries of three types: sentences copied from the students' reading, new vocabulary encountered in any context, and journal entries on topics of the writers' choice. The most striking and unexpected discovery Boyce made concerned the students' interpretations of some of her responses to their writing, which is the aspect of her study that she presents here. Like Ferguson McKay, she became more the kind of teacher she wanted to be through examining the effects of her responses to student writing.

The research, Judy says, "heightened my consciousness of the role a personal relationship plays in teaching. It also reminded me that consideration of one's audience is not important only in a long piece of writing; a teacher needs to be aware of the interpretation a student may put on the briefest of written or spoken comments. As in any writing, what the author 'meant' to say matters less than what the reader takes from the text. Finally, doing research of my own allowed me to internalize the concept of 'noticing an anomaly' and of following that up."

The study of commonplace books was Judy's second research plan. Her original proposal to study writing with a word processor became impossible owing to equipment and class-size problems. Now she looks forward to returning to that study. "The case study itself and the enthusiasm with which Glenda and Richard and my fellow researchers received my results gave me the impetus to make a real, if temporary, life change. I applied for and was granted a sabbatical leave for 1986–87. I will have an entire year in which to concentrate on the use of computers to teach writing." She is spending the year at the Harvard Graduate School of Education.

Judy regards her five children (and her grandson) "as the best and most important work I've ever done." She lives with her husband of thirty-four years in Harvard, Massachusetts, where she teaches fifth-, sixth-, and seventh-grade English.

Eleven-year-old Elizabeth wrote in her commonplace book:

Rain has been dripping all day long. I wish it would stop. The rain is just so dreary.

*Dear Reader:*

*Before reading the rest of this article, please comment on the entry from Elizabeth's commonplace book (a kind of journal) as if you are Elizabeth's teacher. Your purpose in writing a comment on the entry is to help Elizabeth develop her idea further IF she chooses to write another draft.*

*Feel free to jot a comment right on this page. Then, as you read on, you will be able to compare your comment style with the one Elizabeth and three of her sixth-grade classmates liked best.*

*Judith Boyce*
*Middle-School Teacher*

Elizabeth wrote her rainy-day entry in the green mottled composition books my sixth graders call commonplace books (CPB for short). Elizabeth and her classmates, all good readers and competent writers, wrote two entries each week. Elizabeth's short paragraph on rain, a topic she chose, was written during the second week of September.

The commonplace book had been an important part of my sixth-grade writing program for two years, but during this third year the experience promised to be different; I had planned a case study, a close look at several aspects of the commonplace book as revealed in four of them: Elizabeth's book, Amy's book, Jason's book, and Michael's book. From my year-long study, I hoped to learn how the commonplace book looked from the students' point of view and to gain a clearer picture of what I felt was a valuable learning tool for composition.

Because I believe, with James Squire (582), that "activity without language does not become experience," the purpose I set for entries in the commonplace book was practice in explicating ideas—ideas sparked by personal experience, by reading, by observation, or by actual classroom activities in any subject area. During the previous two years, I had worked to ameliorate a major problem with middle-school writers: lack of development, an inability to extend an idea beyond a first thought or to let a first thought be a bridge to another, perhaps more powerful idea. My case study, my personal teacher-research project, would give me an opportunity to record differences in the way Elizabeth, Amy, Jason, and Michael developed ideas. Were they using language to turn activity into experience?

I also anticipated interviewing students to discover their views on comments—which comments gave them the most help and encouragement toward a possible, more developed revision. This article focuses on that section of my study, which uncovered an unexpected reaction from Elizabeth.

My vision of the transaction between writer and instructor, perhaps my fantasy, was this: I would comment on entries as if the writer and I were involved in a writing conference. As gently as possible, my comments would nag Elizabeth and her classmates to be specific about ideas, to develop ideas, to say more. My comments, well grounded in advice from Nancy Sommers, from Lil Brannon and C. H. Knoblauch, from Janet Emig, from innumerable researchers, would lead my sixth graders to an increasing awareness of fully developed writing and an increasing competence in producing such writing. Spurred by my comments, Elizabeth, Amy, Jason, or Michael would expand, revise, even rethink their ideas.

Vision firmly in mind and green felt tip firmly in hand (as a facilitative commenter, one must eschew red pen), I commented on Elizabeth's first few entries.

| My Comments | Elizabeth's Entries |
|---|---|
| | In gym last period I played a game of soccer. |
| What does a defenseman do? | Defense is the name of the position I was playing. It is the position in front of the goalie. |
| How does it look? sound? affect your plans? | Rain has been dripping all day long. I wish it would stop. The rain is just so dreary. |
| I have heard just recently that there were others who also believed the world was round; only the more backward people did not. | When I think about it, I would not like to be Columbus. Everyone must have laughed at him. They might have said that he was stupid, because if he tried to sail the world, then he would fall off the edge. Maybe they would snicker and talk about him behind his back. I sure would not like to be Columbus. |

|  | Television is sometimes considered a bad influence for children, but I don't agree. If you watch between one and two hours a day then I don't |
| Do you think the type of program matters? | think it could be harmful to you. I suppose that maybe if you watched a lot of tv then it could be an influence. Personally, I like television and do not see anything wrong with it. |
| What else can be found in a dictionary? | Dictionaries are useful objects. They can be used to find both the spelling and the definitions of many words. The amount of words depends on the size of the dictionary. I think that they, on the whole, are great. |

As I returned the commonplace books the next day, I was reasonably sure that my comments had given Elizabeth concrete suggestions for development of her rather scanty paragraphs. I prided myself particularly on my attention to the content rather than to the writing, just as Don Graves's successful Atkinson teachers advised (Calkins 1985, 195). In addition, I recognized my responsibility to cultivate Donald Murray's "other self" in my students. Even if Elizabeth never wrote new drafts on soccer or rain or dictionaries, she might very well internalize the process of questioning herself as she wrote, using my gentle questions as her model for that other self.

Then I read Elizabeth's reaction to my comments!

I had suggested one morning that students write a few sentences about my comments. "Tell what you like or dislike, or write whatever you wish to say about the green marks I have made in your CPB," I announced. Elizabeth did. She wrote this: "I think that some of the comments in my CPB are bad, and wrong, but I realize that you must do them quickly. I cannot answer your questions by the side anyway, so why do you write them?"

I replied, rather defensively I'm afraid, two weeks later when I collected the CPBs for another round of comment.

I make comments—often in question form—because those are the questions I might ask if we could sit down and have a conference about the writing. I hope perhaps you will be spurred on to do one of these things: 1. Realize how you could have developed an idea further and transfer that to further ideas. 2. Write another entry to explain your answer. 3. Write a composition at some later time and use the questions to help you think what to add to the basic idea. Please think of the comments as from Mr. X [our classroom audience] rather than from an English teacher snarling that you never do anything perfectly!

Once I had recovered from my initial defensive posture—the "Anybody can see what I meant to say here!" syndrome common to writers of any age—I began to wonder about Elizabeth's negative reaction to question comments. A week or two earlier, when I chose four students to study and interview, I had picked Elizabeth for her outspokenness. Now that she had spoken out, I had dismissed her annoyance with an annoyed reaction of my own.

On second thought, if I looked again, if I examined Elizabeth's repudiation of my comments, I might find that it was only the tip of an iceberg. I had read that a researcher looks for an anomaly, the remark or event that "doesn't fit" and so is often worth looking into. Maybe my study was turning up something unexpected. It was time to ask my experts—Elizabeth, Amy, Jason, and Michael—how they felt about comments on their ideas. I needed to begin shaping my vision of student-teacher communication to the reality of student perception.

Elizabeth said, "I don't like it when you ask questions because I never get to answer the questions anyway. So I like it when...uum...when you don't ask questions...when you say something you like or don't like about them." As an example of a comment she did like, Elizabeth pointed to her entry on Columbus. She enjoyed my comment, which actually said nothing about her entry or her writing. What I wrote, I believe, rose from my own engagement with Elizabeth's topic. I was responding to the idea and not to the way it had been presented. Peter Elbow would say I was looking out the window through the pane rather than at the pane (284). Elizabeth was not alone in her reaction.

Amy wrote about Thanksgiving at her house. She said the only problem was "that some of the men like to watch the football game," and she even included a magazine cartoon of Pilgrims and Indians lined up for the kickoff. Thinking to prompt some added information, I jotted, "What do the rest of you do while they watch football?" Amy did not appreciate this comment. She "wanted to stick to this certain fact and if I did this," that is, if she added information, "I could go into this big composition."

Amy didn't express any general dislike of questions, perhaps because her entries were more developed than Elizabeth's and fewer questions popped into my head as I read Amy's ideas. In fact, in the first ten weeks of entries, I wrote only one question (see below) in Amy's book, and Amy thought it was a useful question because "if I rewrite this I will change the way I said it."

---

| **My Comment** | **Amy's Entry** |
| --- | --- |
| Is it a lifesaver if Mr. Clark is now dead? | The artificial heart is a lifesaver. In 1982 Barney Clark received an artificial heart and he lived for about six months. Now, in 1984, William Shrader received one and he is expected to live a number of years. |

> At the rate he is going he may be out of the hospital and into his own house for Christmas.

Although questions didn't particularly upset Amy, she stated unequivocally that she liked other kinds of comments better, especially those "that add to the idea." When pressed, Amy admitted that questions implied a criticism, meant that "Mrs. Boyce thinks you should have put that in" (my words).

Questions seemed helpful to Jason. His entries were sometimes short, undeveloped ones like Elizabeth's. Jason, who has a great deal of confidence and is comfortable with adults, had his own strategy for dealing with question comments. While Elizabeth's frustration centered on questions she never had a chance to answer, Jason just jotted his answer in the margin next to my question and went on his merry way.

| My Comment | Jason's Entry |
|---|---|
| Can you practice the passage ahead of time? YES<br>Can you choose the passage? NO | The Hebrew language is hard to learn. It has taken me three years to learn what I know about the language. I can speak Hebrew pretty well. When I am 13, I will have to read from the Torah on Bar Mitzvah. |

Jason liked "positive comments and some sarcastic ones—usually funny." He pointed out two examples of "sarcastic" comments. In an entry about football Jason had used the word "reciever" (sic). I wrote "i before e except after c," a comment Jason thought was funny. The other "funny sarcasm" was a comment on an entry explaining the requirements for running for the presidency. Jason was amused by "I'll vote for you when you run." My comment to Amy about the "lifesaver" was probably in the "funny sarcasm" category, and for good language students like Amy and Jason, such remarks might have facilitated possible editing, although most of my question comments did not appear to facilitate possible revision.

Over a span of twenty-two weeks, my comments in the four books under scrutiny ranged from applause—"clever idea!" or "excellent factual entry"—to long responses like one I jotted when Michael wrote about collecting pledges in the campaign against multiple sclerosis.

**My Comment**

Lesson 1: People are friendly. Lesson 2: People are not so friendly when actual money is involved. There is a saying, "Promises are cheap," which seems to fit here!

**Michael's Entry**

When I was collecting for money for multiple sclerosis many of the people who pledged were nice about giving me the money, but others gave me a difficult time. Some said they would mail it and some just didn't want to give the money they had pledged. I didn't want to tell the people who had pledged that they could mail their money because it seemed that they would forget. When somebody didn't want to give the money to me I luckily had my dad with me so he could tell them that I wasn't coming back. After I got home later that night I had collected most of the money, but I still don't understand why people who pledged money for charity gave me such a hard time when I came to collect it.

The most successful comments, the ones students liked best, were those in which I was just another human being rather than the teacher. Amy said, "I like the comments where you tell what you did or what you think." The example she pointed out was a comment I wrote on an entry about Amy cleaning her playroom. She told of dusting and packing old books she plans to save "for my own kids." I wrote (and Amy approved), "I have an attic full of old books I am saving for my grandchildren. Some I had when I was twelve and my children read them. They are like old friends."

Like the comment to Elizabeth about Columbus, this remark about books is one I might make in a casual conversation, not necessarily in a school setting at all. Comments that, according to Michael, "give your [meaning the teacher's] ideas about something" or, in Amy's words, "add to the idea" were definitely the most popular with sixth graders. But, these comments are the hardest to make.

Conversational-tone comments come hard because the teacher has to take a risk. I had always written occasional comments of this type, but there was the nagging worry that a student would think, or even say, "What do I care about Mrs. Boyce's cat or her children or the time she collected money?" I had never experienced such a reaction, but until I discussed comments with Elizabeth, Amy, Jason, and Michael, I worried that my sixth graders were merely too polite or too kind to let me know of their lack of interest. Now I wonder if students are just as hesitant to put their ideas down. It is conceivable that my willingness to take the same risk students do—the risk of meeting with indifference—is one reason they like conversational comments.

I have learned quite a lot about audience in my discussions with sixth graders. Often, as I commented on commonplace books over the years, I thought I was being the perfect process commentator—gently, through skillful questioning, nudging writers toward turning idea entries into essays. Elizabeth (bluntly) and Amy (sweetly) hinted that they read my questions as criticisms, as saying, "Why didn't you include this?"

Elizabeth's frustration at not being provided with a vehicle for answering questions was probably fueled by a need to answer what she perceived as unjust criticism, although Elizabeth said that she thought I wrote questions "so you wouldn't sound as if you were criticizing." In fact, none of the four students was willing to state baldly that he or she felt criticized by question comments, but there was a definite consensus on comments they did want: thoughtful comments about the subject at hand, preferably comments I made as a fellow human rather than as a teacher.

As the year and my case study rolled on, I began to consider ways to revise my comments. If questions might foster hostility, then I would stay away from questions as much as possible. Beyond that, I searched for a strategy to promote written dialogue so that Elizabeth could answer my questions, I could answer hers, and both of us could defuse defensive reactions.

One of the advantages of teaching for a living is being able to start over again each September. The mistakes one made last year can, each new fall, be avoided. So, next year I will stress personal engagement with student ideas. Then I will suspend self-consciousness and risk putting my feelings and my outlooks into written comments. When a question is my first thought, I will try to reword it as an "I wonder" statement, keeping in mind that "the distinction [between facilitative and directive comments] lies deeper than superficial comment form" (Knoblauch and Brannon 1984, 129). Through these revisions, prompted by Elizabeth's first comment to me, perhaps I can nudge next year's sixth graders into writing more, into developing their ideas.

To provide vehicles for answering and asking questions in writing, first I will require revisions of CPB entries on a more regular basis. Knowing what students like and knowing what will prompt the best revision in terms of development are not necessarily the same. I will continue a method that proved useful with the same sixth graders in a reading class last spring, an exchange of letters à la Nancie Atwell, a Maine teacher whose eighth graders wrote to each other about novels they read. It seems likely that such an exchange in writing class might be worked out, perhaps encouraging students to write about their own writing process and the problems they had while writing.

My next year's fantasy is forming right now. It will go something like this:

An eleven-year-old Elizabeth will turn in her CPB on September 20. I will comment on fewer entries this year because each comment will be longer and more thoughtful.

---

| | In gym last period I played a game of soccer. Defense is the name of the position I was playing. It is the position in front of the goalie. |
| I love really violent rainstorms, though, especially if I have a good book to read during them. | Rain has been dripping all day long. I wish it would stop. The rain is just so dreary. |
| | When I think about it, I would not like to be Columbus. Everyone must have laughed at him. They might have said that he was stupid, because if he tried to sail the world, then he would fall off the edge. Maybe they would snicker and talk about him behind his back. I sure would not like to be Columbus. |
| I like television, too. Sometimes when I am tired I watch junk like "Love Boat" because I don't need to concentrate. I don't like violence, though. | Television is sometimes considered a bad influence for children, but I don't agree. If you watch between one and two hours a day then I don't think that it would be harmful to you. I suppose that maybe if you watched a lot of tv then it could be an influence. Personally, I like television and do not see anything wrong with it. |
| Good browsing material. | Dictionaries are useful objects. They can be used to find both the spelling and the definitions of many words. The amount of words depends on the size of the dictionary. I think that they, on the whole, are great. |

---

When I return the books, I will ask the children to write me a letter describing what they remember of their process (I won't use that word if I can help it) as they wrote their entries. I will also direct students to write a reaction to my comments and tell which entry they would choose to revise.

Elizabeth will write in this vein:

Dear Mrs. Boyce,

When I tried to write ideas in the CPB, I couldn't think of anything to write. You said to write the first entry about something factual instead of just saying something that happened in school so I wrote about the soccer game, but I didn't feel like explaining the whole game. Everybody else in class knows anyway.

Then when I needed more entries because you were collecting the book today, I looked around my family room. I saw the TV so I wrote about that. Then I saw the dictionary. I think it is hard to write about ideas. I would rather write kind of a diary.

I liked what you said about television. I never thought a teacher would watch "Love Boat"!

I am going to revise my entry about rain. Can I write a poem about a rainy day? I might tell all the things I do on a rainy day, like watch TV and read and go out and build dams.

Sincerely,

Elizabeth

I will answer Elizabeth's letter. I will assure her that a poem will be fine, and I will say something about rain or about rainy-day activities or both. Maybe I'll say something about my cat. Who can predict a conversation? Whatever I say, if I communicate, one human to another, my twenty-five Elizabeths will be on their way to longer, clearer, more developed writing.

Sometimes my visions turn into reality.

## REFERENCES AND RELATED SOURCES

Atwell, Nancie. "Writing and Reading Literature from the Inside Out." *Language Arts*, V61:N3, March 1984, 240–52.

Bissex, Glenda. *GNYS AT WRK: A Child Learns to Write and Read*. Cambridge, Mass.: Harvard University Press, 1980.

Brannon, Lil, and C. H. Knoblauch. "On Students' Rights to Their Own Texts: A Model of Teacher Response." *College Composition and Communication*, V33:N2, May 1982, 157–66.

Calkins, Lucy. "Learning to Think through Writing." In *Observing the Language Learner*, edited by Angela Jagger and M. Trika Smith-Burke. Urbana, Illinois: IRA/NCTE Publication, 1985.

———. *Lessons from a Child*. Portsmouth, N.H.: Heinemann Educational Books, 1983.

Elbow, Peter. "Teaching Writing by Not Paying Attention to Writing." In *Fforum*. Upper Montclair, N.J.: Boynton/Cook, 1983.

Emig, Janet. "Writing as a Mode of Learning." *College Composition and Communication*, V28:N2, May 1977, 122–28.

Fulwiler, Toby. "Journals across the Disciplines." *English Journal*, V69:N9, December 1980, 14–19.

Harker, Judith O., and Judith L. Green. "When You Get the Right Answer to the Wrong Question." In *Observing the Language Learner*, edited by Angela Jagger and M. Trika Smith-Burke. Urbana, Illinois: IRA/NCTE Publication, 1985.

Knoblauch, C. H., and Lil Brannon. *Rhetorical Traditions and the Teaching of Writing*, Upper Montclair, N.J.: Boynton/Cook, 1984, chap. 6.

———. "Teacher Commentary on Student Writing: The State of the Art." In *Rhetoric and Composition*. Upper Montclair, N.J.: Boynton/Cook, 1984.

Mier, Margaret. "Teacher Commentary on Student Writing in the Process-Oriented Class." *The Leaflet*, V48:N1, Winter 1985, 30–33.

Moran, Charles. "Reading Student Writing." Talk delivered to National Council of Teachers of English, November 21, 1982.

Murray, Donald. "Teaching the Writer's Other Self: The Writer's First Reader." *College Composition and Communication*, V33:N2, May 1982, 141–56.

Newkirk, Thomas. "In Defense of the Teacher as Audience." *The Leaflet*, V84:N1, Winter 1985, 50–56.

Price, Gayle. "The Case for a Modern Commonplace Book." *College Composition and Communication*, V31:N2, May 1980, 175–82.

Sommers, Nancy. "Responding to Student Writing." *College Composition and Communication*, V33:N2, May 1982, 148–56.

Squire, James. "Composing and Comprehending." *Language Arts*, V60:N5, May 1983, 581–89.

# CHAPTER 9

# Rx for Editor in Chief

*Jane Richards*

Jane Richards chose to focus her research on a classroom problem she had been unable to solve: placing the responsibility for noticing and correcting mechanical errors on students. Her complete study, from which she drew this article, presents more detailed information about the editing strategies she employed in her high school English classes, about the two students she followed most closely, and about the responses of the other students in her classes. "The year I spent on the research project was the busiest but most rewarding of my career," say Jane, who is continuing to look closely at individuals who have serious problems with mechanics. She also continues to look to her students for information about ways to improve their learning. "I am more positive about teaching now, and I know how to get assistance with problems. Go to the source— the students." Since describing her case study at an in-service conference in her school district, Jane has also talked more with teachers in other departments about writing and begun some collaborative projects.

Jane decided to be a teacher when she was twelve years old. She graduated from the State University of New York at Oswego after studying year-round for three years.

Before teaching high school English, she taught kindergarten and almost all the elementary grades. When her husband was stationed in France, where their elder son was born, she taught at an army engineering depot. For the past twenty-one years she has taught at Marathon High School, a small rural school in New York State.

For thirty years I've been suffering from a chronic disease. I've kept it a secret, assuming there was no cure. I went through the routine of going to school every day, but I knew I was spreading the disease to my students: I had failed to teach my students how to reduce spelling and punctuation errors.

Last summer I was determined to relieve subsequent feelings of guilt and failure. Editing papers with road maps of red ink hadn't helped the students; I was beginning to suspect that editing had to be the final responsibility of the writer. To remedy my malady, I signed up for a writing institute offered by Northeastern University at Martha's Vineyard. In addition to other subjects, I opted for a case-study course taught by Glenda Bissex. I posed the following question as my case-study topic: How can I encourage students to be responsible for their own punctuation and spelling errors?

Members of the case-study class were supportive, and Glenda was optimistic. What could I lose? For years I had tried every known antidote: teaching rules, distributing lists, circling errors, deducting points, even ignoring mistakes. Nothing worked. I had to encourage students to proofread and correct their own errors. I planned to observe my two eleventh-grade classes and then to focus on two individual students. Charting student progress in response to various teaching strategies was my project approach.

Before school started, I read articles about structuring groups, error analysis, and proofreading techniques. In past years I had asked students to look over their papers, but I had never devoted instructional time to demonstrating editing methods. Students did not understand the reasons for correcting errors, nor did they understand the process of editing. The first day of school this year I shared my concerns, told my students what I was trying to do, and asked for their help. Their response was very positive.

During the first weeks of school, structuring groups was important since most students were not used to working together. At first we discussed questions about literature and planned oral reports in groups. By November, when I started the writing workshop, students were more comfortable working together. I asked students to choose their own topics, write rough drafts, read each others' work both aloud and silently, comment on papers, revise their own papers, and edit writing assignments for spelling and punctuation errors before final papers were due. In the first editing group, I asked students to underline each other's errors with the understanding that it was the writer's responsibility to correct them.

After the first editing session, I drew two conclusions: many students were not conscious of spelling or punctuation errors in their classmates' papers, and most students did not rewrite a final draft.

Before the next editing session, we discussed reasons why correct copy is necessary. I typed dittos that contained mechanical errors; students corrected misspelled words and punctuated sentences correctly. I taught minilessons about comma and semicolon rules. We talked about certain spelling problems and how to look up words in the dictionary. The next session was more successful. Dictionaries did not just take up space; students began using them. Students found more errors, and a few more students rewrote their assignments with the understanding that they would not receive a grade deduction for a late paper.

At this time I distributed a questionnaire about spelling and punctuation errors. In their responses most students indicated that they realized the purpose for rules about mechanics, but only half the students said they knew the rules. About two-thirds of the students reported that they would ask someone how to spell a word instead of looking it up. A number of students admitted that they could not tell whether a word was misspelled, and more than half of the students said that they misspelled the same words over again.

To prepare for the next session, I shared the results of the survey with both classes. Subsequently I refused to spell words for them. I looked up words with the students, but I no longer tolerated their dependency on me as editor in chief. Students read their papers aloud, which helped them punctuate sentences according to meaning. Several students said that they recognized misspelled words when they read their own paper aloud.

The next phase of the project involved selecting two students for close observation. Tom, the first student, was bright and articulate in class discussions. Yet in writing assignments he wrote quickly and handed them in without proofreading. This attitude was representative of about two-thirds of the class. Tom continued to respond in this way until he started to write on a word processor. Then he also entered several essay contests: the American Legion essay contest, the Scholastic Writing Contest, and the *Time* essay contest. His attitude about writing changed between November and February because he felt that editing with the word processor eliminated the drudgery of rewriting entire assignments. He started paying much closer attention to mechanical details. Because he was writing for an extended audience, his *Time* essay was carefully written, revised several times, and proofread by the editing group. Before sending in his story, Tom asked another student to proofread it, and she found two more errors. His obvious growth as his own editor was a solid confidence builder. Tom's improvement was unusual. Evaluating his progress in June, Tom stated, "Thanks to the faith of one teacher and the new computer age I have changed from a 'writing avoider' into a full-fledged creative writing addict."

The other student, Doug, was chosen because he made at least twenty spelling errors in a two-hundred-word essay. He needed help desperately. I recommended placement in a writing lab where he could be given individual instruction. He agreed to the additional remediation. He continued to make errors, however, when he wrote in class, even though he could have used the dictionary. When the writing-lab teacher, Kathy, helped him, he turned in papers with very few misspelled words. Kathy and I conferred about his progress and agreed that Doug should take more responsibility for his own errors. I told Doug that corrections were up to him, and Kathy reinforced this in the writing lab. At the end of the year, when I asked my students to indicate individual progress made in spelling and punctuation, Doug agreed that although his spelling had improved only slightly, he now realized that he was responsible for his errors.

Not only did these two individuals make progress, but many other students in both classes made fewer errors as the year progressed. By year's end, students were proofreading their papers even before submitting them to the editing group. On the New York State Regents comprehensive exam, students made fewer spelling errors than in previous years on the essay and composition tasks. Finally, much to my suprise and his delight, Doug passed the regents.

Graduating from the job of editor in chief has helped me establish better rapport with my students. They grasped the idea that mechanical errors inhibit the flow of ideas. Editing others' papers and their own helped them understand the necessity for correct copy. During that year I looked forward to correcting papers because there were fewer misspelled words, and because I had transferred the responsibility of correcting errors to the writers. By June, students were saying that they enjoyed writing instead of dreading it.

No, I am not cured—just in remission. The epidemic, however, is under control.

# PART III

# On Becoming a Researcher

# CHAPTER 10

# *T*eachers Talk about Their Research: A Round-Table Discussion

### Edited by Richard H. Bullock

What were the rewards and trials of doing this research? How did the act of researching affect these teachers' classrooms? Their views of themselves? Their relationships with other teachers? From their own experiences, what advice would they give teachers who are just starting out to do research? These are some of the questions that were candidly discussed when the case-study group met informally with Richard Bullock and Glenda Bissex to talk about their year's experience before presenting their research results more formally. Teachers talking about their research sound very much like teachers talking about their teaching, but from a new level of awareness and confidence, and with a new courage that frees them to face and learn from their failures as well as their successes.

Several of the speakers in the following discussion have already been introduced in the comments preceding their papers. (All the authors of the year-long case studies except Carol Avery were at the round table.) The new voices are those of Jacqueline Capobianco, Peggy Sheehan, and Eileen McCormack.

Jacqueline Capobianco took what might be called at best a challenging teaching position and turned it into a research opportunity. "My topic came out of group changes that were being forced on the upcoming eighth grade because of decreasing enrollment. I wanted to see the effects that might occur when boys who were labeled 'special' were placed in a regular classroom situation." Although she was teaching seven classes a day—some two hundred students in all—Jacquie made time to follow the development of two of her former students from a small writing class as they moved into a much larger class, which she also taught. "I planned to use the writing process as a tool to help their transition. Not only did the boys make it successfully into the eighth grade, but I too was rewarded. Now, six months later and at a new school and a different level, I am still using what I learned."

Married and the mother of three children, Jacquie received her B.A. in English from Southern Connecticut State University and is pursuing graduate work in writing at Northeastern University. She has taught English and writing for six years, five at St. Thomas Junior High in Southington, Connecticut, and one at Holy Cross High School in Waterbury. Jacquie is also a dancer, having studied for three years at Juilliard, where her teachers included José Limon and Martha Graham. Dancing and writing, she believes, are expressions of a similar creative process.

Peggy Sheehan has taught English composition, literature, and developmental reading at Post College in Waterbury, Connecticut, for eight years. Since she has worked with many students who speak English as a second language, she found that a close observation of several of these students was a natural choice for her case-study project. "Keeping a journal, recording conversations and conferences, analyzing students' writing, and observing their behavior in the classroom with their peers and with me has shown me a different side of the teacher-writer relationship. This research had made me more aware of the students and their needs; but this is an ongoing process. I have not stopped doing research because my case study has been completed. I find myself studying new students and charting their progress." A further effect of Peggy's case study was to provide convincing enough evidence to reverse the college's practice of grouping ESL students together for writing instruction.

Peggy lives in a big old house in a small New England town with her husband, three teen-age children, and her parents. She holds a bachelor's degree from Seton Hall University and a master's in reading from Southern Connecticut State University.

Eileen McCormack is a fifth-grade teacher who was convinced that traditional reading skills could be taught through a workshop approach to writing. Her students not only wrote stories but also wrote about their reading. Her case study documented the learnings of two of her fifth graders. "My question—'How can the writing process improve students' reading skills?'—encompassed many weeks and hours of taped conferences. I look back on this year as a learning time for both my class and myself. I see the need to use tapes and confer as a very important part of the writing process for both the students and the teacher."

A native of South Buffalo, New York, Eileen made her home in Lockport when she began her teaching career thirty-two years ago. For the past nineteen years she has taught fifth grade at the Charlotte Cross School in Lockport, where she lives with her husband and three children, and teaches without skills worksheets.

*Richard Bullock:* Having spent the better part of a year doing your research and writing it up, what gave you the most satisfaction?

*Jane Richards:* I think the results. Mine were very, very positive. My question was, how can I help students take responsibility for their own errors, for correcting their own errors in spelling and punctuation? And I worked on the editing part of the process and tried to give them strategies that would improve proofreading. Then I chose two students to work with, to write about—plus the two classes. Because I was so conscious of it, they became superconscious, and it evolved throughout the year that they became more and more aware. In many cases their errors diminished, and on the Regents' exam there were far fewer errors than my students had ever had before. I think it was because they realized the importance of it.

*Jacquie Capobianco:* When you said the importance of it, do you mean it was because they knew they were being watched?

*Jane:* Well, I would say, "We're going to do this; I'm involved in a case study," and I would talk to them about what we were going to do and why. I don't think I ever did this before, anywhere near to the extent that I did this year. I would ask them how they thought something worked, and they would tell me; they were very frank about it. Also, the editing groups were specifically designed for the case study, and if editing took ten minutes, okay—if it took the whole period, okay—whereas before I would just say, "Okay,' edit!" and pass out the dictionaries.

*Glenda Bissex:* Jane, when you said that the most satisfying aspect of your research was the results, I thought maybe you meant the results in terms of the paper, but what you were obviously talking about was the results in terms of the change that occurred in your classroom.

*Jane:* The process of doing the research and writing the paper was very important, because I wouldn't have gotten the results in my classroom if I hadn't worked through the different strategies.

*Glenda:* I think it's exciting that the results were tangible in that classroom, because when researchers who come into a classroom talk about the results, they usually mean what came out in terms of their theory or whatever and not that it necessarily changed anything that was going on at the time.

*Jane:* Oh, it did. I really can't pinpoint it any better than that—I wish I could. It wasn't magic or anything; we worked very hard. It was the awareness.

*Liz Cornell:* I think I know what you're talking about. In my project I was trying to find out what kind of effect poetry had, how it affected first-grade children's language, reading, and writing in the classroom. My theory is that if children are exposed to an extensive amount or intensively to poetry, then they just start writing. You don't need something that the teacher sets up, because they hear it . . . they start expressing themselves poetically. I always expect my students to start writing poetry spontaneously in the late winter or early spring. This year the poetry writing started in October. In nine years of teaching, it's always happened in late winter or early spring, and this year it started in October; so I have the feeling that the very fact that I was concentrating on it made the difference in what was happening in the classroom.

*Jane:* Did you read a lot of poetry to them?

*Liz:* I read a lot, and then their reading is poetry. We use a lot of poetry every single day for their reading. So it just started happening.

*Glenda:* What for some of the rest of you was the greatest source of satisfaction?

*Jacquie:* I think the greatest satisfaction that I had was in the writing of the thing in the end. When I got to the point that I could sit back and look at everything I'd compiled and put it all together in the format that I'd finally decided on, I found a great satisfaction.

*Richard:* Was that in terms of finally coming to grips with all of it?

*Jacquie:* Seeing it all together and saying to myself, "This is it; now this is what I've been working toward all year long and it's finally all come together." Before that I had been collecting along the way; all of a sudden I had to bring it all together.

*Richard:* Yes, it's as if when you're immersed in the process...

*Peggy Sheehan:* It didn't make much sense at that point; I was thinking that I don't know what I'm going to do with this, I don't know how it's going to fit together, what I am going to do with the end...I was collecting and storing and keeping track, but then, when I finally had to put it all together, I felt so much better about it.

*Jacquie:* I had somewhat the same reaction as Peggy, but aside from that I was most pleased with the satisfaction of how much I learned as a researcher: I had two boys for two consecutive years, part of a group of five remedial students being mainstreamed into a regular eighth-grade class. I chose these two randomly, without any real reason why I chose them, except that I knew they were going to be with me again. They had the exact same training for two years and ended up at opposite ends of the pole—one completely succeeding and being promoted, and the other one accomplishing very little. Yet they were given the exact same opportunities. So I came to the realization that children have to be treated as individuals. You cannot classify them in a class; you have to listen to them and know where their problems are, and treat each one as an individual as best you can in the classroom.

*Jane:* Do you know why the one child couldn't do it?

*Jacquie:* He was not a motivated child; he wasn't emotionally mature enough to handle a large group. He still needed individual attention, and when I had the opportunity to give him that individual attention, he responded to me, but in a large class I couldn't give what he wanted.

*Richard:* Susan, does anything that Jacquie was saying relate to some of the things you were saying in your study about learning styles?

*Susan Kaplan:* I was looking at myself and talking about learning theory. I talked about people, and children in particular, being unique and the uniqueness of the learning process. If I had to talk about satisfactions, I couldn't just pick out one. One was discovering that what I was doing was not just a bunch of baloney, which is pretty much where I was when I started. I think I succeeded in not having to pay a psychiatrist or analyst and discovered an incredible amount about myself. That's worthwhile. I am not unhappy, in a large measure due to the case study, about going back to teaching next year. The case study has excited me and made me think more about learning and different approaches I can use in the classroom, and that's great. I was definitely burned out before I started.

*Richard:* Then it "saved" you—I mean the research actually . . .

*Susan:* I don't want to give it that much credit. I don't ever want that to be a quote: "Saved by a Case Study." [Laughter] But every summer I get excited about lots of things; you'll have to talk to me again in November or February and see where I am then. I haven't had a chance to test out some of the things I discovered through myself and a lot of the reading about learning theory—how that'll all pan out in the classroom.

   Another satisfaction is that I really feel part of the profession. I really understand what I'm reading now and where it's all coming from. A lot of it was hooey as far as I was concerned, and not because I didn't understand the concepts but because the concepts were not meaningful to me. I feel connected now. At a conference I attended I could see other teachers who did not understand what was going on and could not see the relevance. I've got a whole different perspective now and that is exciting, and I like that feeling.

*Richard:* Ferguson?

*Ferguson McKay:* Well, my trouble is that everything everybody else said applies to me. If I'd had a leave of absence this year I'd agree with Susan that case studies are good for reentry trauma or whatever you want to call it. The first thing I thought of when you mentioned that we were going to talk about what was most satisfying was what Susan just said—the sense of being more professionally connected, more professionally aware, relevant, interested. Doing research is probably the most satisfying thing I've done in a long time; it's very, very hard work, but the kind of hard work that doesn't feel like hard work while you're doing it. But everything else is true, also, that everyone's said here, so I see no need to repeat it. I talked with Glenda earlier about how I thought that I had no real evidence for the fact that I was teaching my class better. And she said, "Well, of course you are; you're paying more attention to it. You're thinking more clearly about what ought to happen in it." I didn't get any direct feedback on my teaching, but it differed from previous years. I did have the feeling that I knew better what I was doing and that the students were more involved in it. The only evidence I had of that is that I read all the papers after the end of the semester and grade them—there are no grades until after the last class—and normally about one-third of my students will come and pick up their papers voluntarily, sometime within a year after the course was over. Well, everybody picked their papers up in two days this time. Everybody. And I could not account for it except that the course had gone better. They tended to keep their writing, whereas my files are full of writing that goes back ten years now from people who haven't picked it up. So I think maybe that is one indication that something is going better.

*Richard:* I think what you're saying leads into one of the other questions I wanted to ask, which was: Just what did doing the case study do to your teaching?

*Ferguson:* I didn't expect this to happen, but as soon as I began working [in a class on research techniques led by Lil Brannon] with her research on the story "The Prop" by Gene Garber, it came over me that, my god, I'm teaching my literature courses the wrong way. Instead of teaching them the way I think writing courses ought to be taught, I'm still teaching them in the traditional way that I learned in grad school. There's this big gap between my philosophy of teaching writing and what I'm allowing myself to do in the lit. class. And in two days it's come over me that I can't go back and do that again. So I'm now trying to write a paper for her in which I redesign the lit. class along lines that I can live with. This is one effect of doing a case study and then coming down [to the Martha's Vineyard workshops] and getting involved in somebody else's research—either I've got to change my teaching or I'm going to quit teaching, because I just can't do it the way I've been doing it. I can't stand it. That's one of those feelings that comes over you all of a sudden one day—"Oh my god, this is terrible, what am I going to do?" But it's interesting because what I'm doing is not disapproved of by anybody. Nobody at my school says I'm a bad teacher, that I ought to quit, or that I'm a lousy conductor of a lit. class—I'm doing what everybody else does. [Murmurs of agreement]

*Peggy:* I know. When I first started coming to the Vineyard, I was doing probably what you've been doing all along and I had to shift modes also, and I'm the only one doing what I'm doing. All the other English teachers are doing what everybody else does, you know, the traditional way: give students the modes, here's the argumentative paper, and the samples, and they read the samples and then write a paper. I'd love to go back and say, "Hey, look, you're all doing it wrong, let's do it this way," but I'm not about to, since I'm the youngest and low man on the totem pole; I won't rock the boat.

*Ferguson:* Oh, I wouldn't either. I wouldn't go back and say I was doing anything differently, because they'll either think you're crazy or they'll want to fire you. Seriously, it's not a joke. It's a threat to your professional survival that you see things differently.

*Peggy:* Fortunately I'm in a situation where, because I teach remedial students and I'm the only one who teaches reading, I'm the expert. So they don't question what I do. My techniques have filtered down into writing because I have been successful. I keep saying, "Well, you know, pretty soon we're not going to have any more remedial students. Does that mean I'll not have my job anymore?" And my supervisor keeps saying, "No, you don't have to worry, you're the only one who could do this, you're the only one who gets results." I know it's because of the way I'm doing it. I enjoyed doing the research. When I heard "research" before, I thought "empirical"—keep statistics, have a control group—and it turned me off completely. I didn't want any part of that. I enjoyed doing this.

*Jane:* It's fun research.

*Peggy:* Yes. Truly.

*Jane:* I couldn't wait to correct papers—to see if they had fewer errors. Seriously! To see if they had fewer misspelled words. I had a terrific load of papers to correct, since I have four—what we call Regents'—classes, and I had a lot of papers during the week. But it was wonderful to see the change in some of the kids. Some of them had the same problems that they began with in September, but many of them would make, oh, a couple of misspelled words in a paper. Around December or January, they wouldn't. They would look the words up, and they would be much more careful.

*Jacquie:* Are these seniors, or can you look at the same children if you do it again?

*Jane:* I'm going to have the two that I worked with in my case study this year.

*Liz:* So you can see if there's a carry-over.

*Jane:* Yes, and I'm going to help them diagnose their own misspelled words to a greater extent. I'm looking forward to working. That's another thing: I'll always do classroom research. I don't know whether it will be as well documented as this, but I will always have a question that I will work on, and, like you, I want to do some work on my own.

*Liz:* Do you find it a lot of extra hard work?

*Jane:* Oh yes. I did. I spent vacations and weekends, hours and hours, on the case study.

*Liz:* I was wondering how you did it that made it such fun. I thought mine was really difficult. Maybe it was because of what I was trying to do and I couldn't do it so well. I don't know. I was trying to capture something like a photograph, only I was trying to do it in the words of the children. And I found it very difficult.

*Jane:* Well, I did too, because the process of what I was trying to do was just in bits and pieces and segments and I couldn't see them going together until I sat down at the word processor in April. I just couldn't see how it all would fit.

*Judith Boyce:* That's what I found the most valuable—when I sat down to write and really looked at what I was looking at, which was a thing I call a commonplace book, a kind of journal. When I started writing it, I came up with things I hadn't thought of, so that writing it up made me realize some things about the way I commented on their journal entries. When I wrote up what they said to me in interviews, I realized that there was a point there that I hadn't even thought of when they were talking to me. When I put it together, I came up with ideas.

*Ferguson:* I'd have to agree with that. Writing it up was not the most satisfying experience for me, but perhaps the most important. It made me understand what on earth it was all about. I've also got your problem, Jane. Every time I look at a problem in teaching, I've got another research question. It's just overwhelming.

*Glenda:* Eileen, what about your experience?

*Eileen McCormack:* I'm perfectly delighted. I had marvelous results with the children, the parents. I've had things happen that never happened before. I've learned so much. My central question was, how can the writing process improve reading skills? And since we use a basal reader which is loaded with skills, I changed my whole method of teaching around and had the children focus in on three things. When they got a story to read, first they read it for enjoyment, then they wrote down the things that they liked about it. Then they came in to the group and discussed why they liked the story. The second assignment might be to read the story again and find the author's techniques. Again, they wrote about it and we discussed it. And the third time would be to find facts. I eliminated all the dittos that went with the reader; I didn't do one ditto.

Also, I tape-recorded my students as they talked about their writing, and I wouldn't teach again without using tapes. I'd listen to the day's tape at home, and I might bring it back the next day and have them listen to it, and then they'd say, "Oh! Did I say that?" and go back and make another change in their writing.

*Ferguson:* What would happen if somebody did a research study in which students have a conference; then at some later time, say three or five or seven days later, have them come in and listen to the tape of the conference? Not in place of another conference, necessarily, but in addition to it.

*Eileen:* One of my students and I were talking and I said, "Remember the last conference?" And he said, "No, I didn't say that." I said, "Why don't you listen to the tape again"? And he replied after listening, "Gee, I'd better put that in." Another thing is, the tapes didn't bother them. I used a little tape recorder, and I'd put it down, and they'd just go right on working. The attention they gave to their work was unbelievable! I'd go into the class, and they'd already be at their places. They'd be sharing, they'd have their folders—they knew what they were doing. I didn't have to ask them to start working because they were into it already, before I even started.

*Richard:* Did the rest of you find that your students were cooperative subjects that way?

*Jacquie:* Oh, yes.

*Jane:* Yes. I would ask them if they would come down to the library to meet me during a study period to talk to me on the tape and they always said, "Oh, sure." They never said, "Eehh, I've got homework," or anything. They were doing it on their own time. And they were all perfectly willing to do it.

*Richard:* Ferg, when you were adding to what Eileen was saying with your suggestion that people repeat conferences, or listen to tape-recorded conferences, it struck me that, in a sense, that's what many of you experienced with your own research—when you were talking about pulling things together, and during the writing, things began to make sense. I wonder if any of you would care to comment on your own increased self-consciousness and being much more aware through the case study not only of what your students were doing but also of yourselves as teachers, as speakers, as interactors with your children and with other teachers. Did you become aware at some point that you were watching yourself as much as you were watching your students?

*Judith:* When I listened to the tapes of myself interviewing the students, I saw that that's something I need to work on. I needed an interview technique so that the children were talking. I was talking too much in the interview.

*Jane:* As the year went on, my students didn't need me in the editing groups. I wandered around and helped when I could, but they were pretty self-sufficient.

*Ferguson:* I've been using a tape recorder much more than I was before because I found that it makes me honest. You don't really understand what you've heard somebody say until you listen to it two or three times. What really helps is making a transcript. You've got to pay attention to what's on that tape. I listened to my tapes, copied them out, and wrote comments on them, either the day they were made or within a few days thereafter, but usually the day they were made. Then I went back and reexamined them and reinterpreted them later on while writing the paper. And the second interpretations were not the same as the first. The interpretation I made of the conference in the afternoon, when I'd done the conference in the morning, always caused me to see the conference totally differently from the way I'd seen it when I was meeting. So I started to be forced to be honest about what I was doing. I was deceiving myself about what I was doing. I had a whole series of ideas about what the effect of this or that procedure was which half the time weren't right. Seeing that is threatening and exciting at the same time.

*Richard:* I think you hit on a central term there: the threatening nature of looking at what you're doing and seeing your actions more objectively. That's akin to any other aspect of your self-image; looking at yourself and trying to be blunt about it can be very threatening.

*Ferguson:* I had one girl of the six I studied whom I couldn't work with effectively, and I found out after a while that, without realizing it, I really disliked her. Then I discovered that I disliked her because her weakness in writing was very similar to mine. Was that a shocker! After that I got along better with her and she did better. I had to see I had a hang-up there before I could get beyond it and teach better.

*Peggy:* When I came last summer I showed Glenda the students that I thought I would be working with, and there was one student in particular that I was doubtful about working with. He was so far below what we consider minimal and norm that he certainly wouldn't be successful. I certainly wouldn't look good as a teacher if he didn't improve, and I just didn't know how much time I was going to invest in this kid. So in September, when he was not in my English class, I was relieved. As it turned out, he sought me out in October, and I probably spent more time with him and found him to be more successful than the other two. The prospect of working with him, though, was too much of a task—it was too threatening to me as a teacher: would I be successful with this kid?

*Liz:* I think that doing the research is actually a reflection on the teacher as far as the school district is concerned. Some unusual things happened to me. This year the LD specialist and reading specialist worked in the classrooms instead of taking children out—I've been struggling against that for quite a while—but they came in during my writing time and worked with us in writing, and they were really excited. Now they are going around to other classes, working with writing. And this summer for the first time we had a writing workshop for one week as an in-service in our school district. I think it's hard to say, because I don't have the actual evidence, but I believe that there's a respect for what I'm doing that hasn't been there before, even though I think it's very much what was going on before. Somehow people looked at it differently this year, maybe because they thought I was taking myself more seriously.

*Glenda:* Do you feel more respect for what was going on in the classroom?

*Liz:* I'm really excited about it . . . yes, I guess so. When I look at the information I put together, I feel really good about what's been happening.

*Jane:* I do too, but I'm like you—I've been doing this wrong for years. That was probably the biggest, first revelation and I knew it, but I didn't know what to do about it.

*Susan:* My research was focused on being self-conscious. Being conscious of self and really thinking about that term is at first most uncomfortable. And then I had to find ways to work through how to make learning manifest. So I was reading about journals, and I discovered different articles about annotation and double-entry notebooks. Then I realized how these work. Bruner, I think, talks about "going meta"—metaposition—as being the whole difference between really accelerated learning and your regular old Joe Schmo. I have all these things I had never considered before. And now I have all these different strategies to learn how to learn, or to look at your own learning and become conscious. I've been assigned this coming year to teach a study-skills class, something which would normally be the ultimate *ughh* . . . However, I could actually really get excited about study skills now. I haven't looked at any of the new materials because I haven't been teaching that at all, but any old materials I've seen are awful—I mean, the outlining process, and other things that turn kids right off. But I have a whole slew of strategies that are not available in any of those materials that I could start compiling to be my own study-skills course, that I think kids could really use. And I'd love to see how they react to it. Study-skills course? Sure! Plug me right in there, Principal! [Laughter]

*Ferguson:* You can meet yourself coming down the hallway a lot of days next year. And when it happens, don't think you're going out of your mind. Realize that it's one of the consequences of doing this kind of research. It's a cheap shrink.

*Susan:* I don't understand this.

*Ferguson:* Haven't you ever met yourself coming down the hall? "Oh my god, there I am, that's me"? This kind of research makes you aware of yourself—because it gives you some internal support, some increased self-respect; it makes it easier to look at yourself. You're not so afraid, or threatened, by the revelations that come. I do a lot of writing about what comes into my mind, and I went from one or two pages of writing to eight to ten pages at a sitting in order to handle the stuff that's been coming, at least over the last two months. Ever since I started pulling the research together, really looking at it, I've been looking at me, too. And some people might be frightened by that. I love to do it, but if a person gets alarmed by it, they should simply be told, "This is great," and given some support when it happens.

*Eileen:* This year went so well for me that other people have caught on to it. My principal, for instance, is establishing a publishing house, and she's acquiring a VCR. She has given me a lot of support.

*Glenda:* Maybe that's a question we could get into. What were your needs for support, what kept you going during this, and what made it difficult? What were the hard times?

*Eileen:* I never would have made it without my principal. She has listened and listened, she has backed me right up. She's marvelous.

*Jane:* As far as other colleagues are concerned, my superintendent said, "I think your case study is very important and you should share it with the other English teachers." And my principal asked me to talk to the other English and history teachers about it at the beginning of the year and to explain it at the superintendent's conference. This was something that never happened at school before that I know of.

*Richard:* Do you have inklings of why it never happened before?

*Jane:* Well, I don't think that anyone was that aware; I think that the superintendent knows enough about what's going on in education to realize that case studies are being undertaken all over, and I think that he was very pleased that I was doing it, although he'd never directly tell me.

*Glenda:* What about some of the rest of you? Where did you find support—emotional, intellectual, professional, whatever kind you needed?

*Ferguson:* I needed it, but it wasn't there.

*Glenda:* —or if you didn't. This is sounding like paradise, and maybe it's misleading to talk only about the highlights.

*Jane:* I found support from the kids. [Murmur of agreement] They were very, very supportive. In fact, they would ask me how it was going and what the results were. They were so excited about writing, they kept me going.

*Eileen:* That's what really keeps you going: the kids.

*Ferguson:* I'd agree, Jane, that a certain support came from the attitude of the class. I had a lot of mixed messages from the institution. For instance, I applied for a sabbatical for the fall, so that I could do this and some other research, and they gave the sabbaticals to other people, because they didn't think staying on campus to do research was of any significance. On the other hand, they gave me the money to come down here and study because I said I was going to get a degree, and I'm quite sure that the degree was the main thing that persuaded them to hand out the money. I realize I'm lucky to get that, but I get these two-sided messages from my administrators.

*Liz:* My family is very supportive; through all the reading and all the writing that I did, my husband was right in there listening. My daughters have young children, and they were very much interested in what was happening. My son-in-law is a poet, and he was interested. They were wonderful.

*Judith:* I feel a little bit like Ferg: I didn't talk about it. I did send a letter to my department head and my superintendent at the beginning, and they said, "That's fine, that's great." But I did not talk about it much with the other teachers. All I said was, "I'm working on a paper," but if I had used the word *research* and said I was a teacher-researcher, they all would've said, "Unh. What is Judy doing now! What's the matter with that woman?" The eyes would have rolled. And so I kept very quiet about it.

*Ferguson:* I have to be careful not to say I like teaching or to be too enthusiastic about students. It doesn't go over.

*Richard:* With your colleagues, you mean?

*Ferguson:* Yes, because the prevailing talk is war stories up and down the hall. If you come across very enthusiastically they don't like it. So I just don't talk to them about it.

*Liz:* At our school we have to have a plan for professional development that we have to submit to the principal in the fall of the year. It was very simple for me because the research project satisfied that very easily. Then, also, at the first faculty meeting we have to share with the rest of the faculty what it is we plan to do that year, so it was very much out in the open at the beginning of the year. People were interested. They wanted to know how things were going, and now there's a decided, growing interest in poetry in the whole school.

*Jacquie:* I got no support from my colleagues. They all thought I was nuts for doing my case study, because they all felt we had enough work to do.

*Jacquie:* Aside from my students, I did get support from one of the sets of parents. She was very active in the school, and she would very often come and meet with me and inquire, not about her son but how my research was going. Her question every six weeks or so kept that fire going under me; it said to me, "Don't quit; there's someone here that's interested." The mother of the other subject couldn't have cared less. In fact, I think she completely forgot that I asked permission to do the study. She was hesitant at first, when I asked permission, and when I spoke with her and conferred with her, she just never really cared. This whole attitude came through in her son as well, while the other boy's parents were behind him a great deal.

*Peggy:* Glenda's letters helped me, too. And the questions she asked.

*Liz:* Our group [of teacher-researchers in Vermont, led by Glenda], too, was supportive. That was really helpful. I think that in my next involvement in research, I'm going to use the group even more, because I know more about how to go about using it.

*Peggy:* Probably one of the biggest things I've taken away from this is that I want to do more. I didn't want to stop here. I'm looking to examine other things now. I think as a teacher there's always something you can look at; there's always a problem, another facet that you may have let go by the wayside before that you could work on.

*Ferguson:* While we're talking about support, we shouldn't leave out what I was going to get to, and I think you've already gotten to, Susan: a lot of support comes from just feeling that you're doing something that means more to you than anything else you're doing—inner support, that's what kept me going.

*Richard:* A related question that we should get to is, besides lack of support, what could go wrong?

*Judith:* You can throw away your first design and start over. That's what happened to me.

*Jane:* You can bite off more than you can manage. That's what I did. I concentrated on not only two students in one class but on two classes.

*Eileen:* I had three students when I started but I dropped one.

*Jane:* I had three, too.

*Ferguson:* I started with six for fear that I'd lose two, and I didn't lose any. It just piled up on me.

*Eileen:* When I got all three in September, they all had "For Sale" signs on their houses. And I lived with this fear!

*Jacquie:* I had initially planned on three youngsters and I did not get permission to do the third boy. His parents would not allow it. You might run into that. I don't know what they were afraid of, but I said, "Can't you trust me as your son's teacher?" They just said, "We don't want our son involved in anything like that." So, you might not get support from the family.

*Judith:* Do you think they didn't want him studied by you or they were afraid it would be published?

*Jacquie:* I think it was more that they thought it was going to be published, and they didn't want their name or his name or his situation to be public. I don't know what they objected to, really; I had trouble communicating with them.

*Peggy:* Ferguson, did you have any trouble with the students that you asked? I mean, we're dealing with adults in college who make their own decisions; they're eighteen years old, you don't have to get permission from their parents. I didn't know that my students totally understood what I was doing, but they weren't reluctant.

*Ferguson:* Well, you've got to figure that students don't totally understand anything. That's why they're in school! If you get their trust, it doesn't seem to be difficult after that.

*Peggy:* That's true; after awhile they were most eager to participate.

*Ferguson:* I was going to say that almost any disruption in your life can interfere with the research. It takes all your time, and anything that starts to take extra time will throw you off. I was just lucky nothing happened—or nothing that severe happened.

*Liz:* I had a catastrophe that I thought was going to ruin the whole project, and I wasn't sure I wanted to continue. I was called for jury duty for the month of December. And I had a substitute in my classroom through nine different days. I called and wrote a letter, but I couldn't get out of it. But the poetry was coming in, so to cope I came in early in the morning to listen to my kids read, because I hear them read individually, then I'd take off for the courthouse. Then the substitute would take over. Sometime during this one of my students' poems was mislaid. I was upset because I thought that the substitute had lost the poem. In the process the student became aware of what was going on, and at that point I thought, if this is going to disrupt my classroom, I'm going to stop doing it; it's not worth it. I was fearful that what I was doing was actually disrupting my classroom.

*Richard:* What sorts of things happened, or could have happened with the class-room that could have disrupted the class or disturbed your research? We've talked about external influences that threatened, but as your research itself wheeled along, what squeaks developed or things happened that were disturbing or disrupting, that made you wonder if you were doing what you should be?

*Jane:* I had a few kids who just didn't care, who just were there. Some days they didn't care whether they passed or not. And sometimes their attitude—especially in one class—would be contagious. I had to work to keep the interest up, and to try to encourage them to take responsibility. I had more problems in one class than in the other. I think that the climate is so important and can be ruined by a couple of kids. There were times when I thought, "Where is this going?"

*Eileen:* One problem I had was that Tom, one of my subjects, had the chicken pox for a week. Another problem was that I wanted more time. I spent an hour a day on writing, but the kids would go another hour because they weren't ready to stop.

*Liz:* Do you think we feel more important?

*Eileen:* We get so much out of it. I think that we become engrossed in it, and I think we take our job more seriously; we internalize more.

*Peggy:* We examine ourselves more; we look at ourselves more while we're in the classroom as teachers and see what we're doing, how we're interacting. I think that's a value, if nothing else. It has to be.

*Richard:* What would you say to people who are about to embark, or are thinking of embarking, on the kinds of classroom research that you did? What hints can you offer, what suggestions, what guidance?

*Ferguson:* Most teachers, and I'm certainly one of them, suffer from a lot of professional isolation. We're out in schools someplace where we have very few people to talk to. This kind of research is a great antidote to the sense of isolation. The better feeling you get about yourself—that's been a big help to me. If you're suffering from any kind of sense of being isolated—being out there trying to do something and you have no support system, you're not really sure of what you're doing—this is a great antidote for it.

*Jane:* I'd say not to get discouraged, because the work will progress and open up just like a book. It will happen. But I never thought it would. It took me days and months to eliminate some of the material and then find time to go back over it. That was my most difficult problem—finding time.

*Liz:* So many of us are doing things that many people aren't aware of; even our principals and our superintendents aren't often aware of what we're doing in the classroom. I remember that once, when I called Glenda, she said that she had just been reading a draft of my study. It was one of the most exciting moments I've felt in a long time, because I felt that my story was being told, being shared; it was a wonderful feeling, the sharing! It's just the opposite of feeling isolation. It's a feeling of being a part, and knowing that somebody else is sharing it.

*Susan:* I'm getting the excitement, but I'm not getting the reality here of how the research made you folks feel less isolated. Are you talking about Glenda and her help?

*Liz:* I'm talking about someone hearing my story, the story that I'm telling. Glenda read it. She's the only outsider other than my family who's read it. I don't know about you and your writing, but I write a lot of things that nobody ever reads, and there's a real thrill in sharing something that you think is important.

*Susan:* I absolutely agree, but there's a long period of time between the start of the research and satisfaction, when it seems to me people would still be feeling that professional isolation. I mean, you're working for ten months, and yes, you have that satisfaction at the end of the road, but . . . I did a lot of interviewing of teachers, and over and over again, they talked about lack of support. Teachers would talk my ear off about that. I could hardly get by it. And it's not specifically about research at all; I was trying to talk to them about their learning, and opportunities for learning as teachers. But sometimes I couldn't get through— they were so happy to talk about anything. I found it very depressing, because they were excited about certain things but they had nobody to talk to. That's why I'm asking that question.

*Liz:* Teachers don't have time to talk, especially first-year teachers. When we're finished, we're tired, and we leave. We're exhausted. Even though we get there early in the morning and we're there at the same time, we don't want to talk then because we have things we have to think about and we've got to do. So that's our reason, because we're very, very busy.

*Peggy:* Ferg, why did you say you felt less isolated?

*Ferguson:* Well, I had some contact with Glenda, and some contact with other people; it wasn't at the end only.

*Richard:* In other words, it opened up channels that previously had been closed to you for talking with someone about something of interest to you.

*Ferguson:* I would say I had in my mind a clear understanding that if I didn't finish this research, I couldn't come back and join this group again. Delayed satisfaction is a strong motivation. It was also a matter of pride.

*Liz:* There is a feeling of unity in this group. It very definitely exists, and to belong to it is a good feeling.

*Richard:* Is there anything else you can think of, in terms of practical advice, specific things, general attitudes, that you'd like to pass on so other people would have a slightly easier time of it, or just be able to make different mistakes from the ones you made?

*Ferguson:* That's like trying to tell a pregnant woman how to have her child easier than you did! It has to be gone through.

*Liz:* Next time I would understand better why it's so important to be as clear and specific as possible when you're formulating your question.

*Ferguson:* Gosh, I didn't know how to do that until I got near to the end of the research.

*Jacquie:* The research, the articles, the reading didn't say anything to me until I'd already done the research, and then it reinforced my findings, though not in every case. Some of the readings and articles gave me useful strategies, but others didn't mean a thing.

*Peggy:* I think some of the articles convinced me to be very honest. I've been reading what somebody else observed; now let me tell you what I've observed.

*Susan:* Back to interviewing: anybody who's planning to do interviewing can hardly overanticipate how much time it takes. That was mind boggling. It's much more time consuming than you can anticipate. Also, there are interviewing techniques that let you predict the kind of answers you're going to get and what you're looking for. But I could've used some help. I didn't know how to use the answers I got, to do much of anything with them.

*Jane:* [Donald M.] Murray's second chapter in *Learning by Teaching* was very helpful. It taught me to say things as simply as possible. To simplify as much as possible.

*Judith:* I have a question of the others: How did you decide which students to choose out of a large class? That's one of my biggest problems.

*Jane:* The one I chose was one that had terrible problems from the very beginning. He would have maybe twenty or more misspelled words in one two-hundred- or three-hundred-word essay. And the other one I chose had a very poor attitude about himself. He was very intelligent and articulate when he spoke, but his writing didn't display that.

*Liz:* I had one child in my class last year who was so exceptional that I thought, if I weren't so head over heels with what I'm doing, I would immediately start gathering information on him. He came into the classroom with a speech problem. They tested him for eleven days, and he ended up, they said, with a 78 IQ. But he was reading at the end; he learned to read through poetry, he went on to second grade, and he wrote poetry. When he would read, he was so rhythm oriented that when he couldn't get a word he would tap his foot. I said, "Kenny, why are you tapping your foot?" and he said, "It helps me to remember the word." Unbelievable! He sang his reading. I don't think I'll ever have a child like him again. In his journal, which I've copied, he has four pages which came after I finished my research, where he actually revised this one poem, and it's all there, it's all . . . I looked at this and thought, "Why am I not gathering information about this child?" Again, if that happens and I'm not involved in something more important, I would start immediately.

*Eileen:* You did a whole class.

*Liz:* Yes. I believe in a holistic approach to teaching, and I wanted to have the whole thing there. But this child was so exceptional.

*Susan:* I've been approached by a graduate student at Cornell to talk about teacher research. When I started talking, she said, "You're only talking about English and writing," and I said, "That's all I know about." Teacher research: I felt really stupid. It never occurred to me that I didn't look at anything else, and I had no idea if there are other movements apart from English.

*Glenda:* In English there is Dixie Goswami, one of the very early pioneers, and Mary Kay Healy at Berkeley with the National Writing Project has been very instrumental in this. I don't know about teacher research in other fields, but I know that there have been key people who have been involved in the writing projects who have also become involved in teacher research, and this has really been the source of the teacher-researcher movement. Marian Mohr in Virginia has been another very key person in this, again through a writing project. We need to spread the word to our fellow teachers.

*Susan:* I think many people who are involved in social sciences are doing the empirical type of research and aren't concerned with what's going on in the classroom.

*Richard:* I wonder if part of the teacher-researcher movement stems from writing's lack of clearly defined content—the fact that with writing you aren't dealing with an identifiable body of content. This is probably totally blindsided, but I wonder if there are fewer conflicts and self-conflicts among teachers in history and hard sciences where there is a carefully defined body of knowledge, unlike English, which is so hazy and difficult to define.

*Liz:* Also, if you're doing a phenomenological—listen to that—inquiry, there's writing involved. Since we are interested in writing, and since we are training as writers so we can teach, it's natural that we should be writing about what we're doing in the classroom. Whereas if you're teaching math, you're not writing, and writing is not quite as natural as it would be for an English teacher.

*Glenda:* I don't see why the kind of things that you've done teachers of mathematics or social studies or anything else couldn't do. Looking closely at learners, documenting what is going on in your classroom, interviewing students . . .

*Richard:* I think there's some going on in mathematics, for fairly obvious reasons.

*Susan:* I need that "obvious" spelled out for me.

*Richard:* Mathematics is also a complex set of skills that some people seem to catch on to very quickly and others don't. It's considered a foundation of other sorts of learning, it's highly visible, and if Johnny can't add, people get just as upset as if Johnny can't read; whereas if Johnny doesn't know a particular fact of history, it's difficult to say he has to know this one fact. But if the kid doesn't know 2 + 2, he's in trouble. I think math and English both occupy very privileged positions in the curriculum, because they are cornerstones. As a result, there's more attention focused on them. So they're allied in those ways, even though conceptually they're very different.

*Eileen:* Can we do part two next year?

*Susan:* Yes. What if one of us wanted to do another formal case study? What avenue is there? (Whether I would do this if I weren't getting four credits, there's some doubt.)

*Glenda:* You should be aware that the National Council of Teachers of English Research Foundation has grants for classroom teachers to do teacher research. I think you should apply for one of those if you're at all interested, if not for the money, which isn't a large amount, at least for the recognition that it's important for teachers to do research. Other grants are out there as well.

*Richard:* Publication is another outlet, another reason to do it. And when I say "publication," I don't just mean *College Composition* or *Language Arts* or *English Journal*; there are many regional publications that are looking for essays written by teachers, regional conferences where you can present papers, and even informal groups like the one some of you participated in in Vermont. As Ferg and Liz and others pointed out, sharing your work, letting others know what you're thinking and doing doesn't just add to your professional stature—it feels good.

Thank you all for your frankness and your willingness to talk about your work. It should help other teachers who want to do classroom research and case studies by providing a measure of the comradeship that you all felt was so helpful to you, as well as act as a model for others who will follow your example. Thanks.

*Glenda:* I've learned a lot that I didn't know about your research. I feel so excited and so privileged to have been with this pioneer case-study group. I wish we had a bottle of champagne to shoot up to celebrate it. It's just been wonderful.

# PART IV

# *F*our Short-Term Studies

# PREFACE

# Short-Term Studies in a Traditional Graduate Setting

*Richard H. Bullock*

While long-term studies of the sort exemplified in the first part of this collection clearly hold major advantages for both the research and the researcher, there are situations in which such lengthy studies are impossible. Constraints of time and opportunity, however, should not deter undergraduate or graduate students or faculty from demanding such research as part of their ongoing education as practicing teachers or as students learning to be teachers. The four studies following grew out of such a situation, a graduate course I gave at Northeastern University in Boston during the spring quarter of 1985. Readers of this course's description should not consider it a model, an ideal for the sort of course that would promote teacher research; rather, it is simply one way, and an experimental way at that, in which the principles of teacher research may be imparted.

The course, ENG 3353, Problems in Writing, forms an elective course for Northeastern's three M.A. programs in literature, linguistics and writing (mostly linguistics), and technical writing. Thus the students who would take the course are a mixed bunch, with interests ranging from professional training to general interest, and prior knowledge ranging from extensive to nonexistent. For such a varied class, a general introduction to the nature of writing and a close examination of it seemed necessary.

An additional constraint was the course schedule at Northeastern, which runs graduate courses during the early evening, one day weekly, so that part-time students may pursue degrees without missing work. A class that meets as a group only two hours weekly requires a great deal of independence of its students, who must progress with one-half to one-third the guidance and prodding of typical course schedules. For this reason, I find journals of one sort or another effective means of having students pace themselves through a week's work, rather than slipping into the natural human fault of allowing approaching deadlines to dictate a panicky work schedule.

We began, then, by focusing on the students themselves as writers, learning to see their own writing by writing and examining both what they wrote and how they wrote it. This involved a journal in which students wrote on one page and, on the facing page, commented on their writing, logging their thoughts and actions as they wrote. (For a week-by-week description of the course, see the syllabus and schedule of events following this overview.)

Once they had a clear sense of the nature of writing as seen in their own activities as writers, the students moved into the heart of the course: the study of a single writer, closely observed. Obviously this assignment posed different problems for the students, both in terms of the activities they would have to perform in the course of observing and recording someone else in the act of composing and in terms of, simply, finding a subject, since most had no students from which to draw a suitable subject. Through the generosity of the office of the dean of the College of Arts and Sciences, I was able to offer the writers being observed a small stipend, which I assumed would make the task of writing one or more pieces of prose while being watched and questioned more attractive. As the reports included here suggest, though, the students were quite resourceful in finding varied and interesting subjects, ranging from family members to students and colleagues, a mix that enriched the class by affording multiple perspectives on the writing processes of writers at various ages, levels of ability, and stages of composing.

The observation and reflection period lasted only three weeks, the first five having been taken up with groundwork, background, and self-analysis. At this time students were to continue their progress outward from self to a single other to, finally, a wider audience by working on a more formal research project using published source material and demonstrating not only self-knowledge and observational ability but also familiarity with relevant literature. Most students chose to expand their studies, facing the dilemma that haunts research of this sort: there is seemingly never enough time, for the material—humans in the act of composing—is so rich and fruitful that even a year seems too short, as some of the

Martha's Vineyard Institute writers profess, and a matter of a few weeks only enough to skim the surface.

What surprised and pleased me about the students' work, given the obvious shortcomings of the course, was its quality. That quality, growing out of obvious interest in what they were doing and sincere interest in the subject—or, I should say, their subjects—suggested to me that this sort of research, focusing on individuals as they go about their work, is inherently compelling for students. Unlike the bulk of their studies, which involve abstraction, generalization, and knowledge separated—by time, distance, and the real need for critical perspective—from their day-to-day experience, close observation of themselves and others draws their intellectual lives closer to their lives as students and teachers. By acting as a bridge between the classroom in which they sit and the classroom they command, these studies link theory and practice in ways that neither student-teaching practicums nor sheer experience can do.

## ENG 3353, PROBLEMS IN WRITING: THE COMPOSING PROCESS—HOW WRITERS WRITE

### A Syllabus and Weekly Outline

**Texts**

Ann Berthoff. "Learning the Uses of Chaos." In *The Making of Meaning*. Montclair, N.J.: Boynton/Cook, 1981.

Richard Bullock. "Creativity and Writing." Unpublished ms.

Lucy Calkins. *Lessons from a Child*. Portsmouth, N.H.: Heinemann Educational Books, 1983.

Janet Emig. *Composing Processes of Twelfth Graders*. Urbana, Ill.: National Council of Teachers of English, 1971.

Linda S. Flower and John R. Hayes. "A Cognitive Process Theory of Writing." *College Composition and Communication* 32 (1981): 365–87.

Donald Graves and Donald Murray. "Revision: In the Writer's Workshop and in the Classroom." *Journal of Education* (1980): 38–56.

John R. Hayes and Linda S. Flower. "Writing as Problem-Solving." *Visible Language* 14 (1980): 288–99.

Donald M. Murray. "First Silence, Then Paper." In *Learning by Teaching*. Montclair, N.J.: Boynton/Cook, 1982.

Mimi Schwartz. "Two Journeys through the Writing Process." *College Composition and Communication* 34 (1983): 188–201.

Frank Smith. "On Teaching Writing." In *Writing and the Writer*. N.Y.: Holt, Rinehart, and Winston, 1982.

Nancy Sommers. "Revision Strategies of Student Writers and Experienced Adult Writers." *College Composition and Communication* 31 (1980): 378–87.

William Stafford. "A Way of Writing." *Field* (1970), rpt. in *Fields of Writing: Readings Across the Disciplines*, edited by Nancy R. Comley, David Hamilton, Carl H. Klaus, Robert Scholes, and Nancy Sommers. N.Y.: St. Martin's, 1984, pp. 615–20.

Heidi Swarts, Linda S. Flower, and John R. Hayes. "Designing Protocol Studies of the Writing Process: An Introduction." In *New Directions in Composition Research*, edited by Richard Beach and Lillian Bridwell. N.Y.: Guilford, 1984, pp. 53–71.

### Course Requirements

Student self-analysis/daily journal

Case study of writer

Research project

### Schedule of Activities

(Note: This course, like all graduate courses at Northeastern, met one evening weekly for two hours.)

**Week One:** Introduction to course and its participants. Writing as a creative/cognitive balancing act.

*Journal Assignment:* Open your notebook to the second page. On the right-hand page, compose a piece of writing (anything you like—from a poem to an essay to a report). On the left-hand page, chart your actions—what you did that made the writing happen. Include as much as you can, and look for detailed response. Take notes during the writing, but don't let it interfere with the writing itself—go back and reconstruct. Plan to write at least one full page of writing and an equivalent amount of commentary each day. Bring your journal with you next week with a summary of its contents: what you learned about your own composing processes.

**Week Two:** Discussion of the composing journal: common elements, common threads.

*Journal:* Begin a new piece of writing this week, focusing on what you did *before* beginning to write: what were your thoughts (write them down, either as you get them or afterwards)? When did you think about the piece? How did you think about it? What prompted you to consider such a piece? What led you to create as you did?

*Reading:* Stafford, Berthoff, Bullock, Murray, and Calkins, chap. 21, "Concept Development."

**Week Three:** Writing as creating.

*Journal:* Continue as before, beginning a new piece of writing this week. In your commentary, focus on your *content*—how did you come to write this piece of writing? How did you make your initial choices? How did you move from the first writing on the page to the next? Next, examine your *revising* processes—how did you know that X needed revising? What form did the revising take? Why did you do what you did, change what you changed?

*Reading:* Graves and Murray, Schwartz, Emig, chap. 1.

**Week Four:** The composing process continued: discussion of student processes in context of literature. Introduction to Calkins, Sommers, Flower and Hayes.

*Journal:* This week use your journal to explore the reading. On the right-hand page, write your reactions to what you are reading. The next night, before you begin to read anything new, read and, on the left-hand page, comment on your reactions.

*Reading:* Flower and Hayes, "Writing" and "Cognitive Process," Sommers, Calkins, chap. 9, "Revision?"

**Week Five:** Composing and revising: summary.

*Journal:* Continue reacting to the reading.

*Reading:* Calkins, pp. 3–46; Emig, pp. 45–75; Swarts; Flower and Hayes.

**Week Six:** Case study: concepts and procedures, problems and preliminary discussion.

*Assignment:* Each of you should meet with your subject this week and begin your study.

*Journal:* Use your journal to record your observations of your subject on the right, your reactions and thoughts regarding those observations on the left.

*Reading:* Calkins, pp. 68–101.

**Week Seven:** Tentative study findings: sharing information and problems, pooling resources, finding threads and common elements.

*Journal:* Continue using journal for observation, reactions.

**Week Eight:** Pulling it together: case studies due in final form; distribute one copy to each class member and be prepared to discuss your findings.

*Journal:* Use the journal to explore what has passed in the course so far and how it might be shaped into a research project. Brainstorm, write notes, react to outside or collateral reading, react to your note taking and brainstorming. Write a project proposal, revise it, comment on it. Bring a fully-formed proposal to the next class. Include your project's scope, purpose, methods, sources. And bring too a series of questions: what kind of help do you think you will need (advice, materials) to do this project?

**Week Nine:** Workshop: plan to discuss your planned project and help your classmates with theirs. Our goal: to leave class with firm plans and clear ideas for proceeding, given the time remaining.

*Journal:* Use as you wish.

**Week Ten:** Exploring relationships between the writing process and the reading process.

*Reading:* Calkins, pp. 152–71.

**Week Eleven:** Summary, the wider context: social and educational aspects of writing and its teaching.

*Reading:* Smith.

**Final Exam Period:** Completed projects due.

# CHAPTER 11

# $B$reaking Patterns

*Kathleen Hogan*

While teaching freshman composition this writer studied one of her students, who consistently wrote formulaic narratives regardless of the topic he chose. Only when asked to write on a topic assigned by the instructor did this student need to examine his composing processes and use techniques being taught in the class. From this reaction, Kathleen speculates that while self-chosen topics are often liberating for students, some may find greater challenges, and paradoxically greater involvement, in topics chosen by the instructor that demand more from the student than the student himself would ask.

Kathleen is completing her M.A. in English from Northeastern, where she has worked as assistant to the editor of *Studies in American Fiction*; she has also participated in the Martha's Vineyard Institute of Writing. Kathleen believes that "the act of writing is an enormous act of power and self-expression, and that the way one chooses to teach writing is often an expression of the way one chooses to share that power." She has enjoyed teaching "because it offers a unique opportunity to learn about my own writing by witnessing a student's misconceptions, doubts, and fears about his or her own writing. As an instructor, my students have helped me with my writing as much as I have tried to help them with theirs."

The issue of whether or not topics in the writing classroom should be teacher or student sponsored concerns both researchers and teachers of writing. Donald Murray, an advocate of student-sponsored assignments, explains, "Students will, of course, plead for a life preserver...a topic, any topic, even what I did on my summer vacation—but if you toss it to them they will not learn how to find and develop their own subjects, the basis of the writing process"(2). "Children who can't choose topics...as a steady diet," asserts researcher Donald Graves, "see writing as an artificial act disconnected from their own lives"(1). The effect of teacher-initiated topics, Graves and Murray suggest, is student dependency on teachers for writing subjects. "No talk before writing, no assignments, no story starters, no models, no lists of possible topics— nothing that reveals you think the student has nothing worth saying and makes the student dependent on you for subject matter"—this is the only remedy for students' unhealthy dependency on teachers, says Murray (2). Part of what makes writing meaningful for students is a sense of ownership of their own writing, and when we usurp that authority, a student's control over written language is diminished. The implicit message we send is essentially, "You are empty vessels, lacking experience and substantial ideas; I am an experienced, filled vessel, and therefore I shall supply you with ideas for writing, even if my ideas are not yours." In my teaching of college freshmen, however, I found accepting these assertions difficult. The purpose of this case study, then, is to question the "never assign topics" notion to see if it implies a rigidity similar to the traditional "only assign topics" approach.

Craig, the subject of this case study, is an intelligent, resilient freshman who abandoned civil engineering for history because, he said, his background in mathematics wasn't strong enough; after getting to know Craig, however, as both a case-study subject and a student in my composition class, I discovered that he simply enjoys history. Craig also has an intense interest in military ships, and everywhere in his writing the influence of this interest is apparent.

It should not surprise anyone, then, that when confronted with a young woman and a tape recorder in a strange office, and with the task of writing something—anything—and then talking about it, Craig immediately chose to write a story about a ship. In fact, I wanted Craig to feel comfortable at the beginning of the study, so I suggested that he write on ships or history, since these were the topics he always chose for his class assignments; he was, however, free to choose any topic. Craig's reaction was, "Ships? That shouldn't be much of a problem." Craig explained that he had just been thinking about a ship, the *Normandie*, earlier that morning, so his response was understandable. As Craig set out to write, he said that he first needed to "think about the pictures and then I can reconstruct in my mind what the books have said."

Starting the essay was difficult, Craig said, because he couldn't begin writing until he had generated a first sentence; he needed to "get the sentence that would trip off what I'd be writing the paper on," implying perhaps that once he recalled an idea from his reading and transformed that idea into a first sentence, the paper would write itself. Craig's first two paragraphs on the *Normandie* follow:

> The French have always had a gift for creating oceanliners of tremendous beauty and of advanced design. Their oceanliners were among the most beautiful and popular in the world. Names like "France," "Isle de France," "Paris," and "Normandie" have dominated the Atlantic for most of the twentieth century.
>
> Of all of these names, perhaps the greatest is the "Normandie." From the very beginning when "he" was only an idea in someone's mind "he" was intended to have a special grace that no other ship had as yet possessed.

Craig's writing style is smooth stylistically but possesses a prepackaged quality. In other words, Craig's reading influences not only his choice of subject but his style too.

As Craig composed, he seemed more concerned with form and correctness than in exploring ideas. This behavior could have been caused by the situation— his being the case-study subject and I his teacher and observer. But he mentioned twice that he could "ramble on . . . pages among pages among pages," and that "once I get started it's hard to stop." Still, he was careful to use complete sentences, short, clearly defined paragraphs, and "correct" words and grammar. In short, he was concerned with form and control, not with playing with language. His writerly behavior seemed almost a parody of the traditional model.

By paragraph three of the *Normandie* piece, he stopped writing and explained that he had run into a problem: the *Normandie* he said, was a French ship, and therefore he needed to refer to it as a "he" instead of a "she," even though he was writing in English. (I never asked Craig why he retained the French pronoun form.) Reluctantly, he decided to write a paragraph explaining his pronoun usage, and then told me, "I didn't want to do that. I suppose it's just something I'll have to do for the paper. If something like this came in the middle or during the end of the paper, I think it would be fatal." Craig's statement characterizes his assumptions about written language (or at least it characterizes the assumptions he thinks he should possess). Writing the *Normandie* piece was not an act of playfulness; instead it became a matter of control. Once he wrote words on a page they became permanent, almost as though they were etched in stone. Craig's assertion that if a change or problem arose in the middle or end it "would be fatal" is a clear indication that this attitude affects his notions of revision too.

As time ran out, I asked Craig how he would complete the paper if he had more time. He replied, "The *Normandie* being built. The *Normandie* in its career. The *Normandie* in war and the *Normandie's* sad end." According to Craig, this outline had "been in my head for years and years just waiting to get out." Craig's writing seemed to be a reproduction, both in style and content, of what he had read in books; Craig's earlier comment, that he needed to "think about the pictures and then I can reconstruct in my mind what the books on ships have said," explains perfectly why he wrote what he wrote and the way he wrote it.

Since Craig seemed secure in writing on ships and less challenged by writing on topics he chose, I decided to try restricting his choices; I asked him to change his focus from ships to his relationship with his cousin Rich, who he had said shares his interest in military history. Surprised, Craig responded, "My cousin! He's another person I could ramble on and on about." Again Craig voiced apprehension about "rambling," yet this time he didn't try to control it as much and was less anxious about getting the "right" first sentence than he had been in the *Normandie* piece:

> Many of my relatives have often remarked how my cousin Rich and myself appear more like brothers instead of cousins, I can see why they would say that. At a glance, we look quite similar. In the past we have fooled each others' parents, our friends, and even our Sunday school teachers.
>
> Besides our physical appearance, we are quite similar in our interests. Both of us are quite interested in military history, although in recent years he has concentrated more on land-oriented things (such as the army) and I tend to "drift out to sea." Although we share many more interests aside from military topics, the military has always been our favorite subject to dwell on.
>
> I suppose the reasons behind this difference in interests have to do mainly with our background. I spend a lot of time on Cape Cod and Boston, and as a result, my interests have focused on things oriented with the sea.

Craig goes on to say that his cousin Rich, by contrast, spends most of his vacation in the "forested regions of New Hampshire, which explains why he has more or less stayed with things that deal with the land."

In general, Craig was much more flexible in writing about his cousin. "I wrote down the first sentence just to see what it would look like," he said. For the first time I saw him cross out words, stare out the window, grapple with a topic. But though he became more playful and tentative, he "ran right into a wall. It's funny. You start writing . . . you've got it all in your head; then it's like going right off a cliff; it stops right in the middle of the sentence too. It's frustrating." What Craig experienced is natural: the discrepancy between what's in the writer's mind and what's on the page. But Craig didn't recognize the naturalness of such a problem and became blocked. A close look at what he wrote reveals a lot of repetition of both style and content: "quite similar," "quite similar in our interests," "quite interested in military history." Later, when I asked Craig about his difficulties, he said that his usual strategy of telling a story in "chronological order," which he used for the *Normandie* piece, couldn't work with a piece on his cousin: "[The *Normandie* is] more cut and dried. You can look at the history books and follow the facts. . . . This is something that's happening in my everyday life. There's no book that has it in black and white." In other words, Craig had to think actively and make sense of the subject by himself, something he obviously felt uncomfortable doing.

In our third interview I asked Craig if he could revise the piece he had composed on his cousin, but he seemed reluctant. Either he sensed that the writing was too general, which it was, and so wanted to avoid developing it; or he didn't know how to develop an essay comparing his cousin's interests with his own because he felt, in general, more comfortable writing personal or historical narratives. (A third possibility is that the situation of the case study did not lend itself, for Craig, to writing such a piece.) Instead of revising the existing piece on his cousin, he took out a new piece of paper, used the first paragraph from the original, and retold a story about how his cousin's physical resemblance to him "almost got us into quite a large amount of trouble."

> It was a Sunday in his hometown of Stamford, and we had just gotten out of a rather long and boring church service. I suppose it wasn't too bad for him because he knew how his church ran services, but I was rather run-down from it all, since I didn't know what was coming next and I had no idea of how much longer the service would drag on.
>
> After the service, the church was going to hold some kind of fair or something to that effect. The idea of being in another confined area for another indefinite period of time made me shrink back in horror.
>
> I expressed these feelings to my cousin Rich, and I was happy to see that the feeling was mutual. We decided to "slip out" of the church and go off somewhere for an hour or so.
>
> Once we were outside, we agreed to go to the railroad tracks a short distance away. We had discovered the tracks about a month earlier when we were skipping one of his Sunday school classes after yet another long church service, but that in itself is another story.
>
> Once at the tracks we were at a loss as to what to do next. The tracks themselves were on a bed that was approximately thirty feet above where we were standing. Since we came there to see the tracks we went up the embankment and started to walk back and forth over the rails, trying to think of something to do.
>
> I came up with the idea of placing pennies on the rails so that a passing train could flatten them. After putting the pennies on the tracks we climbed down the embankment and waited.
>
> After about ten minutes my cousin decided to go back up and cross over to the other side of the track bed. I stayed where I was (I was never the adventurous one of the two of us and I felt uneasy about going across the rails) and watched a group of signals nearby.
>
> I'm not sure if I actually saw the signal, but I felt deep down that it was coming.
>
> I shouted out to Rich, and he turned around. As he was doing so he froze, made a weird noise, then started to run as if he had kicked over a hornet's nest. He half ran, half jumped down the enbankment and nearly ran me down as he came down. Shortly after a commuter train plowed through at high speed.

Feeling somewhat shaken, we agreed that a boring fair might be better than being permanently affixed to the Stanford–New Haven trackbed. Upon returning to the church, we were greeted by Rich's mother, my Aunt Mary. Aunt Mary and I don't get along that well (I won't get into that—it's another long story), and the fact that she caught us away from the fair didn't exactly get us on her good side.

If there was a lesson to be learned from that episode, we didn't learn it. We still do things that aren't exactly what we should be doing. To be honest, I don't think we'll ever learn.

This piece was different from the original; it wasn't about Craig's cousin as much as it was about their experience together. I wondered why Craig didn't pursue his first topic—what he and his cousin had in common and what they didn't—even though he gained self-awareness by writing it. "I never really thought about it until now . . . but I suppose it makes sense why our interests are the way they are and why they tend to differ slightly. Actually, it's more why they differ than why they're the same. When you write about it you gotta think about it; it comes out." By contrast, when I asked Craig later about the railroad piece, he said, "I wrote it as it happened, as we went through it . . . I really didn't decide how to end it; it ended itself." A pattern emerged in Craig's writing: whenever he felt unsure of a topic, or if the order seemed ambiguous, he resorted to "chronological" order.

Craig's reliance on retelling narratives makes good sense in his immediate situation—as a case-study subject who must produce writing. But Craig was also a student in my class, and the same pattern emerged in his class assignments. My goal as his teacher was to nudge him away from narratives about ships, the same goal that underlay my study.

In our last interview I presented Craig with two choices. One was to revise his piece on his experience with his cousin and the other was to write a response to a newspaper article. He reread his essay and concluded that it "served its purpose." The newspaper article, titled "Students— Conservative, Fearful," had been read and discussed in class two days earlier; briefly, it discussed the perception that college students are not interested in foreign or domestic politics because they are obsessed with training for professional careers. For these students, education is not an act of inquiry but a means to entering law or medical school, an attitude rooted in Watergate and the oil crisis of the 1970s, which planted a deep fear of economic insecurity among the children of those years. In class and in our interview, Craig was extremely reluctant to talk about the article. "I don't know if I could write too much about that . . . because I really don't have any opinion on it either way, really." Craig reconsidered the first choice—revising his story—but still felt that revision wasn't necessary, so he agreed to write about the article.

I left Craig alone for fifteen minutes to grapple with the topic. When I returned, he admitted that he had gotten "backed up by this thing" and tried freewriting, a technique he had never tried before. He had written: "I don't know what to think about the article. I agree that what the writer is saying is quite true, yet I don't know how to develop that agreement into anything that could remotely resemble an organized piece of writing." I asked Craig about his turning to free-writing and he said, "Well, I don't think I would have done this strategy had I not read that book you assigned [Donald Murray's *Write to Learn*]."

Craig's difficulty in responding to the news article is, however, understandable. He felt threatened perhaps, by the article's message during the class discussion, and now he was being asked to write about the news article as a case-study subject. Even so, writing freely, which for Craig consisted of composing complete sentences and short paragraphs, allowed him to achieve significant insight: that he did have opinions on the article and that it did apply to his life. He then revised his free-written piece:

> The article "Students—Conservative, Fearful" has given me a sense of "personal conviction." At first glance, I thought the article was right on target; it exposed all of those students who "put up a front" of conservatism and did nothing about it. As I read on however, I realized that it was on target not because it exposed all those other "pseudo-conservatives," but because it exposed me.
>
> When the article's author mentioned the Brown University students I immediately remembered seeing that incident on television. That is what "woke me up." I saw it on *television*, not in the newspaper or in a conversation. . . . I fit the author's description of the students who were "intellectually handicapped."

I realize it is possible that Craig came to this awareness because he thought that he ought to (although there had been enough disagreement among the students in class that Craig could have felt comfortable taking another position, at least there). He explained that although he had thought about the article after class, he never connected its theme with his own life: "This is something I didn't really realize until this week when you introduced the article, actually until I free wrote . . . I'd thought about it but I hadn't made the connection until now."

Overall, Craig seemed resentful and uncomfortable with freewriting. When I asked him about it, he replied sarcastically, "[Freewriting has] quite a lot of flexibility." "Sometimes too much?" I asked. "Yeah," he replied. For a writer who warned me that he could "ramble on and on," Craig's apprehension seemed curious. It suggests that he "rambles on" only about subjects he knows well—ships and personal narratives—and on subjects that grow from an implicit narrative pattern.

Ironically, it seemed that the less Craig wrote on topics of his own choosing, the more he learned about himself and the more he grew as a writer. He even admitted, "Before I didn't have any idea how I'd write on [the article]. . . . I'm moving in the proper direction, anyway." Yet, although Craig had generated two pages of writing on the article, he turned down my suggestion to use this as the start of a paper for the next class assignment. In class the next day Craig announced that his next paper would be "about a certain fleet of ships," and since my class policy was to allow student-initiated topics, there was little I could do beyond suggesting that he expand his subject matter.

Craig's response challenged my previously firm conviction that students should always choose their own topics. It became clear both in the taped sessions and in the classroom that Craig would use the open-topic situation to limit his challenges, and so limit his growth as a writer rather than expand it. After all, Craig seemed to impose more rigidity on his writing when he chose the topic than when the topic was chosen for him. His resistance to branching out into unknown territory could be counteracted not by freeing him from artificial constraints but by requiring him to expand his range of subjects. That he came to understand the news article's message (even it he didn't really agree with it but only thought he should appear to) reveals where writing and learning converge; it also shows his breakthrough as a writer. When cornered, he had to recognize and try a new approach, freewriting. As Mimi Schwartz argues, what brings writers success is their willingness to recognize when they are stuck and to have a repertory of strategies to choose from (106). Because of the artificial environment of the case study, Craig was forced to do this; on his own, and in class assignments, he would fall back on retelling personal narratives or reproducing stories about ships.

Craig's approach to writing is common. His problems with writing, however, must be compared with those of another student in my class, Dave. Presented with the challenge of creating writing without an assigned topic, Dave produced a piece of writing that left the entire class spellbound. He later showed me a paper on George Orwell's *1984* that he had written for another course; it was stilted, disorganized, and painful to read. That topic had been assigned by the teacher, and it became obvious to me that the policy of having students choose their own topics is right for some students and should not be abandoned.

My point, finally, is that my experience with Craig and other members of his class leads me to think that any broad policy on essay topics—either that they should be student generated or that they should be teacher generated—should be tested against the specific needs of the writers in the classroom. In other words, whatever policies a writing teacher adopts must recognize that each student in a writing classroom has different needs, and one approach is unlikely to work for all. As Lucy Calkins concludes in *Lessons from a Child*, although writing development is talked about "in general," it always happens "in particular" (7). Thinking of writers as individuals deemphasizes the role of the teacher; it suggests to the writers that the responsibility of learning to write must come from them. Freed from being the focus of the course, the teacher can wander around the room, giving nudges to those like Craig and space to those like Dave.

## REFERENCES

Brannon, Lil. "Toward a Theory of Composition." In *Perspectives on Research and Scholarship in Composition*, edited by Ben W. McClelland and Timothy W. Donovan. New York: MLA, 1985.

Calkins, Lucy McCormick. *Lessons from a Child*. Portsmouth, N.H.: Heinemann Educational Books, 1984.

Graves, Donald. "Break the Welfare Cycle: Let Writers Choose Their Own Topics." *Fforum*, Winter 1982, pp. 1–6.

Murray, Donald. "First Silence, Then Paper." In *Fforum*, edited by Patricia L. Stock. Montclair, N.J.: Boynton/Cook, 1983.

Schwartz, Mimi. *Writing for Many Roles*. New Jersey: Boynton/Cook, 1985.

# CHAPTER 12

## *L*aura

*Kathy Calkins*

In this study a junior high school English teacher explores differences between reflective writing—writing that obviously holds meaning for the writers—and obligatory writing—pieces written to please others. Using her daughter as her subject, she examines both self-generated and assigned writing from the dual vantage points of distanced observer and parent to try to see what teachers can do to elicit from their students writing that the students themselves care about.

Kathy, a mother of three teenagers (and "a horse, five cats, and a dog"), returned to Northeastern at thirty-five to finish a degree in elementary education and reading. She teaches literature and Latin at King Philip North Junior High School in Norfolk, Massachusetts.

I can't stand many more pieces on "My Trip to the Shopping Mall" or "Jane's Pajama Party." How do you get students away from these canned, impersonal topics and into a more reflective vein? To explore that question, I chose to study my daughter, Laura, as she wrote two poems, one written spontaneously and the other written at my request.

Laura, my daughter, is fifteen and a half as of this writing. She has always been intensely emotional—the kind of child who had tantrums in the aisle of Stop & Shop and needed a spanking to break through her screaming outburst. With Laura, her bad feelings seem to be her most intense; happy feelings she can evenly control. Laura has a learning disability that affects her spelling, penmanship, and general neatness. She has always been very frustrated and angry with this handicap.

Laura has been writing poems since she was in second grade. The poems are all reflective, self-generated, and always written when she is alone. She did write one poem in fifth grade which was teacher directed as to subject (pollution), and it won a state prize. Here is an excerpt:

THE FOREST

A wild animals home
A place that has
    deer
    trees
    meadows
    and lakes

But man built houses
    roads
    cars
    stores
    and signs

Dams were built to block the
    water ways so that the
    fish
    beavers
    turtles
    and others

Can not get across the
    dams
    bridges
    docks
    and piers. . . .

Please try and help save
    animals
    plants
    trees
    and our world

I've always felt it was her only "Dick and Jane" type of poem, its sentiments growing out of canned attitudes, attempts to please the teacher, instead of deeply felt emotions.

Laura has written few required compositions in school, and she always involves me with ideas and proofreading. During the seventh, eighth, and ninth grades, Laura's writing was very sparse, maybe five poems a year. But this year, as she goes through the tenth grade, there seems to be a bumper crop, at least one poem a week. I'm wondering if these poems are mature tantrums, her way of dealing with intense negative emotions. If writing has given her this substitute, what a valuable form of catharsis it is for her!

Our first session, which consisted of an interview, focused on a recently written poem, "I Can't Find Peace":

> I can't find peace
> In this world of mine
> I'm a prisoner
> Of my own design
>
> I want to escape
> And I want to be free
> But I can't do that
> Until I can see
>
> My world seems bright
> And life is long
> But still I'm restless
> And it feels all wrong
>
> The fire within me
> Is burning bright
> But somehow I just can't seem
> To get it right
>
> I see the sun
> And try to hide
> But the image is fading
> As if it has died
>
> I curse this evil
> And look for the help
> But I can't kill the beast
> Because the evil is myself

I began by asking, "Why did you write this poem?"

*Laura:* I write poems when I have such bad feelings that I feel like I have to punch something or someone. [Pause] It's like eating; you have to do it.

*Me:* Who do you write for?

*Laura:* I write for myself. It's because I have to. [I've noticed a change in Laura's publishing. She used to keep her poems private for a week or so and then show them to me. Maybe she didn't want to let go of her frail self too soon. Now she often shows me a poem on the same night she writes it. Then the poem functions as a key to a discussion about her feelings. Many nights, we've sprawled on her bedroom floor and talked about the feelings in the poem.]

*Me:* How do you choose your theme?

*Laura:* I write about how I feel at the moment. If the feeling is very strong, I write easy. The weaker the feeling, the harder it is to find the right words. Sometimes I just give up if it's too hard.

*Me:* Do you ever go back and finish those pieces?

*Laura:* No—I throw them out.

*Me:* Do you think about the form of your poem? I've noticed your stanzas are different lengths.

*Laura:* No, I don't really think about that. I guess I skip lines like a paragraph.

*Me:* Do you read your poems as you go along or at the end?

*Laura:* I usually read the lines out loud as I write.

*Me:* How do you know when the poem is finished?

*Laura:* When I have nothing left to write.

*Me:* Then do you feel satisfied?

*Laura:* [Pause] "No...empty." [Tantrum over?]

The flow of the discourse during the session looks deceptively smooth on paper; that was not the case. Laura paused before she answered each question. I had to be careful to give her plenty of time to think. I'm sure she never really thought (or cared) that her writing had a process.

Laura's reflective poem doesn't seem to me like something that could be written in the classroom. First, she needed to be alone, and second, she had to write when the feeling was intense, not scheduled. The expression of intense feelings, especially in the teen years, may need to be kept private. I do assure my students that their writing folders are just between us unless they specify otherwise. But who says that they want to share these feelings with me? How do they know they can trust me?

I began our second session by asking Laura if she could write a poem for me now, about anything. She replied that she couldn't pick a subject because she didn't feel bad. I waited while she played with a flashlight and started to sing. After what seemed like ages, I made some title suggestions. She chose one and wrote:

HANK

He's always there
No matter how I feel
No matter what's gone wrong
I can always count on him

People say horses are dumb
Maybe about some things
But so are they

People are always changing
from black to blue but
Hank never does and
he's always there

People like lie and make
you feel bad but Hank
doesn't do that he doesn't
know how

Hank's a friend that I
can trust and there will
Never be a human I can
trust as much

Laura wrote two stanzas very quickly. She paused and wrote a third stanza. She reread what she had written. She tipped the paper, looked out the window, skipped a line, wrote another smooth stanza. She stopped and reread the whole poem and then wrote stanza five with no pauses.

This teacher-initiated poem is like most of the writing I read in my students' folders. Yet I know Laura can write with sincere and original feeling, and I'll bet my students can too. How do I get them to this point? Or can I get them to this point? Do I have the right to try?

In a third session I asked Laura to write a teacher-directed short piece. Again she had trouble finding a subject, but she finally chose a recent event:

I could feel Hank's heart racing as we waited for the hounds, evey mocle in his entirer body was tense. As the hounds apporoched us Hank began to dance. The rain had finally stoped and the sun was starting to come out. We heard the call of the bugle and the howl of dogs the hunt had begun. We turned off the road and on to a narrow dirt trail I had a hard time keeping Hank under control he wanted to run. We kept having to stop every few minutes because the hounds were getting all strung out. the heavey rain in the morning had washed away the scent of the traq. I heard someone yell "jump ahead" so I pulled Hank up and got him ready just in time to see the fallen log. Hank flew over it and up the slope on the other side. We stoped again to regroup the hounds. by this time both Hank and I were sweatting but there was still more.

Soon we were off again, galloping down a windy dirt road. I could tell Hank was tiring because he was more responsive to me. I settled him down to a nice easy canter and kept him there until I heard the hounds howling in victory. They had found the scent.

This piece was written in about fifteen minutes. Laura paused several times and looked out the window, but her writing appeared to be fairly painless. She did get frustrated at one point because she had trouble with the spelling.

Like "Hank," this was another average piece of writing—and this was Laura's feeling also. Laura said that she didn't like either piece of writing done in our sessions, but she had no interest in revising either of them. I know that the Hunting piece that Laura wrote could have elicited some real feelings from her; the whole experience for her was a nightmare—she came home from the hunt looking like a ghost. She had thought she was going to be killed. Why didn't that emotion come through in her writing? She certainly has the talent.

Maybe the subject was too cool. If that's the case, how could a classroom teacher rekindle that kind of feeling in her students? Draw students out about their feelings and experiences? Maybe. The other day during writing, one of my students asked me what she could write about. I suggested dancing because I had seen her dance in the *Nutcracker*. She came back in ten minutes with a very detached piece. She wanted my help. Maybe that would have been the time to discuss her feelings as a sort of prewriting. Maybe discussion is partly the key to eliciting reflective writing: create an atmosphere of safety and trust where kids are comfortable to discuss their feelings, then give them time to write.

It does appear to be possible to set a mood that encourages reflective thinking, then reflective discussions, then reflective writing. As is true of most discoveries, I happened on this process of encouraging writing quite accidentally—or maybe instinctively. In my literature/writing class, I had been trying to encourage students to write from firsthand knowledge, the write-what-you-know principle. We read orally an excerpt from E. L. Doctorow's novel *World's Fair*. The piece was a first-person narrative of the narrator's boyhood memory of his semiannual shopping trip with his mother. The piece was perfect because it drew out from all of us the feeling, "Ah yes, I remember that." The author released in our minds the thousands of little sights, smells, and sounds of the dreaded Shopping Trip with Mom. My students were all vying for floor time to talk about their experiences. After an excited discussion period, we switched to pencil and paper and began to write. I could sense the class's atmosphere and felt that "Jane's Pajama Party" was about to receive a crushing blow—and it did.

I expected to read many "Shopping with Mom" pieces, and there were quite a few. They were warm and alive. The range of the writing, though, went far beyond that; it included the death of a family member, parents getting divorced, jealousy over a new baby, and a scary hospital stay, to name a few. The unifying ingredient in all these pieces was the depth of the reflective writing. None of them had what I call the "list" quality:

**1.** I went to the store.
**2.** I bought some cereal.
**3.** I went home.

Some of the pieces were a bit rough, some were written beautifully, but they all felt and throbbed, and they were all written *in a classroom.*

To unlock the reflective writing abilities of my students, I had found a trigger to get them started. In a noncontrived situation the trigger might be an emotional song, an old photo, or a bedraggled teddy bear. Thinking back to Laura's poem, I realized that she always wrote her real pieces with Pink Floyd playing in the background and incense filling the room. In a contrived situation like a classroom, the trigger seems to be composed of four ingredients: a comfortable room climate, the reading of a well-written reflective piece that is geared to the experience level of the readers, a follow-up time for shared discussion, and a quiet, unmeasured time with pencil and paper (I've noticed that my students are startled, then annoyed when the bell rings to signal the period's end).

How ironic! Laura told me in our interview a year ago that "if the feeling is very strong, I write easy." She obviously spoke for all my student writers. I should have listened to her more carefully. I probably would have found the feeling-release trigger more quickly by design than a year later by accident. I felt like the doctor who doesn't listen to his patient, but spends a great deal of time taking complicated tests. Finally he comes to a diagnosis he could have made much sooner if he had listened. I have learned a valuable lesson. If you want to teach student writers, you must talk to student writers, and you must listen to student writers. "Jane's Pajama Party" comes through when feelings are too weak. "The weaker the feeling, the harder it is to find the right words. Sometimes I just give up if it's too hard."

# CHAPTER 13

# Observing a Would-Be Novelist

*Patricia Hanlon*

This essay by a student learning to become a teacher explores the composing processes of an adult, an amateur fiction writer struggling to bring his mental constructs
into narrative form. This struggle divides itself into fluent brainstorming sessions, during
which the writer discovers insights and links that deepen his characters, and much
more difficult revision sessions, during which his preconceptions about readers' demands hinder his ability to compose or even to explore alternatives.

Patty Hanlon, who lives "near the salt marsh in Gloucester, Mass.," with her husband
and three children, completed her master's degree in linguistics and writing at Northeastern in 1986 and was awarded a one-year teaching instructorship as a result of her
performance on her comprehensive examinations. Her essay grows naturally out of her
long interest "in the puzzles of language and knowing."

Robert is a thirty-one-year-old designer and builder of houses who creates stories in somewhat the same way that he plans clerestory windows and workable kitchens. "It just comes," he says, speaking of ideas both for house design and for a novel about a middle-aged man and his severely disabled wife. Robert's house blueprints translate reliably (most of the time, anyway, depending on the vagaries of local zoning boards and subcontractors) into wood and glass and plaster; there is a close relationship in the building process between thought and artifact. He is less certain, though, of the process by which one turns "movies in the mind" into "finished writing for other people to read."

The body of writing this case study concerns began with a "daydream or maybe a dream; I don't remember which exactly" about Joel, the central character. "My mind went to work right away, filling in details and making things happen—Joel would be an aeronautics engineer, going through a midlife crisis. I thought up a very specific house for him to live in—it was a particular house in my parents' neighborhood. Then I decided that Joel's wife had been in a terrible car accident that left her completely disabled, and *that* opened up the plot in all kinds of directions. I sort of told myself the story—not every last detail, but some of the basic plot."

According to Robert, he has always had this ability to entertain himself by making up stories. "I think of them at odd times—while I'm driving, maybe; cutting up firewood, taking a shower." But it had never occurred to him until recently to translate one of these stories into writing. I asked him where this new-found desire to write had come from.

"I guess I'm a pretty confident person, and that must make me willing to try things I'm not supposedly 'professionally qualified' to do. When I built the house [his own house, as opposed to those he has since built for clients], I knew I could figure out wiring and plumbing and masonry even though I'd had no training for it. You just use common sense and read some instructions and figure it out. Writing fiction is just another challenge like that; something I've always wanted to try out."

Robert allowed me to study several dog-eared brainstorming notebooks, as well as a computer diskette that contained a few attempts at more finished text. "When I write longhand, it's more likely to be stream of consciousness," he explains. "On the word processor, I'm more aware of it being writing for other people. I've only done a little of that so far." And it is true that the bulk of Robert's story writing has been in what James Britton would term the "expressive" mode. "You finish one stage of writing before proceeding to the next. I'm still figuring out the plot, so that's why I've mostly just written it in loose form in the notebooks—just written it to myself."

Robert's explanation of what he does while writing in this "loose" form is quite interesting. He writes, in a journal entry:

I'd like to believe that there's an "essence" of the story already existing somewhere. Sometimes I feel like I'm getting "warmer," getting closer to the real thing. Sometimes when I'm not writing I see faces and hear voices, like watching a movie. Then I'm seeing it in its essence. If I can just get enough of that essence down, I can transcribe it later. So if this model is sufficient, I can write this story just as if I were transcribing it, seeing it take place. The more models like this I can find the sooner (and easier) the story will be written. I become the journalist of an invented reality.

Robert's idea that the story already exists in its "essence" is reminiscent of a classicist, mimetic theory of art; he implies here that his story, like a Platonic form, is a preexisting totality. If this is so—if minds simply, as Ann Berthoff has put it, "have" ideas and stories and poems that they subsequently "put into words"—then the writing process ought to be fairly straightforward, a simple copying down of what already exists fully grown in the mind.

Yet Robert readily admits that the act of writing is far from simple, echoing such theorists as Donald Murray, who has stated that "writing is a significant kind of thinking in which the symbols of language assume a purpose of their own and instruct the writer during his composing process"(3). Robert acknowledges, for example, that his writing not only records but also generates ideas, sometimes in unexpected ways:

> The movies in my head tend to be Bergmanesque—very visual—and, rather than plot, there's a mood—sorrow or greed or whatever—expressed in visual sorts of ways. But if I sit down and start writing, my mind will pursue it deeper and deeper. In this scene about his getting high [Joel tries marijuana in an attempt to fit in with some hip young acquaintances], I felt like I could write on that for pages and pages. I kept getting more specific, and the more I wrote, the further I got from the original idea [from the "essence"] of where I thought I'd end up.

Although Robert may wish for the unambiguous role of transcriber, what he actually does as he writes is clearly far more complex. His ideas do not hold still to be "gotten down" on paper or computer screen; like rabbits, they beget numerous new and unexpected ideas. And his texts give clear evidence of a complex and always shifting array of cognitive processes.

A brainstorming piece titled "Story Ideas: Pool," for example, begins with simple telegraphic jottings: "wife is injured, possibly paralyzed, unable to communicate," a brief transcription of the picture—the "essence"—in Robert's mind.

Switching gears, Robert moves to consider the overall structure of the novel, writing a directive to himself: "much could be revealed by inserting short chapters comprised entirely of her stream of consciousness." He has surely read novels in which this device is used, and knows that the wife's inner thoughts will be both of interest in themselves and an effective way of introducing material that would otherwise have to be given "straight" by the narrator.

Robert next fiddles with more specific possibilities for the wife's interior monologues, possibilities that appear to be not mutually exclusive but rather steps in a progressive revelation—one gained as he writes—of who the wife is and what she will do:

She could reveal her own bitterness, or perhaps joy; she could recall the past and fill in important details of their earlier life, and she could make astute observations about her husband's present behavior. She could speak as his conscience while his is inactive. She could pray. She could reveal bizarre thought patterns common to intelligent people who cannot communicate.

In another rapid cognitive shift, Robert takes on the role of reader (shown by his use of the word *we*), trying out some specific ideas about the wife, and then introduces another character, apparently *ex nihilo*, who links husband and wife and provides a crucial twist to the plot:

> We could discover that she is actually able to communicate with a typing machine or with help from a word chart and a person to nod or blink at. She may communicate his conscience to him and bring him back to himself, but when he finally falls in love with a wonderful woman his own age (perhaps her therapist or someone from her church who comes to visit regularly with the children, or the one who teaches her to communicate!) then she realizes that there is only one way to make them both happy (him and the other woman) and she takes her own life, perhaps by drowning herself in the pool!

The exclamation points indicate the excitement of discovering connections between elements of the story that Robert couldn't have foreseen without having put pencil to paper. Like Robert Frost, he discovers as he writes things he didn't know he knew.

The swimming pool, for example, is an important part of Robert's original "seeing" of his story: "I envisioned a middle-aged guy trying to become young again by investing in expensive things, like this enormous pool he had built in his back yard." The pool recurs unexpectedly in the passage above, in an ironic way Robert hadn't originally planned on.

Having discovered what could be the end of his story, Robert describes the events leading up to the wife's suicide. His use of the present and future tenses indicates that he is still writing for himself (all his attempts at finished text are in the narrative past tense), as does his use of the word *perhaps*:

> She makes certain that her suicide will work. She encourages Joel and girlfriend to go away for a while, perhaps sending them on an errand. She has a power chair and she knows that the battery will send her straight to the bottom of the pool. Perhaps she could get stuck or the battery will run down and she will have to find another way to get herself into the pool, one which will demonstrate even more will power.

As the piece progresses, it becomes less tentative, moving gradually from the notes-to-myself genre toward something very much like narrative prose (note that in the last line of this passage, Robert lapses into the past tense):

> He [Joel] recalls Billy, their first, as an infant and how beautiful they both were in the hospital bed. The girl comes out of the kitchen at this point and sees him under the

pear tree wiping tears from his eyes. He looks down to hide the tears and sees the wheelchair ruts in the dirt. His eye immediately follows them to the patio. Two thin mud lines pointed to the pool.

What James Britton has called "shaping at the point of utterance" seems a good description of what Robert does in these expressive pieces. As when he mulls over room configurations and window proportions, he feels free to trust last-minute hunches and intuitions about the way things might felicitously go together. Britton argues that successful writers are able, even when attempting reader-oriented prose, to adopt this kind of fluency, and that they "continue to rely on it rather than switching to some different mode of operating" (62).

Yet the ease and confidence of Robert's brainstorming pieces contrast greatly with the difficulties he encounters in attempting to create "writing for other people to read." While working at the word processor on the first few "real" pages of his story, Robert spends much time pausing, drumming the keyboard, inspecting spots on the wallpaper. Such markers of writerly frustration do not often stimulate Robert's muse, do not often lead to fresh insight or significant revision.

Surprisingly, though, Robert does not perceive a gap between his two "modes of operating." "It's a difference of degree, not a qualitative one," he says. "It's sort of like putting three coats of paint on a house. You're doing the same job over and over again, only it gets a little more refined in the later stages."

Asked to clarify what he means by "a little more refined," Robert is noncommittal: "Well, I guess you're writing to satisfy some idea in your head about what sounds good. I check things over to see if they're consistent, if they make sense. I don't like to see myself using trite figures of speech, so I would change those as soon as I noticed them. Also, typing [using the word processor] always tends to make me more aware of what my sentences look and sound like. That definitely makes a difference because I can see so clearly what I've just written. I'm much more likely to try to make a finished copy than when I'm writing longhand—I don't see my words so much then."

This awareness of what words "look and sound like" (despite Robert's claim that he doesn't really have different modes of writing) does seem to diminish his ability to play freely with an emerging text. When brainstorming, he feels at ease with and is able to exploit a multiplicity of data, but his approach to writing for others is, as Janet Emig has put it, to march doggedly through Georgia. To be sure, Robert does make changes as he writes, but nearly all of these are fine tuning of diction and syntax. He seldom makes changes above the sentence level.

For example, he begins typing the word *married* in a sentence, but immediately changes it to *wed*. "*Married* has a double meaning," he explains. "You could either be the groom or the minister, and *wed* can only mean the groom." Another pause after he has written a complex, multiclause sentence: "Would *after* make it more logical than *with*?" Not surprisingly, many of Robert's pauses occur at the juncture between clauses, as in "a grin which—" (pauses, drums fingers on keyboard). Often he rehearses possible subordinate clauses or predications in his mind before selecting one, but he seldom scraps the entire superstructure of a sentence, much less that of an entire paragraph, and starts over.

Although Robert does not state it explicitly, it is clear from textual differences between his two modes of writing that he expects prose for others to express complex interrelationships among ideas by means of multiple subordinate clauses. This passage has, in contrast with the loose and relatively simple language of the brainstorming pieces, a variety of such constructions:

> At 1:00 he was to appear in court for what he hoped would be the last time to win a two million dollar lawsuit against Quick Serv, Inc., manufacturers of the "Open-Sez-Me" automatic garage door opener, which had dropped his garage door while Betsy was backing their VW beetle convertible out of the garage. The canvas top was up at the time, but "Open-Sez-Me" automatically put it down. Betsy's head was split from ear to ear. She survived, but all that remains of her former self is a grin which betrays neither intelligence nor emotion.

Perhaps the complicated patterns and rhythms of these constructions cannot help but have a stifling effect on fluency, on "shaping at the point of utterance." Once typed, such sentences may seem, to Robert, to take on a forbidding inevitability that precludes much further tinkering.

According to Richard Bullock, who commented on this study,

> It's easy to see here that Robert does not trust his writing, and thinks there must be an approved "social" style—one doesn't answer the door in one's pajamas, no matter how comfortable they are, I suppose. The key to his improving may lie in developing that trust—in brainstorming extended passages and then revising them, instead of attempting to craft reader-oriented prose from the start.

With time and practice, though, Robert—who, after all, has a robust confidence in his ability to "figure things out"—may well be able to adapt the ease and playfulness he uses in brainstorming to the sterner task of creating the worlds and words of fiction.

## REFERENCES

Berthoff, Ann. "Learning the Uses of Chaos." In *Reinventing the Rhetorical Tradition*, edited by Aviva Freedman and Ian Pringle. Conway, Ark.: L & S Books, 1980.

Britton, James. "Shaping at the Point of Utterance." In *Reinventing the Rhetorical Tradition*, edited by Aviva Freedman and Ian Pringle. Conway, Ark.: L & S Books, 1980.

Emig, Janet. *The Composing Processes of Twelfth Graders*. Urbana, Ill.: National Council of Teachers of English, 1971.

Murray, Donald. "Writing as Process: How Writing Finds Its Own Meaning." In *Eight Approaches to Teaching Composition*, edited by Timothy R. Donovan and Ben W. Mc-Clelland. Urbana, Ill.: National Council of Teachers of English, 1980.

# CHAPTER 14

# A Writer Composes Aloud: Tracing Cognitive Processes in Writing

*Jennifer Hicks*

This author designed and analyzed a structured protocol involving an adult, an instructor in writing. Following the model for writing as a cognitive process outlined by Flower and Hayes, her analysis suggests that rather than being "hierarchically organized" (where prewriting, drafting, and revising tend to be distinct stages involving only some parts of the writing process), writing is best characterized as a hierarchical spiral, in which writers use each part of the writing process during each major stage in an organized and recurring pattern. Moreover, her study indicates that the "monitor," the element Flower and Hayes believe controls the various composing processes, is the focal point for those processes, an insight leading to specific pedagogical strategies for teaching writing.

Currently a part-time instructor of writing at Northeastern, Jennifer has taught freshman composition for six years and has worked as an assistant to Northeastern's coordinator of introductory writing programs, and as the writing-curriculum coordinator for a junior high school. She "enjoys watching students become excited and involved with developing their own ideas."

Recent research in the process of composing seems to indicate that Linda S. Flower and John R. Hayes's cognitive-process writing model (1981, 370) is the most accurate representation available of how people write. In an attempt to determine just how accurate it actually is, I analyzed the record of a writer as she composed orally to investigate the process involved in composing aloud. What I discovered leads me to believe that knowledge of a writing model can benefit students and teachers alike. What we must focus on, however, are the reasons behind how the process works.

The cognitive-process model of writing developed by Flower and Hayes attempts to illustrate the writing process as a set of hierarchically organized mental processes. After much study involving many writers, these researchers decided that there are three major aspects of the activity known as the writing process.

The first major aspect they call the *task environment*, which consists of everything outside the writer. The rhetorical problem, the task itself, and the text in the process of being produced are components of the task environment.

The second major aspect of the model is the *long-term memory*, which Flower and Hayes define as consisting of the author's stored knowledge, his or her awareness of writing structures, and the audience.

The third and most intricate part of the model is called the *writing processes*. These are divided into three parts. One governs the author's *planning* and includes the generating and organizing of ideas as well as the setting of goals. A second governs the *translating* process, whereby the author begins to take abstract ideas and put them into words on paper. The third, the *reviewing* stage, governs the evaluation and revision of the writing. This entire set of processes is overseen by a *monitor*, a sort of manager that determines at what points the writer progresses from one process to another.

Flower and Hayes believe that the *writing-processes* unit affects and is affected by the *task environment* and the writer's *long-term memory* (1981, 370).

## RESEARCH QUESTIONS

Three general questions focused my research:

1. How do all the stages in the cognitive model interact?
2. Is there a portion of Flower and Hayes's model that takes precedence over all others?
3. How can this model benefit the pedagogy of writing?

## STUDY SUBJECT: EILEEN

Eileen is twenty-eight years old, has a master's degree in English, and teaches writing to underprepared college freshmen. She has been teaching for nine months and entered the profession after having owned and operated her own legal title-search business for two years.

She approaches the teaching of writing very seriously and has come to believe that the backbone of good writing is the thinking that is put into it. Thus, she begins her classes by trying to teach critical thinking. She involves her students in arguments based on one-word clues. For example, on the blackboard she will write *music*. Her students then must decide what music means. Is it rock 'n' roll? Is it playing an instrument, listening to the stereo, attending a concert? The class considers all the answers they generate, and then each student must decide on a focus for a paper on music.

Her results are impressive. At the end of the course the majority of her students are able to put forth a clear and logical argument for something they believe in. So, by starting with thinking, Eileen ends up with relatively good writing from students who have not done much thinking through writing before being exposed to her class.

Consequently, Eileen's belief that thinking is of paramount importance plays a large role in her writing process, as we shall see later in the considerable amount of time she spent brainstorming on her topic.

## CASE-STUDY METHOD

### Design

My study consisted of two two-hour sessions during which I observed Eileen composing aloud. I focused on the prewriting and drafting processes during the first session; during the second I was mostly interested in revision.

Because time was a limiting factor, and because I wanted to avoid having Eileen write a piece dredged from memory, I designed an assignment. The assignment, which was typewritten, read: "You have two hours in which to plan, write, and revise a paper based on the word *Education*. Please think aloud while you do this, but do not analyze your thoughts."

Eileen met with me at a prearranged time, sat down, read the assignment, and began work. There was no preliminary interview, and at the end of the first two-hour session no mention was made of what would happen in the next session. I tape-recorded the first session and sat in the room observing her work.

I also taped the second session, but the assignment was different. Before this meeting I typed out what Eileen had written during our first meeting; this included any revisions she had made. When she came to the second meeting, I simply told her to revise her work.

## Protocol Analysis

A protocol analysis is simply the analysis of what transpired during the two sessions. The protocol itself is the transcript produced from these two sessions, including spoken and written thoughts.

Once I had transcribed the sessions and had my protocol in hand, I applied the ideas of Swarts, Flower, and Hayes for parsing (56–65), using a coding system to categorize Eileen's work into what she said, what she wrote, and what she read.

After doing this, I diverged a bit and tried to create a "map" of the actual processes I observed. To do this, I analyzed each aspect of Eileen's writing behaviors and tried to put them into Flower and Hayes's model: planning, translating, and reviewing. For example, in the early stages of the first session, Eileen said:

> The juice you get in, ah, from now at this point, I'd go out and run out and check the juice can. Or I'd call somebody up on the phone and ask what kind of juice there is. A juice, lemonade container. No. No, it's gotta be a jar with screw top. Ah, candy wrappers. No. Uh, the students here . . .

I characterized "from now at this point, I'd go out" as *planning*. Ideas that began as statements but were written down, such as the initial "the juice you get in," were considered *translating*. Finally, utterances that she read from her writing as well as statements that made a judgment on them ("No. No") were considered *reviewing*.

I then linked these pieces of the protocol in diagram form to see if any processes were dependent on others, if any had to occur before others did, and if there were indeed distinct stages in the writing process. I also looked at how frequently the various relationships between aspects of Eileen's activities occurred.

## RESULTS AND DISCUSSION

Unfortunately, the protocol revealed that the writing processes that Eileen used were probably not typical of her writing style. An early statement ("Well, let's see if what I teach my students works") indicates that the process I observed was, at best, a relatively new one for her. Most likely, conscious brainstorming was not something Eileen had tried before in her writing. Thus, Jack Selzer's idea in "Exploring Options in Composing" (276–83) is worth considering: authors do indeed have more than one style or process in their composing repertoire. This notion is important from a pedagogical viewpoint: we would be wrong to teach the writing processes as static. We must instead let students understand that the entire writing process is flexible and malleable and can be adjusted by the writer to suit different types of writing or writing situations.

As I tried to validate Flower and Hayes's cognitive-theory model of the writing process, I found that it came close to being accurate, at least for Eileen. The environment in which the writer writes and the writer's long-term memory do influence the writing processes, as Flower and Hayes suggest. In turn, as the writing process continues, the writing itself influences the long-term memory by bringing more stored information to the front of the author's mind.

Eileen's activities while writing suggest that the writing process may be characterized as a spiral. Flower and Hayes use the phrase "hierarchically organized" (1980, 396), but the term does not appear quite accurate, since it suggests a linear progression. While organizing and generating information are indeed subprocesses of planning, as Flower and Hayes suggest, their implication of a step-by-step path up the hierarchy does not explain Eileen's progression.

During the prewriting stages, Eileen used all aspects of Flower and Hayes's cognitive model, but the majority of her activities focused on two aspects of the model: the task environment and the writing processes. And, in the writing-processes unit of the model, Eileen focused her attention primarily on the generation of information. In a hierarchy Eileen would have left the stage of planning and moved to the next. Instead she kept returning to it. This indicates a spiral movement through the stages. Also, during the drafting stage, her focus lay in planning—generating and organizing, translating, and long-term memory. In her final stage of revision, she concentrated on review. What this can tell us is that the composing process does have a hierarchical order, but the order includes all aspects of the model rather than just the writing-processes part, which includes prewriting, drafting, and revising. While this has a linear order, the boundaries overlap, as the writer moves from drafting back to prewriting and then to revising. At the same time, the writer interacts in important ways with long-term memory and with the task environment. It is important to keep in mind, though, that during all this movement from one activity to another, the process is moving forward; something is always being added to the writing: thus the notion of a spiral.

## THE SIGNIFICANCE OF THE MONITOR

Flower and Hayes describe the monitor as the overseer of the writing-processes segment of the cognitive model. Eileen's composing activities, with their complex spiraling through all aspects of cognitive processes involved in writing, though, lead me to believe that the monitor is instead the place where all processes begin and end. Rather than merely controlling "the sequences of the writing processes," as Flower and Hayes suggest (1980, 392), the monitor is really the *mind* of the author, the part that creates and influences writing. It is this that we need to focus on.

The monitor does indeed let writers know how long they have to complete a task, as Flower and Hayes assert. For example, at one point Eileen said, "Okay. Enough freewriting." This illustrates a type of control the monitor exerts. More important, though, the monitor is the foundation from which all stages of the writing process emanate, not just one-third of the factors involved. Flower and Hayes are concerned solely with the monitor's effect on the author's style; is the author interested in producing a perfect first draft, or is he or she initially productive but haphazard? This limited interest in style is not enough, for the monitor also affects what the writer will make of the task environment, or how she will utilize her long-term memory. To illustrate, let us look at this excerpt from Eileen's protocol:

> [After spending several minutes talking to herself about a particular group of students she had just met with] It's really driving me crazy and they don't think and it's driving me crazy. But, I'm getting there. They're willing to try it. And I'm just trying to think how do you instill . . . how do you instill the desire to learn? Ooh! I'm on!

In this episode it is apparent that Eileen is making simultaneous use of her long-term memory, her task environment, and her writing processes. She is calling on her long-term memory by remembering the way she teaches. She is also generating ideas for an essay. In addition, by asking herself a question, she is subconsciously aware of an audience that she will later write for. Because of these simultaneous occurrences, she finds the focus for her paper. And it is the monitor—her mind—that controls all aspects of this activity.

A bit later Eileen demonstrates how the monitor and the long-term memory interact:

> [Reads] "The first week of the quarter focused on freewriting and brainstorming." Okay, I have designed my course based on the principle that writing is a means of communicating one's thoughts and ideas. . . . [Writes] "The first week of the quarter focused on freewriting and brainstorming. From there we discussed at great length focusing on a topic."

Reading back to herself the first sentence triggers Eileen's long-term memory, and the next few sentences reveal her looking back at the way she structures her classes, and why. This recollected knowledge then spurs her to continue.

Although Flower and Hayes's model allows for the occurrence of these exchanges, their model inaccurately portrays the monitor's function. Instead of being embedded within the writing-process part of the model, the monitor should emerge and become the focal point, the orchestrator of the entire cognitive process.

To better understand the role of the monitor, which can also be thought of as the author's mind, it is helpful to divide the monitor into two segments and label them according to Sondra Perl's (1980) concept of projective and retrospective structuring. In other words, reflective thought, or at least thought associated with the writing topic, is needed in order for writers to get an idea of where the words are to lead. This type of thinking is what Perl calls "retrospective" and is necessary in order for writers to call up their "felt sense." This "felt sense" can best be defined as that gut reaction or instinctive knowledge that writers experience when they *know* that something is working. The projective aspect of the monitor is the grammar teacher in all of us, the part of us that wants to create a favorable impression and so is concerned with correctness and form.

An example can best illustrate the twofold nature of the monitor. While drafting, Eileen generated an idea about evaluating students:

> A description. An evaluation a well as an assessment. An assessment of each student. An assessment as well as an evaluation. No. Evaluation of each student as well as an . . . [Pause] Oh, I had the word. As well as some recommendations which would, which may be helpful and . . .

In the pause, which lasted twenty seconds, Eileen was in the retrospective mode of her monitor. She felt the need for quiet—for time to think and reflect. This retrospective structuring enabled her to discover a word to express her meaning. Immediately after the pause she said, "I had the word." This vocalization tells us two things: one, she had been in but was now out of the retrospective mode; and two, she was now in the projective mode, aware of the need to portray her meaning accurately to her audience. Even the change from "which would" to "which may" demonstrates action on the part of the projective monitor attuned to the needs of its audience.

The retrospective aspect of the monitor can be seen especially in Eileen's statement, "No, I have to think for a minute." What follows this statement is of particular interest, because she was quiet for twelve minutes, during which time she wrote four pages of notes that later formed the foundation of her essay. A clear example of the projective aspect of her monitor can be seen immediately after this retrospective episode, when she says, "Who am I writing this for?" and then expresses her concern over the structure that her piece of writing will take.

So, that brings us to dissonance: the author's inner self quests for meaning (Berthoff), while the author's other self searches as a reader might for correctness, readability, and economy (Hirsch 1977, 74–89). Thus each segment of the author's monitor interacts with and influences not only the written words but also the thoughts that create and revise the words. For this reason, the monitor is of utmost importance in any cognitively based writing-process model. It considers the task environment; it dredges up long-stored knowledge; it determines the time allowed for each writing stage; it thinks, creates, and finds the meaning for which it searches. It is the key to the process of composing.

## CONCLUSION

Flower and Hayes's cognitive model, with the expansion of the monitor's role to that of the focal point of all writing activities, can help steer the pedagogy of writing. It can give teachers insight into the composing process, and it can indicate to them at which stage or segment of the process an author is having difficulty. Realizing the divided concerns of the monitor, teachers can encourage students to better utilize their retrospective structuring abilities to produce "real" writing, the kind that shows thought and insight. Teachers can also help students learn to take advantage of their own creativity in writing and initially ignore concerns for correctness, which tend to impede the creative processes. Then, consciously separating the two aspects of the monitor, teachers can develop students' abilities to use projective structuring to shape their writing with a clearer eye toward the needs of their audience.

## REFERENCES

Berthoff, Ann. "Learning the Uses of Chaos." In *The Making of Meaning*. Montclair, N.J.: Boynton/Cook, 1981.

Calkins, Lucy. *Lessons from a Child: On the Teaching and Learning of Writing*. Portsmouth, N.H.: Heinemann Educational Books, 1983.

Flower, Linda S., and John R. Hayes. "A Cognitive Process Theory of Writing." *College Composition and Communication* 32 (1981): 365–87.

Hayes, John R., and Linda S. Flower. "Writing as Problem Solving." *Visible Language* 14 (1980): 288–99.

Hirsch, E. D., Jr. *The Philosophy of Composition*. Chicago: University of Chicago Press, 1977.

Perl, Sondra. "Understanding Composing." *College English* 31 (1980): 363–69.

Selzer, Jack. "Exploring Options in Composing." *College Composition and Communication* 35 (1984): 276–84.

Swarts, Heidi; Linda S. Flower; and John R. Hayes. "Designing Protocol Studies of the Writing Process: An Introduction." In *New Directions in Composition Research*, edited by Richard Beach and Lillian Bridwell, 53–71. New York: Guilford, 1984:

# PART V

# Afterword: Beyond the Writing Class

# AFTERWORD

This book is a demonstration of the inseparability of teaching and learning. It is also a demonstration of courage: the courage to scrutinize what we do as teachers, as Ferguson McKay has done; the courage to look at ourselves as learners and consider what that might imply for our classrooms, whatever the challenges to implementing it, as Susan Kaplan has done; the courage to look both critically and sympathetically at the learning process of someone close to us, as Kathy Calkins has done; the courage to respect ways of learning that are different from our own and from what we have planned for in our curriculum, as Carol Avery has done; the courage to hear how we are perceived by our students, as Judith Boyce has done; and the courage all these researchers have shown to look at what might have gone unexamined and to speak in their own voices about what they have seen with their own eyes.

Because this book celebrates the opening up of a search rather than an arrival, it has no conclusion. The teachers who have finished their case-study reports find that they are just beginning their researching. As other teachers join them, teacher research will surely move in new directions and spread across the curriculum. In lieu of a conclusion, then, we offer a case study, completed in the second year of the case-study course, by a teacher who, in both her teaching and researching, struck out in a new direction.

# CHAPTER 15

## Circles within Circles: A New Perspective on Writing about Art

*Alice DeLana*

Alice DeLana had taught high school English at Miss Porter's School in Farmington, Connecticut, for twenty-six years when she took on a very different teaching assignment—art history—which also became the focus of her research. In one sense it wasn't so different, because of the way she decided to teach the course. Her study asks the question, what is the effect of employing writing-process techniques (prewriting in class; peer conferences; repeated sharing and publication of ideas generated by reading, observation of slides, and class discussion) in an art history class? In this elegantly designed study DeLana observes the development of three students from three perspectives: her analysis of their writings in relation to the goals of her course, the students' ability to comment on the writings of their peers, and the comments of other students on the writings of these three. DeLana's study is further distinguished by a creative use of language and image that while truly appropriate to her subject is unusual in a research report, as is the joyful spirit of her discoveries.

Alice was coeditor of *On Common Ground: An Anthology of Hartford Authors* and has published numerous articles, including a monograph on Lydia Huntley Sigourney, published in conjunction with the 350th anniversary of the founding of Hartford, Connecticut. She is a graduate of the University of Michigan and holds the Pauline Foster Reed Teaching Chair at Miss Porter's School. She and her husband are the parents of two children.

Because readers may be less familiar with the literature of art than with the works referred to in the other case studies, we have included Alice's splendid annotated bibliography.

This case study documents my attempts during the academic year 1985–86 to actively engage in writing across the curriculum—that is, to apply the techniques and procedures of writing process to a discipline other than English. In my case the discipline was art history, a subject that requires students to commit to memory great quantities of immutable fact, to look with open eyes, to see not only what instinct leads them to but also what instruction shows them, and to write about what they see. In the writing exercises, a certain amount of technical jargon is necessary, and so a significant percentage of class time and reading time must be spent in defining terms and looking at examples. Also, in the writing exercises a certain amount of personal interpretation is permissible, so guidelines for acceptable modes of expression have to be established.

In the course of the year, the students and I established a set of five goals and then worked towards making them less goals than givens. By the end of the year, the five points were simply taken for granted by most of the students, virtually all of whom experienced a sense of having developed a true voice for their personal observations and convictions.

This paper attempts to provide a framework for the conscious application of writing-process techniques to art history; to report upon the specific transformations observed in the writing methods and skills of three students; and to assess the effectiveness of incorporating writing-process language, techniques, and expectations into a discipline other than English. This is a paper about writing across the curriculum. It is entitled "Circles within Circles" because the root of the word *curriculum* is "to run a course," to trace in circles, to move around rather than across.

## INTRODUCTION

Like a snake eating its own tail in the margin of a medieval illuminated manuscript, the language of the writing classroom circles through the studios, laboratories, audiovisual rooms, and classrooms of other disciplines before it finds itself and closes the circle of its journey. As it moves, it sloughs off and leaves behind for future reference a number of words that work equally well in various and differing contexts. Words like *sketch*, *depict*, *portray*, *delineate*, and *construct*, not to mention *balance*, *outline*, and *perspective*, serve similar functions in different settings, some of which focus on the theoretical and philosophical, while others center on the physical and practical. Slipping through the cracks in the jargon of each course, the vocabulary of the writing classroom defines the boundaries of a schoolful of subjects.

Looked at out of context, the words seem to spring from a common source: the artist's studio, where it is assumed that the terms will call forth visual images. It is hardly surprising, then, given that source, that the terms apply so well to the activities of an art history class, where works of art are looked at, analyzed, and written and talked about. In the third part of that three-step sequence, the language of the studio can help to provoke and evoke observations that might otherwise have remained hidden from view, even from the inner eye of the viewer. If speaking is "oral writing," and writing is a "way of making meaning," as Ann Berthoff has observed (41), then the language borrowed from the studio and embedded in the writing of thousands of students, like a quiet snake threading its way through a field of wildflowers, is central to both the process and the products of the act of writing.

If language is central to the effort to discover, uncover, reveal, and share observations and interpretations, then the circle around that center is formed by the recursive quality of thoughtful writing. As Sondra Perl has argued in "Understanding Composing," (Newkirk 29):

> Many researchers including myself have questioned the traditional notion that writing is a linear process with a strict plan-to-revise sequence. In its stead, we have advocated the idea that writing is a recursive process, that throughout the process of writing, writers return to substrands of the overall process, or subroutines . . . writers use these to keep the process moving forward.

In that search for forward motion, the student of art history must continually look at the image. In order to derive meaning from a visual image, the writer must apply language (most likely the language of the studio) to both what the eye sees and the mind observes (most likely the images projected on a screen). The act of making meaning sends the viewer/writer into a series of circular motions designed to circumscribe the subject; most of these motions are ocular as the eye moves from image to page, from upper-right corner to lower left, from most recent sentence to the one first written. Whether moving recursively from edge to edge of an image or from sentence to sentence of a page of writing, the eye of the viewer/writer moves back and forth, round and round.

The difference between this circular mode of behavior in an art history class and the roughly comparable circle in an English class is in the nature of the object being observed and responded to. In English, images are self-generated by the reader/writer. Each reader/writer reads the text, carries on an internal dialogue with the author, and constructs a mental image from the ideas suggested by the words on the page. Then the reader/writer writes. In art history, images only infrequently contain or make reference to visible language. (Certain works of Picasso and Braque and a number of other mostly twentieth-century artists are, of course, exceptions.) Instead, they combine shape, color, texture, and line into visible manifestations of the invisible workings of an artist's mind. Each viewer/writer looks at the image, sees what her eyes and her experiences equip her to see, and derives a mental image from the shapes, colors, textures, and lines on the canvas or the pedestal or the screen. Then the viewer/writer writes.

When the techniques of the writing process as set forth and utilized in the English classroom are applied to the preparation of art criticism, then the language of the studio, in its general and widespread applicability, serves as an important link between the two. Equally important although much less generally used is the language of writing process, filled as it is with words like *prewriting, conferencing, revision,* and *publication* that are employed in specific and limited meanings. When the focus is on writing, *prewriting*—which might mean cave drawings to an archaeologist—means setting down the quick and unformed ideas that first come to mind. *Conferencing*—which might mean discussing a painting's provenance to a team of curators—means bringing together groups of students to read and discuss each other's writings. *Revision*—which might mean giving Michelangelo his due as a colorist to a team of restorers working on the Sistine Chapel—means reworking the early versions of a paper. And *publication*—which might mean printing and disseminating the posters of Toulouse-Lautrec to a huckster who knows when the copyright expires—means sharing the finished piece of writing with a public that may be as small as one teacher or as large as a whole school.

The point is that unlike the language of the studio, which means virtually the same thing from subject to subject and from context to context, the language of writing process contains words that have other meanings within the culture at large. Within the school setting, however, the words of writing process move easily from the writing classroom into the studios and laboratories of other disciplines, maintaining their meanings as they go, silently slipping through the halls.

The circular interplay of words sometimes shedding, sometimes retaining their original meanings as they move from subject to subject repeats in its configuration not only the closed circle of the snake in the margin of the manuscript, but also the link to be discovered between the writing class and any other. The techniques and procedures and language of writing process empower students of any subject by freeing them from the rigidities of past assumptions and allowing them to progress at their own speed from idea to idea, image to image. In the process, writing moves around the curriculum rather than across it.

## THE CROSSING SPACE

It was at the intersection of the idea of "multiple intelligences," as articulated by Howard Gardner in the Science section of the *New York Times* (May 13, 1984), and the concept of writing across the curriculum that I began my consideration of the effect of using writing-process techniques in art history classes. In his article, "Science Grapples with the Creative Puzzle," Gardner makes a number of assertions that shaped my thinking about teaching art history, a subject I had not formally studied since 1958. Gardner maintains, for example, that "the most proficient artists work at their craft with a speed and facility which can astonish naive observers, but we all achieve analogous kinds of facility after sufficient practice in driving a car, planning dinner parties, or writing letters of recommendation." (28). I wondered what would happen if the words *writers about art* were substituted for Gardner's word *artists*. Narrowing the range, I wondered what would happen if *my students* were the substituted words.

Could students who had (1) never studied art history, (2) never consciously thought about how they looked at or saw what their eyes perceived, and (3) never written papers that mixed analysis of an artist's work with their own perceptions of it become so "proficient" that they could compose their thoughts and papers with "speed and facility," not to mention wit and accuracy and honesty? Could students be helped to develop those skills by being asked to prepare rough drafts, to share them with others, to revise, to rewrite, and then to publish in some form? In short, could art history students benefit from the lessons of writing process?

The juncture of Gardner's ideas about the many and various activities of the mind with the many and various aspects of writing across the curriculum provided a metaphor for my thinking about what I hoped to do with and in and for my classes. The juncture became for me a "crossing space" (to use a term straight out of Gothic architecture), a nexus of limitless possibilities and accepted procedures, of language and sensory impressions, of form and idea. Connections and crossings became the focus of my thinking about teaching art history, for in such a course the emphasis is on both looking and seeing, two very different concepts that require different skills, especially when what is being looked at and seen is a visual form that will be described and analyzed in words. Looking depends upon an open mind; seeing depends upon training. One does not necessarily lead into or out of the other. But both, at least in the course that I taught during 1985–86, ultimately led to writing.

## INTO THE FRAY

### September 12, 1985

During the opening days of school in September 1985, the twenty-nine students in the course called Survey of Art History: From Caves to the Present Day circled warily around what they perceived to be the central issues of the course: How much factual material would they have to learn? How many papers would they have to write? Would they have to use big, unfamiliar words? What if they had never really enjoyed going to a museum?

As a group, the thirty of us were gathered together to study the development and evolution of various art forms across a stretch of time from the caves of Lascaux and Altamira to the soup cans of Andy Warhol and the ubiquitous stylized arches of McDonald's. We were all new at the game. Not only that, but of the twenty-nine students, six were underclassmen. I had never taught art history, but in my twenty-six years of teaching English at Miss Porter's School, I had taught at every level from ninth to twelfth grade, and had conducted classes in everything from "Women in Literature" to "The Literary Form" to "Chaucer to Stoppard: A Survey of British Literature." I had also, from 1981 to 1984, taught computer programming in BASIC, a highlight of which—at least for me—was working with students to produce programs that generated haiku, sonnets, and villanelles.

As I planned the art history course, a syllabus gradually emerged that called for some sort of formal written work every six to seven class days, sometimes in class, sometimes out. Daily logs were to be kept, sometimes in class, sometimes out. Writing done in class would usually compare or contrast slides projected during class time; writing done out of class would require descriptions of images so clearly delineated that readers could envision them even though they could not literally "see" them while reading the paper. Different skills would be tapped for different writing assignments, just as new skills for looking and seeing would have to be found, developed, and exercised for the sake of enabling students to use their eyes to discriminate as well as to absorb. The process of developing these skills looked rather like waving a divining rod in the air until some inexplicable force drew it irresistibly toward the goal.

The first papers produced for the course suggested that the divining rod was wide of the mark. Writing about the images of the earliest known works considered art—the cave paintings in France and Spain—the students struggled to find their footing on the slippery ground between reporting facts and articulating opinion. We had decided as a group that the casual phrase "thus we see . . ." would be forever off bounds in the course; we had also said that "I" could be used, but only if it were used authoritatively. Hiding behind "I think" and "I assume" and "I" as subject of a sentence was to be avoided in favor of keeping the focus on the writer's opinions rather than on the writer per se.

After all our class discussions about ways of presenting opinion without spotlighting the opinion maker, it was disconcerting to read the paper Susan submitted. Susan, a senior who had no particular interest in art history, wrote this opening paragraph to a three-page paper:

> While glancing through the pages in this book, I caught my eye on one particular image, this image being that of a bison, and it appealed to me for several reasons. First of all, the image is quite distinct, whereas in some prehistoric works of art, it is hard to distinguish one object from another. Second of all, I find it interesting to see two arrows protruding inward into the bison's belly. It apparently was showing these primitive people's hunting tactics. Lastly, I found this image amazing, because it was

created between 15,000–13,000 B.C. and it's incredible to think how long back art was being developed. All together, this image intrigued me and that is why I chose to examine it more closely.

As her classmates pointed out, the real subject of this paper is "I," not the cave paintings. Susan's reliance on "I" converts even her most factual statements into seemingly unfounded observations. When she says, "I find it interesting to see two arrows...," the emphasis shifts from the fact of the arrows being in the bison's belly to Susan's finding the sight interesting; by constructing this shift, she then requires another sentence to explain her interest.

Despite her excessive reliance on the first-person singular, Susan does show in this paper that she knows well the "proper" way to begin a paper. Somewhere she had learned to introduce her topic, name names, establish a series of points to be developed later in the body of the paper, and conclude the introduction with a summary that leads into the examination of individual points. Susan knew how to construct an adequate paper; she simply didn't know how to express her ideas in vocabulary that did justice to her thinking.

For that same assignment Madeleine, a senior with a long history of museum-going and a genuine interest in art history, wrote this opening paragraph:

> I was struck most of all by the "Hall of Bulls" left wall from the Lascaux Caves in France. Most certainly, it can be discerned that the purpose of this art is to instruct and inform, especially since man who lived in caves in 15,000–13,000 B.C. probably had little or no contact or communication with other humans not in his cave group other than through visual aids. These visual aids consisted of scratches in the earth and paintings left behind on cave walls. The only other communication would be grunts and primitive sounds and hand motions (to point at an oncoming beast, to show the size of the fish that got away) when directly in visual contact with another person. Therefore, to have the intelligence to communicate in the form of artwork is one of the most startling facets of the figures.

How very different this is from Susan's! It is clear that Madeleine—despite the pretentiousness of some of her language and the wide scope of her mind's wanderings—is thinking about both the assignment and the images themselves from a very philosophical angle, rather than the close-to-home approach taken by Susan. Since both were in the same class, that class needed to find common ground on which to stand when committing ideas to paper. As a group, the class came up with the following list of goals to keep in mind when writing papers that combine facts with personal response:

## Goals for Writing in Art History

1. To be personal—even intimate—without ever saying, "Thus we see..." and without using "I" in such a way that it obscures the view.

2. To be honest and direct and forthright with the reader, avoiding the "bogus religiosity" (Berger 1983, 21) that puffs and swells the language of criticism.
3. To be so clear and exact and precise in the passages of description that someone who had never seen the image could accurately imagine it.
4. To keep the dimensions of the commentary within a reasonable scale, avoiding grandiose statements that undercut and diminish the value of honest opinion.
5. To be receptive to and tolerant of not only the novel and unexpected but also the all-too-familiar.

Class discussion produced the list in response to the students' having read not only Susan's and Madeleine's paper but also Marie's. Marie was a senior with a particular interest in writing. Her paper began like this:

> In the primitive painting, "Marching Warriors," dated 8000–3000 B.C. and found in the Gasulla Gorge, there is humor (which I'm not sure is an aspect the artist wanted to convey but which, nevertheless, is seen), and there is also evidence of personality, energy, leadership, response to authority, and unity of men—all qualities of human beings, even prehistoric ones. The picture's inherent message rather than its appearance appeals to me, as it proves that although cavemen probably could not solve quadratic equations, they were just as human as anyone (including mathematicians) we would come across today.

The tone of Marie's opening is entirely different from either Susan's or Madeleine's, and Marie's classmates sensed that difference immediately. In her first lines Marie may not have satisfied point 3 in the list, but she more than satisfied the other four, creating in the process a paper that promised much in its opening paragraph and then went on to make good on that promise in the subsequent pages. Fifteen lines into the paper, Marie described the marching warriors this way:

> The men, led by someone with apparent authority, are moving in perfect union and with exaggerated motivation, their popsicle-stick legs taking giant strides. They seem to radiate animation. Their mood, despite the weapons they brandish above their heads, is quite civilized; they would fit in quite nicely on Wall Street, for all their drive and concentration.

In those three sentences, Marie satisfies point 3.

The students' responses to that first assignment and the papers it produced were predictable. In groups of three students, in which each writer read her paper aloud, asked for responses, and then adjusted her paper (or ignored the suggestions), many students voiced their uncertainty about themselves as writers and as art critics. It is bad enough, one girl said, to have to write about a poem or novel in English, but at least that is a familiar assignment and you can always say, "I don't see it that way." In art history, everyone is shown the same image, so no one can say "Browning's 'Last Duchess' was a redhead" while someone else says, "No, she's a blonde." The work of art is what it is, and every viewer has to accept certain givens of shape, color, texture, and line. The problem is that the language in which those givens are described is fairly specialized and has to be learned with as much care as the vocabulary for the parts of a bean sprout or the characteristics of a sonnet.

As a class we set about learning the vocabulary, seeking ways to compress and intensify the language used to describe and interpret the details and meaning of the observed object. And we observed objects galore, looking at an average of eight to ten slides per day, five days a week. Accumulating information, we also developed a healthy respect for writing as a means of learning what we know. Writing, both in class and out, became the mechanism of testing hypotheses, describing initial responses, modifying those responses in light of subsequent information, and making connections between art and the world around us. The act of writing became an integral part of the process of learning to see what we were looking at.

## IN THE THICK

### February 25, 1986

Even though in September the students in art history agreed with Hermann Hesse that "language is a detriment, an earthbound limitation. . . . [A writer] thinks with envy of the painter whose language—color—is instantly comprehensible to everyone from the North Pole to Africa" (Hjerter, 135), by February they had begun to feel more at home with the language of art criticism. They had also established for themselves as individuals and as a group a far-reaching scheme of things in which the primitive cave art they had studied in September had gradually evolved into Byzantine icons, Gothic spires, and proto-Renaissance madonnas. Along the way, the students had experienced and talked about what Rudolf Arnheim calls the "fascinating interplay in the human mind between the desire, and indeed the need, to comprehend the total range of a phenomenon and the attractive simplicity of static concepts, which pick out some one characteristic of an object of movement and let it stand for the whole" (Arnheim 1969, 178–79).

This tug of war between the vast and the specific, the all-encompassing and the small, was of particular interest midway through the school year. By February the students and I had become accustomed to the specialized vocabulary of art history; we had had a great deal of practice in quick identification of slides (every other week we had a slide quiz of either eighteen slides in forty minutes or nine slides plus a comparison of two other slides in forty minutes); and we had come to take for granted that prewriting, conferencing, revision, and some form of idea exchange would take place whenever a paper was in the works. That assumption was fostered at least in part by the fact that my school is a boarding school, which means that day and night, weekdays and weekends, the students wander in and out of each other's rooms saying, "How're you doing on your paper? Want to hear mine?" Also, the computer room is open twenty-four hours a day, seven days a week, so if a student isn't in her own room working on a paper, she is likely to be typing away on an Apple, seated next to a classmate working on the same topic, both of them composing at the keyboard and then reading sections aloud to whoever will listen.

On February 25, 1986, everyone wrote in class for twenty minutes on her favorite illustration of fifteenth-century Italian art. It was an open-book writing exercise, followed by twenty minutes of swapping papers, assessment by groups of peers, and writing evaluations. Each evaluation was to consider (1) clarity of topic, (2) clarity of detail, (3) coherence of argument, and (4) consistency of focus. In addition, each evaluator was to assess the appropriateness of diction. Susan wrote this in her first paragraph:

In Andrea Mantegna's "Camera degli sposi" ceiling fresco, characteristics of both the artist's individual style and the concerns of the time period are visible. Known as one of the "most brilliant talents of the entire Renaissance" (519) Mantegna creates this ceiling fresco with much joy and emotion. He painted this in 1474 when he was working mainly for the Gonzaga family at their palace in Mantua. His paintings primarily expressed the wonders of court life there, and he often depicted members of the Gonzaga family in them. This ceiling from the "Camera degli sposi" is the beginning of his experimenting with ceiling works that add a new perspective and dimension to these highly decorated rooms.

Responding to Susan's essay, Cecily wrote:

This is a very good description of Mantegna's motives in painting the Newlywed's Room the way he did. She begins with a brief summary of the artist's relationship with his patron and foreshadows the style and subject matter which single him out as a master artist. When she gets to it, she does a good job of describing the scenes he painted. The only thing I could say which might improve the whole paper is to compare the ceiling fresco with another painting or Mantegna's style with someone else's.

The peer response to Susan's paper indicates that both students have come to a point in the course and in their thinking where they are aware of the several levels on which art criticism can be constructed and appreciated. Both Susan and Cecily speak not only of the subject matter of the work under consideration, but also of the reasons behind the work's form and character. Both students keep the focus on the work rather than on the competence of the viewer—which is where Susan's greatest emphasis was at the beginning of the year. Over and over again in September Susan had said "I think' or "I guess"; by February she was writing with much more confidence, and Cecily's comments respond to that increased sense of security and certainty.

In her comments about a classmate's paper, Susan showed less confidence than in constructing her own argument. Where Jenny wrote:

> Verrocchio's "David" is seen in the typical pose of the victor who has successfully beaten his enemy. His weight shifts, and while he places one hand on his hip in a gesture of self-satisfaction and pride, he seems to ignore the head of Goliath which lies, dripping blood, at his feet,

Susan commented, "I would maybe say more specific details would be good here rather than always referring to what he represents." Susan evidently was more struck by the vision of David as "victor" than by the image of the young boy standing above the severed head of the giant; in her concern with interpretation, and because of her own self-doubt, she seems worried about the correctness of interpretation and representation to the exclusion of all other concerns. Nevertheless, she is looking more carefully at both the work of art and the language used to describe it than would have been possible in September.

Madeleine, too, had shifted her focus by February. Her essay began:

> Andrea Mantegna of Padua, painting during the second half of the fifteenth century, is an example of the pragmatic Renaissance artist, using not only geometry and learned skills, but also what the human eye sees. Mantegna especially worked with pictorial illusion and perspective. On the ceiling of the "Camera degli sposi" ("Room of the Newlyweds"), a fresco by Mantegna becomes an architectural illusion, the first *di sotto in su* perspective of a ceiling. Mantegna achieves the illusion of a domed oculus on a flat surface through foreshortening and manipulation of perspective. Through foreshortening, for example, he gives the viewer the impression that the little cupids who seem to lean on the inside wall of the oculus are being looked *up* to. The carefully painted baby feet add to the illusion.

Laura commented:

> I learned a lot about the times and the painter in the first paragraph, but I particularly liked the part where Madeleine shifted from talking about Mantegna to talking about his painting. She made the painting come alive by giving a lot of details. She started with a big overall view and then got specific. If she had had more time, this would have been a very good paper, I know.

That particular peer response might not have done justice to what Madeleine achieved in twenty minutes of in-class writing time, but it does show that members of the class were becoming accustomed to looking for specific aspects and configurations of language within each other's papers. When they read each other's papers, they read for accuracy and honesty and skillful use of terminology, as well as for a feeling that the work of art was given value by the writing.

When Madeleine commented on a classmate's paper, she revealed the same sense of purpose that characterized her own essay. Madeleine wrote this comment about Kathy's paper:

The painting itself is precisely and vividly described, and can be seen in the mind's eye just by reading Kathy's words. No facts of history or biography of Mantegna, though. Good comparison with how Christ is usually depicted—far off, serene—but which depiction exactly is she speaking of?

The specific criticisms and queries were prompted by Kathy's having written the following passage. (Kathy, by the way, was one of the more taciturn members of the class, so what follows is the entirety of what she wrote in twenty minutes.)

> Andrea Mantegna's *The Dead Christ* is an abrasively realistic portrait of the Christ figure laid in the tomb. The perspective in this painting is such that the viewer seems to be standing at the foot of the hard bed which the figure is laid on and looking down on the massive figure and the tormented face. In contrast to other depictions of the dead Christ, the view gives the illusion that the viewer is almost in the tomb itself instead of observing from far off. The way in which the Christ figure is viewed is also revolutionary, for instead of looking from the side at a regal and calm human form, the viewer looms above a massive form whose face is still contorted from the agony of the last throes of death. The drapery across the figure is highly realistic and sharp lines of the fold echo the sharp lines of the muscles in Christ's chest. The figure hardly evokes images of the meek and mild shepherd.

Madeleine's assessment of this one-paragraph essay is, according to the standards set by the class, right on target. In her evaluation, she was to look for clarity, coherence, and focus; she also checked to see whether Kathy's language enabled her to see what Kathy had seen when she looked at the Mantegna painting. Madeleine praises Kathy's descriptions but takes her to task for not setting the artist in his time or the painting in the context of other depictions of the same scene. Madeleine reveals here a heightened sensitivity to the dual nature of art criticism; she is clearly aware that it is not enough simply to describe a work of art without adding a layer of information about the artist and his or her intentions. Without that layer, an essay is less an analysis than a mirror.

Marie chose to write on a work of sculpture; she produced the following passage in twenty minutes:

> *Bartolomeo Colleoni*, a massive equestrian statue by Andrea Verrocchio, shows the lion-hearted, bulldog-faced character of the Renaissance; it reflects the popular idea that through his tenacity, enthusiasm, and spirit, man is the measure of all things.
> Bartolomeo, the man depicted, appears as if he were the man the philosophy was thought up for. Framed with a functional helmet, his fleshy face looms with an intense grimace, his wide-open eyes condemning anyone foolhardy enough to challenge him. His body, likewise encased in armor, conveys the same message; standing tensely in his stirrups, the burly Bartolomeo seems an impregnable fortress. The picture of energetic, tense, no-nonsense authority is made complete in the statue by Bartolomeo's horse, a massive yet graceful creature who seems ready, like his rider, to take on the world. Tough and brave, alert and confident, the combination of the man and his mount, appropriately seem to fit the mold of Machiavelli's Renaissance prince.

> The bulldog strength of *Bartolomeo Colleoni* seems even more apparent when this equestrian statue is compared to others we have studied, *Marcus Aurelius* and *Gattamelata*. While massive and authoritative, the Roman Marcus Aurelius astride his horse is peaceful. He wears no armor or helmet, he sits quietly on his mount's back, he raises a gentle hand in seeming forgiveness of all who see him.

Nipped in the bud by the passage of time, Marie did not round off her essay, a fact reflected in the comment of her classmate, who wrote, "Too bad she didn't have enough time! I would like to have read what she had to say about *Gattamelata*. Even unfinished, though, this is an excellent essay."

The brevity of the comment she received is echoed in the succinctness of the comment Marie wrote on Leslie's paper. Leslie began with an extended discussion of the Renaissance as a "period of time in which man re-found himself and glorified his achievements and his being in art," then progressed to a detailed description of Mantegna's *St. James Led to Martyrdom*.

> The overriding focus of the fresco most obviously is the triumphal arch, whose barrel vault is reminiscent of the Arch of Constantine or the Arch of Titus. Mantegna has placed this arch on purpose, for with the Renaissance's love for the classical times it seems only appropriate that an artist should include something of the past.

Marie seems to focus on this section of Leslie's paper in her comment, which she divided into three sections: background, image, and comparison.

> Background: the Renaissance was a time when (1) man glorified himself and his achievements and (2) ancient arts and sciences became topics of interest.
> Image: good perspective, central figure = classic arch, humans are anatomically correct as well as strong in physique and character.
> Comparison: talks about the use of classic images (i.e., Arch of Constantine look-alike in the painting.)
> This is a good paper!

In this comment Marie makes no specific suggestions about ways in which she thinks Leslie might improve either this paper or her writing in general. Instead, she gives evidence of having been a careful and interested reader, and in her thoughtful, logical consideration of Leslie's ideas, she offers tacit approval and encouragement. It is a response that neatly fits the notion of positive reinforcement that is at the heart of process writing.

In these selections from a set of midwinter papers and the student comments upon them, a marked shift from the uncertainties and self-doubts of September can be seen. The visible, up-front "I" of the earliest papers of the course has taken a back seat to a more confident, more sophisticated third-person point of view. The self-conscious retracings of the same images and ideas have given way to more expansive statements restrained only by the configurations of the works of art themselves. And the extravagant but unfounded "amazing" and "incredible" of the neophyte art critics have been subsumed into equally strong but less inflated wordings. In short, in the February papers the students seemed to feel at home with both the subject matter and the format of art history papers. They took it for granted that their own opinions were valuable, that what their own eyes saw was the true subject matter of their writing, and that responding to art was both a private and a public act.

## AND IT COMES OUT HERE

### May 5, 1986

On the first Monday in May, the class finally reached the twentieth century. From the cave art of 20,000 B.C. through the art of Egypt, Greece, Rome, the Byzantine and Early Christian eras, the Middle Ages, the Italian Renaissance, the Baroque and Rococo, Romanticism, Impressionism, and Symbolism, we had made our way to May and our own century. In anticipation of studying the various forms of modern and contemporary art—and after a number of discussions about the fact that the terms *modern* and *contemporary* are relative, not absolute—the students participated in a long-term project that required them to focus at least minimally (subliminally?) on the twentieth century even as they were spending class time studying the eras preceding it.

In February, at the beginning of the second semester, each student found in her syllabus the fatal words, "Short research paper on one twentieth-century work due in May." By March each student had to have chosen the work of art she wished to write about and to have submitted to me a paragraph or two about what she expected to find out about her work. Each student and I then had a twenty-minute conference in the library about (1) her expectations, (2) my expectations, and (3) the available material. In April each student submitted to a classmate a statement of her own personal response to having thought about a specific work at various times over a six-week stretch, as well as a paragraph about her attitude toward the work itself. Had it changed? Did she see anything in the work that she hadn't seen when she first looked at it? Did the same features leap out at her in April that had leaped out in March? In May each student submitted a three-to-five page paper on "her" work; in no case was the work chosen one that we had discussed in class.

Susan's paper began with a series of quotations. In her continuing effort to use "I" less conspicuously in her writing, she sometimes took refuge in the opinions of others, letting them say first what she would later corroborate by her choice of example. In the course of the year, Susan had practiced constructing sentences that had nouns rather than pronouns as subjects (that was a suggestion from one of her classmates) and had worked to maintain her easy, breezy, colloquial style while making it somewhat less windy. The class felt that she had achieved a style that seemed more mature and less giddy, but she herself felt that she had not yet achieved a balance between personal opinion and an appropriately distanced level of diction.

This is the beginning of Susan's last, formal, out-of-class piece of writing in the course:

> The twentieth century is an era of turbulence and uncertainty for the world is obsessed with the question "What is 'real'?" (de la Croix and Tansey, 806). The question of existence is central to man's confusion as he can find no pivotal philosophy which sets the individual above the mass. He see himself pitted against the world around him, much as Edward Hopper sees modern man's isolation in his painting entitled *Room in Brooklyn* (1932). In it, Hopper vividly captures this sense of being alone in a crowd by depicting a woman facing the world through her apartment window. She looks out on an endless row of windows which stare back at her.

Gone is Susan's reliance on phrases like, "I am amazed to see that . . ." and "I can hardly believe how often . . ." Instead, in this last paper she widens her point of view to include the opinions of others, seeking to become an invisible and articulate observer rather than a very visible and very chatty one.

Madeleine's final paper was entitled "Who and Where the Wild Things Were." It treated the Fauves, a group that—to quote the last line of her paper—"achieved the conjunction of the primitive and the sophisticated, producing works that were startling to the eye, stimulating to the mind, and uplifting to the emotions." Madeleine's paper began:

> The group of painters exhibiting in the Salon d'Automne in Paris in 1905 was dubbed "Fauves" or "wild beasts" by the critic Louis Vauxcelles. A new movement was thus ushered in, a movement unplanned by its participants, and utterly devoid of rules, stipulations, or requirements. The movement, though, was a response to social influences, the influence of the Impressionists, and the instincts and impulses of the beasts themselves. The Fauves were led by Henri Matisse and were held together by common bonds of painting style, political influence, and friendship. They themselves did not name their movement, for they did not consider themselves a formal group.

In the course of the year, Madeleine had concentrated on eliminating the passive voice from her writing, removing easy words like *thus*, *accordingly*, and *therefore*, and on emphasizing facts while maintaining her own highly individual point of view. In her conferences with her classmates, she had been encouraged to use the most vigorous language possible (everyone knew she had strong opinions) and to let her innate sense of humor shine through. When she doctored Maurice Sendak's title "Where the Wild Things Are" to make it fit her paper, she gave evidence that she had taken their advice.

Marie began the year writing well, and she was still doing so at the end. She had been encouraged by the response of her fellow students to view herself as a better writer than she had thought she was, for throughout the year she received applause from everyone in the class. By May, everyone in the class had read everyone else's work, and so Marie had heard praise from all quarters. This is the beginning of her last paper:

> If modern art is the product of modern artists trying to be original, putting all of their time and energy into creating something that has not yet been created in the 22,000 year history of art, then *The Twittering Machine* (1922) is a true piece of modern art, and its creator, Paul Klee (1874–1940), is a true modern artist. As Rosamund Frost states, "A faked Klee is unthinkable." This is so for two reasons that I can see: first, while Klee did belong to the Blue Rider Club (an exhibition group started in 1911), he stayed aloof from any of the other specific movements that were so predominant at the time, and second, Klee's work is a product of his own very personal feelings and private dream-world. Thus, *The Twittering Machine* is not in any way like anything ever done before Klee or most like anything that will come after Klee, because it has all the understatement, primitive childishness, wry humor, and disguised cynicism that are his and his alone, rather than being characteristic of any movement and stereotype.

True, Marie makes a sweeping statement in her last line that cannot be supported by the evidence she has provided in her paragraph, but in every other particular the paragraph is a strong, vigorous, informative, and compelling introduction to a paper. It even makes good use of "I," tucking it in where it will do most good but not advertise itself.

In the final papers of the year, Susan, Madeleine, and Marie showed that they had paid attention to and absorbed the goals the class had set for itself at the beginning of the year. They had sought to be personal in their communication with their readers, but knew that repetition of the first-person singular tends to shift the focus of a piece of writing from the argument to the speaker. As a result, they relied on simple wordings and let facts speak for themselves, avoiding cliches and terminology designed to impress rather than inform. They had sought to be so precise in their descriptions of works of art that their readers could imagine the essential elements of those works without having seen them. As a result, they looked long and hard at those works of art about which they were writing, studying paintings from top to bottom and side to side and considering sculpture from every angle. They had sought to maintain an appropriate scale, so that they avoided pomposity and melodrama. As a result, they found that their most effective arguments were constructed on the smallest points, that they did not need to flaunt their learning, that, as Mies van der Rohe observed, "less is more." And they sought to treat with respect even those works that at first glance looked like something the cat dragged in. A a result, they empowered themselves to laugh at and revalue those works that amused or repelled them, for they had honored those same works with serious consideration based upon research, discussion, intellect, and instinct. If, given a fair chance, a work of art failed to record itself favorably in the viewer's eye, the students spoke of beauty's being in the eye of the beholder and then passed judgment.

Working all year with the five agreed-upon goals in mind, the class reached the end of the school year satisfied that attention had been paid to matters that gave focus to the writing done over the course of the nine months from September to June. Paying attention to those matters had enabled a number of students to clarify and enliven their writing, not only in art history but in other disciplines as well. It can be argued that students in the art-history class were more willing to accept and absorb instruction in and responses to writing than they would have been in an English class simply because art history isn't English. They expect a focus on writing in English and tend to dismiss it because it seems to have no point beyond itself. They do not expect a focus on writing in art history and tend to accept it because it seems to have a valid and valuable point well beyond itself; it is the enabling device that makes it possible to "make meaning" out of an aesthetic experience, to connect that experience with the world of visible objects, and to place an emotional response in an intellectual context.

## COMING FULL CIRCLE

In the beginning was the snake. Embellished with interlacements, a study in contortion, it adapted itself to each of its temporary homes as it slid from classroom to classroom. When it reached the art-history room, it found a hearty welcome, all the more exuberant because the students in that room craved help from any source, so profound were their feelings of inadequacy and self-doubt. By the time the students had made their peace with the requirements of the course and the awkwardnesses of acknowledging and assessing aesthetic experiences in the world in which machines and McDonald's seem to have eclipsed madonnas and mythology, the convolutions of unfamiliar forms and wordings seemed to straighten themselves out into fairly simple admonitions. Writing became pleasurable and instructive because each writer had guidelines in mind for providing a dependable, solid foundation for any paper or exercise, in class or out. And that foundation provides an underpinning for the conclusion of this case study as well: the procedures of process writing when applied to art history work at least as well as, if not better than, they do in English. That is not to say that there is or should be any sort of competition between disciplines to see where the techniques work best, for there is no way to judge such a thing. But it surely can be said that where the central focus of a course is on subject matter with an intrinsic value apart from the form of its presentation, students can engage in prewriting, conferencing, revision, and publication with admirable results. Then, pleased with themselves, they can look the visible snake in the eye and see him for what he is: a creation of the mind of man, brilliantly illuminated and shining with gold.

## ANNOTATED BIBLIOGRAPHY

Arnheim, Rudolf. *Art and Visual Perception: The New Version*. Berkeley: University of California Press, 1974. Although the book focuses mainly on specific principles and aspects of art appreciation and criticism, it does describe—chiefly in the chapter called "Expression"—the process by which the eye perceives. Arnheim speaks of "intellectual inference" (445) as being part of the procedure by which the mind apprehends what the senses grasp.

————. *New Essays on the Psychology of Art*. Berkeley: University of California Press, 1986. A wonderful book! It begins with a glorious color reproduction of Giovanni di Paolo's *Adoration of the Magi* and ends, 325 pages later, with a three-paragraph consideration of "Values Lawfully Determined." What Arnheim means by that is based upon his theory of "target" and "recipient"—that is, artwork and viewer. In the "conditions prevailing in the target and the recipient," he asserts, "the objective properties of the target to be perceived and evaluated are an indispensable component of any such encounter." A viewer/critic/writer who views a work of art is, therefore, subject to the intrinsic qualities (and worth and value) of the work itself, just as the perceptions of that viewer/critic/writer are subject to his or her own frame of reference.

————. *Visual Thinking*. Berkeley: University of California Press, 1969. The most useful chapter for me was "Words in Their Place," which contains the line, "Concepts are perceptual images and . . . thought operations are the handling of these images" (227). Arnheim explores the idea of thinking in words as opposed to shapes or amorphous "feelings," focusing all the while on his belief that "thoughts need shape, and shape must be derived from some medium" (226). The medium might as well be words.

Barnet, Sylvan. *A Short Guide to Writing about Art*. Boston: Little, Brown, 1985. An excellent text! I used it in my course this year and will use it again. Each student owned her own copy, and we devoted six days each semester to working with it directly in class. Best of all, I think, is the chapter on "Analysis," which makes clear the similarity between analyzing a work of art and analyzing anything else. The art world is not an unreal, disconnected cul-de-sac of life; the same principles of logic and reason and intuition and perception hold in the art—or art-history—class that hold in chemistry, medieval history, or Latin. Barnet lists useful questions to ask about any object or concept.

Berger, John. *Ways of Seeing*. London: British Broadcasting Corporation and Penguin Books, 1983. A short (166 pages), sassy, provocative, invaluable book for stimulating ruminations on the nature of perception. Berger's basic contention is that "seeing comes before words" (33), and he explores the relationship between visible images and language in page after page of illustrations, some of famous and "approved" artworks (Holbein's *Ambassadors*, Cimabue's *Madonna Enthroned*, Manet's *Olympia*), some of advertisements (Helena Rubenstein, Tanqueray gin), some of contemporary scenes and celebrities (an IBM office, Greta Garbo, Marilyn Monroe).

————. *The Sense of Sight*. New York: Pantheon Books, 1985. Most of the book focuses on specific painters, paintings, and painting techniques, but the chapter called "The Place of Painting" offers some interesting observations on the impact of the visible world upon the imagination. The opening sentence is, "To be visible is to be present; to be absent is to be invisible," a concept that speaks to the notion that a piece of writing (whatever its subject) is an artifact, something visible. The process, therefore, is an act of creation designed to make visible the ideas and images of a creative individual.

Berthoff, Ann. "A Curious Triangle and the Double-Entry Notebook; or, How Theory Can Help Us Teach Reading and Writing." In *The Making of Meaning*. Montclair, N.J.: Boynton/Cook, 1981. This chapter clarifies and defines *criticism* as "knowing what you're doing and thereby how to do it. Criticism is method; it is practicing what you teach" (41). Berthoff argues that writing is a "way of making meaning," that no one—not students, and not their teachers either—knows what he or she means until forced to try to write it down.

Bronowski, J. *The Visionary Eye: Essays in the Arts, Literature, and Science*. Cambridge, Mass.: MIT Press, 1984. Two chapters are of particular interest: "The Imaginary Mind in Art" and "Imagination as Plan and as Experiment." In the former Bronowski argues that "no work of art has been created with such finality that you need contribute nothing to it" (14), and in the latter he asserts that "the work of art has a quite unique capacity, which is this: by some profound and obscure mode it directs you into the general statement and somehow makes it resound in you as if it were your private property" (133). The book provides an interesting assessment of the relationship between works of art and their audience.

Bruner, Jerome. *On Knowing: Essays for the Left Hand*. Cambridge, Mass.: The Belknap Press of the Harvard University Press, 1982. A theoretical ramble through the thickets of perception, knowing, and knowing that one knows, this book contains a handful of ideas of particular interest. One is that twentieth-century man is fearful that "knowledge will negate the pleasure of innocence" (60). Another is that "in the experience of art, we connect by a grammar of metaphor, one that defies the rational methods of the linguist and the psychologist" (74). A third is that "the cycle of learning begins . . . with particulars and immediately moves toward abstraction" (123).

Clark, Kenneth. *Looking at Pictures*. London: John Murray, 1972. Primarily a very personal and decidedly whimsical discussion of some of Lord Clark's favorite works of art, the book demonstrates the highly individual way in which art can be viewed. The book is of less use as an analysis of the process of viewing art than as a paradigm of what viewing can lead to. Its rationale seems to be that "the meaning of a great work of art, or the little of it that we can understand, must be related to our own life in such a way as to increase our energy of spirit" (15). Clark's spirit dances through the book.

Cooper, Charles R., and Lee Odell. *Evaluating Writing*. Urbana, Ill.: National Council of Teachers of English, 1977. The most useful chapter for me was "Measuring Changes in Intellectual Processes as One Dimension of Growth in Writing," for I was trying to document and assess changes in the ways in which my students approached and moved through the process of writing art criticism. I was particularly interested in measuring developing self-confidence, and Odell spells out a series of operations everyone must perform in order to understand "some chunk of experience" (111). The series of operations includes (1) contrasting, (2) classifying, (3) becoming aware of change, (4) placing the "chunk" in its physical context, and (5) placing the "chunk" in its time sequence.

de la Croix, Horst, and Richard G. Tansey. *Gardner's Art through the Ages*. San Diego: Harcourt Brace Jovanovich, 1980. This is the text used in the course in art history that served as laboratory for this case study.

Gardner, Howard. *Frames of Mind: The Theory of Multiple Intelligences*. New York: Basic Books, 1985. This is the book that the following article was extrapolated from.

———. "Science Grapples with the Creative Puzzle." *The New York Times*, Sunday, May 13, 1984, p. H28. This article plays with Tom Stoppard's play "The Real Thing," using it as a jumping-off spot and touchstone for discussion of the relationship between "crystallizing experiences" and the works they produce.

Gombrich, E. H.; Julian Hochberg; and Max Black. *Art, Perception, and Reality*. Baltimore: Johns Hopkins Press, 1984. Gombrich's chapter is very specifically visual; he focuses on "the perception of physiognomic likeness in life and in art" without analyzing the processes by which the viewer perceives. Hochberg's chapter discusses looking at pictures (static objects) with eyes (movable objects) in a fleeting moment that cannot be recaptured. He makes a connection between active looking and those reading skills that move quickly from a letter-by-letter investigation of a text to a more general perception of what is on a page. Black's chapter asks whether art is an "imitation of reality" or a joint construct of painter's image and viewer's perception.

Hjerter, Kathleen G. *Doubly Gifted: The Author as Visual Artist*. New York: Harry N. Abrams, 1986. This is a wonderful visual and linguistic treat: side-by-side words and images by literary figures not usually thought of as visual artists.

Newkirk, Thomas, ed. *To Compose: Teaching Writing in the High School*. Portsmouth, N.H.: Heinemann Educational Books, 1986. A collection of a dozen essays by the big names in writing process—Perl, Murray, Flower, Tchudi, Atwell, Fulwiler—in which the central issues of the techniques are articulated in succinct, reasonable, and often witty arguments. Taken together, the essays make the case for using writing to make sense of the world around us; individually, they focus on the specifics of using language as a medium of expression.

Roskill, Mark. *What Is Art History?* New York: Harper and Row, 1982. In the very beginning, Roskill asserts that "a work of art is affected by the way in which it is seen, by the label it carries, reflecting how it is rated and what is known behind the label" (9). He then examines specific works and specific artists. The chapter on Giorgione provides especially interesting information about the value of the written word in analyzing an artist's achievement, especially if the word was written during the artist's lifetime.